D0207983

Norman Winegar

The Clinician's Guide to Managed Behavioral Care
Second Edition

Noteworthy
REVIEWS
OF THE FIRST EDITION . . .

" **A** survival kit for practitioners in an era when managed care has taken from clinicians the control of their own practices. Those who read and learn from Mr. Winegar's book will survive and prosper. . . . The book provides the practical, basic knowledge required to understand the current revolution in health care and to respond effectively. All this is presented in a clear, concise fashion that is readily understood."

Nicholas A. Cummings, PhD
Founder, American Biodyne, Inc., San Francisco; Past President, American Psychological Association

More noteworthy
REVIEWS OF THE FIRST EDITION

"**A** solid introduction to the managed care environment itself and to managed mental health care in particular. Its detailed yet concise style is highly readable without becoming overly technical for benefits managers and other health care decision-makers."

Managed Healthcare News

"**W**inegar provides a very thorough discussion of historical developments of managed care and its present-day practice, including HMOs, PPOs, and networks. EAPs are discussed in context of integrating MMHC functions. This book is helpful in marketing to MMHCs, service development, client advocacy, and utilization management."

EAP Digest

"**M**ust reading for clinicians and directors of managed care and EAP programs, benefit administrators, and most importantly, professors of clinical practice who need to immediately apply the wealth of knowledge presented in their courses. This is without a doubt the seminal work on managed care. . . . Winegar's charts and tables make the various models presented realistic. Conceptually, the author addresses the practice implications as well as the critical issues for the future in a thoughtful and searching manner. A truly professional contribution to the development of mental health services, this book is essential in the reading lists of those concerned with delivering and receiving good mental health and substance abuse treatment in the U.S."

Dale Masi, DSW
Professor, University of Maryland, Employee Assistance Program Consultant

More noteworthy
REVIEWS OF THE FIRST EDITION

"**A**n extremely informative guidebook to managed care for clinicians. The book has something for everyone, from the practitioner already employed in managed care settings to independent clinicians in areas where managed care is only beginning to impact their work with clients. . . . Winegar has done an exceptional job of clearly explaining how and why managed mental health care systems work as they do."

Managed Care News

"**T**imely and comprehensive. . . . An excellent primer for arming oneself to survive the revolution underway in the mental health and substance abuse care and treatment industry. . . . All stakeholders will find both challenges and guidance in its pages."

Jaclyn Miller, PhD, LCSW
Director of Field Instruction,
Virginia Commonwealth University

"**H**elps readers see their role more comprehensively in relation to others in a managed care system. I especially like the clear guidelines for adding managed care functions to employee assistance programs, for influencing the utilization management process, for informing client/consumers of their choices, and for surviving in an era of managed care."

Joseph R. Steiner, PhD, ACSW
Professor and Chair,
Occupational Social Work,
Syracuse University

"**A**n invaluable resource for anyone in today's health care field. Winegar provides greatly needed insight into managed health care operations and values. . . . I recommend this book to clinicians, human resource managers, and anyone interested in the expanding role of managed mental health care."

Margaret Kellogg, MSW
Licensed Clinical Social Worker
in Private Practice,
Johnson City, Tennessee

More noteworthy
REVIEWS OF THE FIRST EDITION

"**E**asily the best explication of managed care principles and practices as they are developing in the mental health arena. . . . an excellent resource, one that is desperately needed by independent practitioners who have not had the opportunity to sort out and grasp the complexities of emerging managed care systems. . . . Perhaps the greatest contribution Winegar has made resides in his clear explanation, using detailed examples, of exactly how these systems work."

Larry K. Hill, EdD
*Licensed Professional Counselor
in Private Practice,
Rock Springs, Wyoming*

The Haworth Press, Inc.

**NOTES FOR PROFESSIONAL LIBRARIANS
AND LIBRARY USERS**

This is an original book title published by The Haworth Press, Inc. Unless otherwise noted in specific chapters with attribution, materials in this book have not been previously published elsewhere in any format or language.

CONSERVATION AND PRESERVATION NOTES

All books published by The Haworth Press, Inc. and its imprints are printed on certified ph neutral, acid free book grade paper. This paper meets the minimum requirements of American National Standard for Information Sciences–Permanence of Paper for Printed Material, ANSI Z39.48-1984.

The Clinician's Guide to Managed Behavioral Care

HAWORTH Marketing Resources
Innovations in Practice & Professional Services
William J. Winston, Senior Editor

New, Recent, and Forthcoming Titles:

The Clinician's Guide to Managed Behavioral Care

(Second Edition of *The Clinician's Guide to Managed Mental Health Care*)

Norman Winegar

The Haworth Press
New York • London

© 1996 by The Haworth Press, Inc. All rights reserved. No part of this work may be reproduced or utilized in any form or by any means, electronic or mechanical, including photocopying, microfilm and recording, or by any information storage and retrieval system, without permission in writing from the publisher. Printed in the United States of America.

The Haworth Press, Inc., 10 Alice Street, Binghamton, NY 13904-1580

Library of Congress Cataloging-in-Publication Data

Winegar, Norman.
    The clinician's guide to managed behavioral care / Norman Winegar.–2nd ed.
        p.   cm.
    Revised ed. of: The clinician's guide to managed mental health care.
    Includes bibliographical references and index.
    ISBN 0-7890-6012-4 (alk. paper)
    1. Managed mental health care–United States. I. Title.
RC465.6.W556 1995
362.2'0973–dc20   95-45916
                                                         CIP

FLORIDA GULF COAST
UNIVERSITY LIBRARY

CONTENTS

ABOUT THE AUTHOR

Norman Winegar, LCSW, CEAP, is the Regional Director for Professional Practice for MCC Behavioral Care in Richmond, VA. Mr. Winegar has been a clinical administrator in the managed care field for over ten years and is a frequent presenter and trainer on this and related topics. He is the co-author of *Marketing Mental Health Services to Managed Care*, also from The Haworth Press.

Acknowledgments

This book is aimed at providing counseling professionals and others interested in the delivery of mental health care services to Americans an overview of managed behavioral care systems and strategies. It is hoped this book will contribute in some small way to the improvement of services received by American consumers and toward an increased partnership between the payors, providers, and utilizers of valuable mental health care resources.

I would like to thank the following individuals for their contributions and assistance in the preparation of this book: Dr. John Bistline, Dr. Nicholas Cummings, Dr. Ralph Earle, Dr. Larry Hill, Dr. Roderick Hafer, Margaret DeCarlis, Dr. Michael Freeman, Rick Kinyon, Dr. Dale Masi, Dr. Joseph Steiner, Joseph Strahan, and Susan Feltus who reviewed an early draft of a chapter concerning the legal aspects of utilization management. I am also indebted to the following organizations for their assistance: MCC Behavioral Care, the National Association of Social Workers, the Employee Assistance Professionals Association, the American Association of Private Psychiatric Hospitals, Inter Study, Marion Merrell Dow, the American Managed Behavioral Healthcare Association, the National Committee for Quality Assurance, and the Department of Health and Human Services.

Finally, special thanks to Susan Sheridan, MS, LPC, who helped revise early drafts and to Eden Alexander, MSW, who has long encouraged my interests in the delivery of behavioral care services.

Introduction

A revolution has changed how mental health and substance abuse treatment services are delivered to most Americans. It has affected the practice of most behavioral care clinicians in both private and public sector settings. It has helped transform the private psychiatric hospital industry and has reshaped and revitalized community-based outpatient care. The revolution is Managed Behavioral Care.

Today more than any time in the past, both practicing clinicians and students anticipating a career of service in the treatment field must be knowledgeable about the current practice environment and armed with strategies needed for successful competition. This book enables the reader to understand the operations, values, and philosophies of managed care systems while discussing the strategies clinicians need for successful practice in an increasingly changing and competitive area of health care.

This competitive environment in the behavioral care field was recently highlighted by Michael A. Freeman, MD, President of the Institute for Behavioral Healthcare and founder of the *Behavioral Healthcare Tomorrow* journal.

At the current time there are approximately 250,000 licensed mental health clinicians in the United States, or approximately 1 per 1,000 Americans. By contrast, most HMO mental health programs rely upon 1 mental health clinician per 5,000-6,000 members. Most managed behavioral carve out firms, which in the past have maintained broader provider panels, are increasingly shifting referrals to behavioral group practices. What does this mean for the average clinician? As Americans continue to drift into organized systems of care, there could be a surplus of as many as 80,000-100,000 licensed mental health professionals across the country. The pressure on mental health clinicians who wish to stay in business will be intense.

MBC has changed traditional practice in numerous and diverse ways. Most concern increased accountability and structure. Alternative fee and pricing arrangements, the organization provider networks, the hiring of specialized clinicians and clinical managers, the development of practice standards, redesigned employee benefit plans, new models of Employee Assistance Programs, the variety of utilization management technologies and processes, and an emphasis on outpatient solution-focused treatment are only a few of MBC's change strategies.

As an emerging growth industry, MBC is frequently a source of confusion and consternation to practitioners, managers, consumers, and purchasers. At its worst, it is perceived as an intrusive, confusing impediment to or interference with clinical practice. At its best, MBC is a partnership between providers, MBC firms, and payors in providing quality, cost-effective care to consumers while ensuring that benefits for such services are preserved.

This book will enable the reader to understand the fundamentals of Managed Behavioral care operations, the market for these services, how clinicians and facilities can integrate themselves in the increasingly "managed" practice environment, and MBC trends in coming years. Appendixes provide the reader with useful supplementary information, including an up-to-date listing of the nation's over 600 HMOs as well as a directory of America's leading MBC specialty firms.

Throughout this book, the term Managed Behavioral Care, or MBC, will be used to describe these entities. These firms may provide direct services to clients, provide services indirectly through Provider Networks, or may only manage mental health and substance abuse benefits.

The term "member" is frequently used throughout as the descriptor for the individual consumer of managed care services. "Client" and "patient" are used interchangeably. The term "provider" is a generic one, referencing any practitioner or clinician rendering services.

The book aspires to contribute by providing information about

MBC systems, their impact on practice in the mental health, substance abuse, and Employee Assistance fields, and how professionals can continue to serve their clients, while prospering professionally in a time of radical change in America's mental health delivery system.

REFERENCE

Freeman, Michael A. (1994, October). (Personal Communication.)

Chapter 1

What Is "Managed Care"?

Managed care is a term that elicits a variety of reactions from health care professionals. Some practitioners feel anxious, confused, or bewildered as they try to provide traditional care to clients while coping with a maze of acronyms, undecipherable insurance jargon and procedures, and unclear or distasteful "business" concepts that have invaded clinical practice. Others feel resentment or even anger at managed care firms—resentment toward systems that seem to constantly question their clinical judgement and autonomy, and anger toward perceived threats to their professional livelihood. Many clinicians who have fought hard for increased access to counseling and therapy services for consumers are angered by what they see as managed care's roadblocks to individuals and families receiving such care. They point to waiting lists, "gatekeepers" (who may not be clinicians), and excessive paperwork as obstacles to treatment imposed by managed care systems in an effort to restrict or deny services.

Other groups are concerned about managed care as well. Employee assistance professionals, accustomed to directing clients to particular treatment modalities and providers, are now confronted with relinquishing that role to others when managed care systems are involved. Hospital-based treatment staffs face declining admissions, reduced lengths of treatment stays, and radical restructuring of traditional programs due to the influence of managed care. Graduate students in the counseling professions wonder whether or not their education is preparing them for the actual practice environment of the coming decade. Many students and clinicians even question if "private practice" as it has been historically defined will survive in the future. They wonder how and if their "practices" will interface with managed care systems. What new strategies, skills, and innovations will they need to employ to be successful in the era of managed care?

Meanwhile these concerns and questions take place in the larger health care environment in the 1990s—one in which insurance behemoths are purchasing their own specialty managed care/employer services companies; where unions initiate work stoppages over employer benefit issues; where the federal government is experimenting with managed care systems for its CHAMPUS members, while policymakers debate greater federal involvement in controlling health care costs; where consumers are turning to HMOs and other managed health care alternatives as the cost of traditional health insurance products escalate. Rather than wish for a return to simpler times when counseling and treatment services were purchased on a "fee-for-service" basis and client choice reigned supreme, counseling professionals and others are being challenged to learn about managed care systems and how their influence on practice will increase in the years to come. By doing so they will be better prepared to prosper in changing times while fulfilling traditional roles of service delivery and client advocacy.

ESSENTIAL FACTS

Managed care, or, as it applies more specifically to our discussions, Managed Behavioral Care, is a term applied to a variety of strategies, systems, and mechanisms that have as their objectives the monitoring and control of the utilization of mental health and substance abuse services while maintaining satisfactory levels of quality of care. MBC has as its focus the marshalling and coordinating of the appropriate clinical and financial resources necessary for each client's care. Essentially, managed care clients' needs are matched to appropriate treatment resources, and then the delivery and outcome of these resources are monitored. Managed care developed a significant presence in the 1970s and made important impacts in the mental health and substance abuse treatment fields in the 1980s. MBC will revolutionize America's mental health care delivery system during the 1990s.

There are three basic facts about managed care today:

1. *Managed care is here to stay!* It will not go away. Its impact on treatment patterns and reimbursement systems will only increase in

years to come. Managed care has already made impressive in-roads into the health care market and it continues to grow. According to industry publications, enrollment in America's 540 HMOs grew in membership to about 49 million Americans in 1993, an increase of over **10 percent** from the prior year. Almost one in five Americans are enrolled in an HMO, easily double that number are involved in some sort of employer-sponsored managed care product. HMOs were headquartered in every state except Alaska, West Virginia, Vermont, and Wyoming. A large majority of employers offer HMOs as a part of their health care benefit menu–an attractive option to many Americans. These numbers do not include the millions of consumers who are involved in other types of managed care systems, either through their employers or through insurance carriers. Nor do they reflect the several million Medicaid and other public sector consumers who are increasingly moved through managed health care systems.

Some have advocated for Federal intervention in health care in such ways that would eliminate managed care, HMO, and insurance companies in favor of a government-run health care system financed through taxes, not insurance premiums. The spectacular failure of President Clinton's health care reform legislation and the subsequent 1994 election results, together with the continued embrace of managed health care by the private and public sectors, seems to have dimmed the hopes of those who favor greater governmental administration of the health care industry. Clearly, consumers will receive care, and practitioners will continue to deliver care through managed care systems in ever increasing proportions. Managed care structures, including HMOs, are the rule not the exception.

2. *Understanding managed care systems, philosophies, and dynamics is essential for successful clinical practice in the future.* Today more than half of America's physicians conduct at least part of their practices in association with HMOs. Still others are associated with Preferred Practice Organizations (PPOs). Clearly, managed care systems have exerted tremendous influences on physicians during the last decade, and their influence will extend deeper into the allied health professions in the 1990s. Successful counseling professionals, agencies, and facilities will be those whose practice patterns and programmatic offerings are most attractive to managed care systems.

3. *Managed care is not the problem in health care today.* It is a response to the problem confronting consumers, providers, and purchasers alike: rising health care costs, especially that segment of costs associated with the mental health/substance abuse treatment field. To many employers this "grey area" of health care seems particularly in need of "management."

The nation spent over $884 billion or about $3,300 per person for health care in 1993 or about 13.9 percent of the Gross Domestic Product. One of the fastest growing segments of costs have been mental health and substance abuse treatment services. Employers and employees through private health insurance plans bore the largest share of these costs, while taxpayers absorbed the next largest portion of the national health care bill through Medicare, Medicaid, and other government-administered programs. Table 1-1 delineates this information further, while Figures 1-1 and 1-2 deal with 1991 data.

Because about one third of health care costs are paid by taxpayers, the rise in costs has helped to maintain the deficit in Federal spending and to place increasing burdens on state governments as well. One of the themes of President Clinton's ill-fated 1994 effort at health care system reform was that health care costs were driving government spending faster than the growth of the economy. Rather than wait for federally mandated reforms, numerous state governments have initiated waivers from regulations concerning Medicaid funds and are introducing managed care systems to the public sector at a rapid pace. Table 1-2 details federal and state/local government health care spending trends.

BACKGROUND:
DEVELOPMENTS THAT SET THE STAGE
FOR MANAGED BEHAVIORAL CARE SYSTEMS

Introduction of Prepaid Health Care

Three historical developments helped shape today's application of managed care to the psychiatric and substance abuse treatment fields. First was the gradual development of prepaid health care coverages. The most prominent feature of these systems was that the consumer paid one monthly fee and then received all health care services from selected providers at little or no cost.

TABLE 1-1. National Health Expenditures as a Percent of Gross Domestic Product, Selected Years

Year	% of GDP
1960	5.3%
1965	5.9%
1970	7.4%
1975	8.4%
1980	9.2%
1985	10.5%
1986	10.7%
1987	10.9%
1988	11.1%
1989	11.5%
1990	12.2%
1991	13.2%
1992	13.6%
1993	13.9%

Source: Letsch, S.W. et al. *Health Care Financing Review,* Winter 1992, Vol. 14, Number 2, and *HHS News Release: National Health Expenditures for 1993.* Nov. 22, 1994.

Even though the first rudimentary examples of prepaid health care coverage came in the first decade of this century, the major breakthrough for Health Maintenance Organizations (HMOs) occurred in the late 1930s and early 1940s. Industrialist Henry J. Kaiser and physician Sydney Garfield established the first HMOs in Oregon and California. They served the health care needs of Kaiser's employees. These organizations were very successful in the cost-conscious World War II era. From these efforts came the Kaiser-Permanente Health Maintenance Organization, the nation's largest group model HMO. (See Chapter Two for discussion of HMOs and HMO models.) Kaiser-Permanente flourished first in Northern and then Southern California. Later HMOs made their appearance in other parts of the country and were particularly successful in the Minneapolis-St. Paul area of Minnesota and in Wisconsin.

FIGURE 1-1. The Nation's Health Dollar in 1991

Where it came from

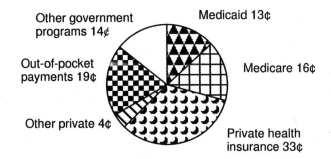

Other government programs 14¢

Medicaid 13¢

Out-of-pocket payments 19¢

Medicare 16¢

Other private 4¢

Private health insurance 33¢

FIGURE 1-2. The Nation's Health Dollar in 1991

Where it went

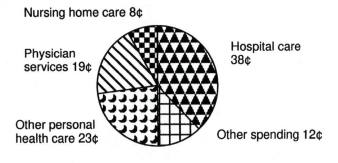

Nursing home care 8¢

Physician services 19¢

Hospital care 38¢

Other personal health care 23¢

Other spending 12¢

NOTES: "Other private" includes industrial inplant health services, non-patient revenues, and privately financed construction. "Other personal health care" includes dental, other professional services, home health care, drugs and other non-durable medical products, vision products and other durable medical products, and other miscellaneous health care services. "Other spending" covers program administration and the net cost of private health insurance, government public health, and research and construction.

SOURCE: *Health Care Financing Review,* Winter 1992, Vol. 14, No. 2.

TABLE 1-2. Government Health Spending as a Percent of Total Government Spending, Selected Years

Year	Federal Government	State/Local Government
1960	3.1	7.8
1965	3.9	7.6
1970	8.5	7.8
1975	10.0	8.5
1980	11.7	9.9
1985	12.7	10.8
1986	12.9	11.1
1987	13.5	11.6
1988	14.1	11.9
1989	14.8	12.3
1990	15.3	12.9
1991	16.7	14.1

Source: Letsch, S.W. et al., *Health Care Financing Review*, Winter 1992, Vol. 14, Number 2.

Still, by 1970 less than three million Americans in fifteen states belonged to HMOs. The label of "socialized medicine" and the opposition of physician and hospital groups had hampered their growth. It was the Nixon administration who gave impetus to HMO growth through its support of legislation that "federally qualified" an HMO and mandated its offering to employees in the geographic area it served. Called the HMO Act of 1973, this law required that employers of twenty-five employees or more must offer an HMO option, if an HMO is in operation in their locale, and if requested by the HMO to do so. During the Carter administration, Health Education and Welfare Secretary Joseph Califano simplified the HMO qualifying process and HMOs began to expand. There was a sizable jump in enrollment in the early 1980s and growth continued, though at a slower pace, in the latter part of that decade. The industry as a whole struggled financially during the 1980s as it attempted to control or slow down rising health care costs. Some, mostly smaller, poorly capitalized HMOs failed, while others were purchased or absorbed by larger organizations. By 1990 a financial turnaround had been achieved in the industry. Analysts predict that while the number of HMOs will drop in the 1990s, there will be continued growth in membership overall. Additionally, the success of HMOs spurred the development of other managed care systems such as PPOs which compete for membership. (See Chapter 3.)

Just as the 1973 HMO Act had far-reaching effects on the development of HMOs, the 1974 Employee Retirement Income Security Act (ERISA) was to facilitate growth of managed care systems as well. Even though this act was primarily aimed at pension equity, ERISA contains a provision allowing self-insured groups to be exempt from most state regulations pertaining to mandated health insurance benefits and mandated provider requirements.

For example, until recently most HMOs charged premiums to employers and employees based on "community ratings," that is, based on the projected cost of services provided to the entire HMO membership, not a single group of employees. Under ERISA, a large employer may choose to fund insurance coverage only for its own employee population. In this way the employer hopes to take advantage of its own efforts to maintain a healthy work force. By not funding and participating in the larger pool of insurance groups, it hopes to achieve cost-savings. Self-insured employers have great flexibility in designing benefits. For self-insured employers, insurance carriers serve only to administer the program. Employers sometimes use Third-Party Administrators (TPAs) for this function, as well. During the 1980s, self-insured employers proliferated. Today, ERISA provisions continue to influence how health benefits are designed and administered. (See Chapter 7 for a further discussion of ERISA.)

Growth of Private Psychiatric Hospitals

Responding to reimbursement system changes and changes in societal attitudes, the development of private, for-profit, psychiatric and substance abuse hospitals and treatment units was a second factor in the development of managed care systems in the mental health area. These facilities grew rapidly in the late 1970s and throughout the 1980s. The development of the Diagnostic Related Groups (DRGs) as a funding mechanism for Medicare inpatient medical care indirectly helped to spur this development.

In 1975 the DRG system was developed at Yale University and included 467 diagnoses. The federal government began utilizing it for Medicare patients as a cost management tool, a means of sharing financial risk with hospitals. Under a DRG system, a schedule of maximum payments for hospital care is developed for each diagnosis. The hospital is reimbursed for this amount, regardless of the actual length of the admission. For example, if diagnosis "X" is covered for four hospital days, but the patient is well enough to be discharged after three days, the hospital is still reimbursed for four days of care. Likewise, if the patient is so ill that five days of hospital care is required, the hospital will only be reimbursed for four days.

DRGs, a form of managed care, were used for medical/surgical hospital care but were not applied to psychiatric diagnosis, due to the lack of professional consensus about treatment of various disorders. They did impact hospital management by indirectly incenting hospitals to expand into the area of mental health and substance abuse care. These hospitals and specialty units in general hospitals proliferated in the late 1970s and throughout the 1980s.

Another factor that stimulated the growth of inpatient psychiatric facilities were changes in statutes concerning the housing of minors with adults in correctional facilities. As society decided that many troubled teenagers should not be housed in existing correctional facilities, psychiatric hospitalization often became a more attractive and humane alternative (while still fulfilling much of the social control function that was desired by parents and the judicial system). Between 1982 and 1986 the percentage of adolescents as a portion of the population as a whole declined, but the incidence of hospitalization of teenagers went up 350 percent!

Thus, by the late 1980s, most larger communities had several competing inpatient-based substance abuse or adolescent treatment units providing intensive and very costly care. These hospital-based units became large employers of nonphysician counseling professionals. They marketed toward Employee Assistance Program staff who could direct referrals to them. They also formed lucrative formal or informal arrangements with psychiatrists who were expected to admit their patients to these units for the milieu treatment of the inpatient environment. Often the fees derived from inpatient care became an important income source for psychiatrists, overshadowing their outpatient practices.

Expansion of Counseling Professions

A third development, paralleling the other two, was the proliferation of counseling professions that were licensed by state boards and were reimbursable by insurance carriers. Prior to the 1960s most insurance carriers reimbursed services provided by the nation's relatively small supply of psychiatrists. But during the twenty years between 1960 and 1980, society's attitude toward therapy for emotional and substance abuse problems changed. The number of counseling professions and professionals expanded. Led by the American Psychological Association (APA) and the National Association of Social Workers (NASW), these professions successfully lobbied for legal recognition as providers of treatment services. By 1977 psychology had achieved regulatory status in all fifty states. At this writing, social work is regulated in forty-eight states, while professional counselors have achieved recognition in thirty-three states. Marriage and family therapists and clinical nurse specialists have statutory recognition as mental health providers in fewer numbers of states. Many of these professionals have successfully developed private practices and achieved a broad appeal to consumers. Some promote the "cost-effectiveness" aspect of their respective professions, comparing their charges in a favorable light with those of psychiatrists.

While these professions found popularity among consumers in the 1970s and 1980s, insurance carriers equated the proliferation of providers with increased service utilization and, in turn, increased costs. Insurance carriers passed on these increases, or the risk for them, to the ultimate private purchaser of health care services—employers.

RISK: THE DYNAMIC THAT DRIVES MANAGED CARE

Risk, when used in its simplest connotation, refers to responsibility or liability for payment for services. Before the advent of health care insurance, an individual was fully at risk for payment for his or her own health care needs. If the individual had an illness or accident, he or she paid a provider (usually a physician) for the unit or units of treatment received. (See Figure 1-3.)

FIGURE 1-3. The Patient at Risk for Health Care Costs

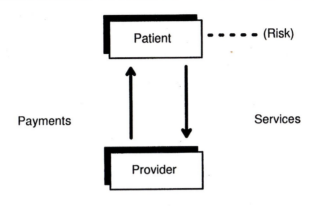

With the development of indemnity health insurance and its proliferation during the 1940s and 1950s as an accepted "benefit" of a job,
employers took on a large portion of this risk for payment. The employer paid a premium to a health insurance company who then reimbursed a provider (usually a physician or hospital) for care provided to
a patient (the employee or family members). This traditional indemnity
insurance system maximized consumers' ability to choose the provider
or facility from whom they would receive services. It also tended to
motivate providers to focus on customer satisfaction while conducting
more services, since reimbursement was based on number of services
performed. As utilization (number of services performed) grew, insurance companies would periodically reevaluate their costs and charge
higher premiums to the employer. As employers purchased policies
from insurance companies that included coverage for mental health
and substance abuse treatment they took on greater risk for the cost of
services delivered by the various counseling professionals and inpatient treatment facilities. In this system, insurance carriers functioned
as passive claims payors. Consumers selected the provider while the
providers selected and delivered treatment services, which were ultimately funded by the employer through premiums paid to the carrier.
Consumers contributed through their payroll deductions and "deduct-

ible charges" but employers contributed the majority of the total insurance costs. (See Figure 1-4.)

As health care costs rose in the 1980s, employers increasingly felt themselves in an uncomfortable bind. Faced with a more competitive environment, they struggled for means to contain the escalating impact of health care on their profits, while searching for ways to provide adequate care for their employees' mental health and substance abuse treatment needs. Led by IBM in the early 1980s, most of the nation's large employers developed or expanded their Employee Assistance Programs (EAPs). Many, already utilizing managed care in the forms of HMOs and PPOs, turned to these organizations as models to address the quandary of how to provide adequate care while containing the escalating mental health and substance abuse care costs. The MBC specialty firm came into existence to meet this market's needs. (See Figure 1-5.)

FIGURE 1-4. Indemnity Insurance: Employer and Carrier Share Risk

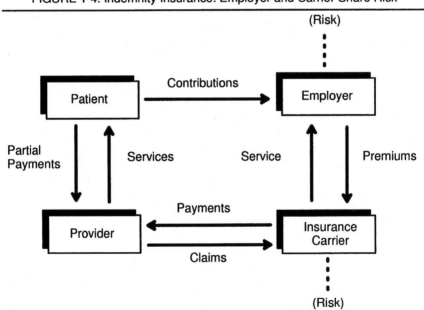

FIGURE 1-5. Sharing Risk Through Managed Care

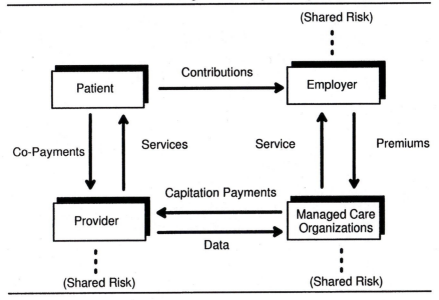

BIBLIOGRAPHY

Bloom, J. (1987). *HMO's. The Revolution in Health Care.* Tucson, AZ: The Body Press-HP Books, Inc.

Califano, J. A., Jr. (1986). *America's Health Care Revolution.* New York: Simon and Schuster, Inc.

Cooper, A. L. (1990). Providers and managed health care. *HMO/PPO Trends, 3*(1), 5-9.

Cummings, N. A. (1990). The credentialing of professional psychologists and its implication for other mental health disciplines. *Journal of Counseling and Development, 68,* 485-490.

Garcia, A. (1990). An examination of the social work profession's effort to achieve legal regulation. *Journal of Counseling and Development, 68,* 491-497.

Group Health Association of America. (1990). *1990 National Directory of HMO's.* Washington, DC: Author.

Health Care Financing Review, Winter 1992, Vol. 14, No. 2.

Health Insurance Association of America. (1989). *1989 HMO User Satisfaction Study.* Washington, DC: Author.

Health Market Survey. (1990, May 14). Washington, DC: Interpro Publications Inc.

HHS News Release. (1994, Nov. 22). Department of Human Services.

Letsch, S. W., Lazenby, H. L., Levit, K. R., and Cowan, C. A. (1992). National health expenditures, 1992. *Health Care Financing Review, 14*(2), 1-30.

Mahoney, J. (1987, May). EAPs and medical cost containment. *ALMACAN,* pp. 16-20.

Marion Merrell Dow, Inc. (1990). *Marion Managed Care Digest-HMO Edition.* Kansas City, MO: Author.

Marion Merrell Dow, Inc. (1994). *Managed Care Digest/HMO Edition.* Kansas City, MO: Author

Chapter 2

Managed Care Basics:
Health Maintenance Organizations

Managed Behavioral Care systems have been largely derivations of and outgrowths from Health Maintenance Organizations and Preferred Provider Organizations, and MBC entities utilize many of the technologies, values, and structures inherent in these organizations. Moreover, HMOs represent a major market for MBC firms, which manage the HMO customer's mental health and substance abuse services. A familiarity with the fundamental operations of HMOs and PPOs provides the background necessary for understanding the developments in Managed Behavioral care.

Health Maintenance Organizations (HMOs) number over six hundred in this country today, and provide health care to thirty-five million Americans. HMOs are large, complex, highly regulated businesses that can operate as for-profit or nonprofit entities. Unlike traditional health insurance carriers, which function largely as claims payors, HMOs both deliver and finance health care. They also differ from traditional carriers in that they provide preventative services and have as part of their focus the "maintenance" of health, not just the treatment of illness. HMO membership grew 10.5 percent in 1990, a major increase after two years of sluggish growth. Analysts predict HMOs will continue to grow in the 1990s as new products are made available. (See Figure 2-1 and Table 2-1.)

The trade association for the HMO industry is the Group Health Association of America (GHAA). It publishes a periodical about the industry called *HMO Magazine*. GHAA's address is listed in the Resource Directory section of this book. GHAA can provide a

FIGURE 2-1. HMO Enrollment, 1986-1990

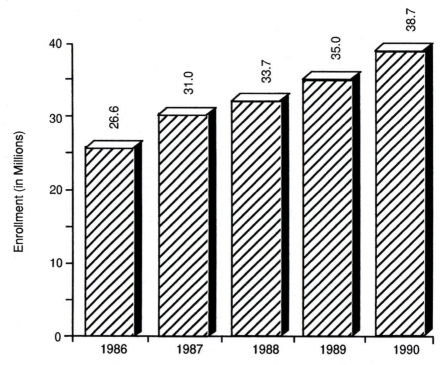

Source: *Marion Merrell Dow Managed Care Digest/HMO Edition,* 1991, p. 7.

range of information about its member HMOs and the industry in general.

The leading managed health care research and policy analysis institution is the nonprofit InterStudy Center for Managed Care Research (see the Resource Directory for InterStudy's address). InterStudy provides business managers, policy makers, analysts, and clinicians with current data about HMO trends and developments. It publishes *InterStudy Edge,* a widely read quarterly publication.

HMOs provide services (medical, dental, pharmaceutical) to their subscribers, called "members," on a prepaid, fixed fee basis;

TABLE 2-1. HMO Growth Trends, 1986-1993

YEAR	NUMBER	ENROLLMENT IN MILLIONS
1986	632	26.5
1987	707	31.0
1988	659	33.7
1989	623	35.0
1990	610	37.5
1991	581	40.3
1992	562	44.3
1993	540	48.9

Source: *Marion Merrell Dow Managed Care Digest/HMO Edition,* 1994, p. 7.

that is, members pay for services through fixed, monthly premiums. These premiums are usually less than those of traditional indemnity health insurance coverages. (In 1989 average family HMO premiums were $265.50 per month, while individual premiums averaged $99.20 per month.) At the time of service, members may pay an additional charge, a copayment. This copayment is usually quite small ($3.00 to $5.00 or so) for basic health care visits or for prescriptions. Copayments to specialists may be substantially higher. Instead of looking to the HMO to reimburse health care expenses that have already occurred, as in the case of indemnity insurance plans, the member looks to the HMO for the actual provision of health care services. Meeting deductibles, filling out and filing claim forms, and waiting for reimbursement checks to come are eliminated. In return for this simplified financial system, members must depend on the HMO to provide adequate access to quality health care services. Figure 2-2 shows how HMOs function, while Table 2-2 contrasts HMO operations with indemnity insurance benefit plans.

FIGURE 2-2. How HMOs Function

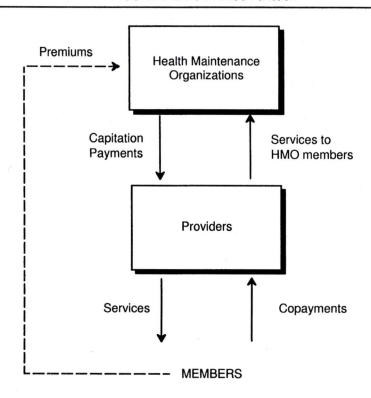

THE CENTRAL ROLE OF THE PRIMARY CARE PHYSICIAN

In medical HMOs the Primary Care Physician (PCP) is the focal point of service delivery. In these organizations, the physician serves as a coordinator (case manager) of health care services, providing care when needed and referring members to others when specialized services are required. His practice serves as the point of interface between the member and all covered health care services. The PCP also functions as a gatekeeper, ensuring that treatment resources are used appropriately. Using his medical judgement and expertise, the PCP determines what type and what level or inten-

TABLE 2-2. Summary of Managed Health Care Systems

	Traditional Indemnity	Modified Indemnity	PPO	IPA/Network/Group HMOs	Staff HMOs
Provider Panel	Consumer selects any provider →	→	Selected providers, with out-of-network choices	Pre-Selected Providers →	→
Consumer Choice	Complete freedom of choice →	→	Incentivized Choice	No Choice →	→
Utilization Review Procedure	None	Precertification of Admissions →	MIS Profiling, Concurrent Review →	→	→
Provider Payment	FFS →		Discounted FFS	Capitation	Salary
Practice Settings	Community-based, independent practice →	→	→	Mixed	Clinic Setting
Consumer Payments	Varied deductibles, claims reimbursement →	→	Reduced copayments, claims reimbursement	Copayments	Copayments

23

sity of care is necessary. (Both these roles, case manager and gatekeeper, are duplicated by specialists in managed behavioral care systems as they pertain to mental health and substance abuse services.) In return for the advantages of HMO membership, patients give over to the PCP a degree of choice in health care decisions that is retained by subscribers to other non-managed health benefit plans.

The way in which physician services are organized defines the HMO model. What follows is a description of how most, though not all, HMOs utilize their physician providers. When a new member joins an HMO, he selects a PCP from the available panel of physicians (usually family practitioners, internists, or pediatricians). Each month thereafter, the selected PCP is paid a fixed, monthly amount for that member and all other HMO members who have selected the physician to be their PCP. The physician then becomes responsible for the provision of all the medical services, preventative and remedial, that were offered to the member by the HMO contract.[1] Regardless of how much or how little primary care the PCP delivers to the member, he receives the same capitation payment each month.

In addition to the capitation payment, the PCP typically receives an allowance for specialist care, inpatient care, or other referral services. This is called the "referral account." (Mental health and substance abuse care may or may not be included in this account.) The PCP "authorizes" reimbursement for a specialist to provide care, paying for the care through the referral account. That is, the member must first be referred by the PCP before accessing this specialty care. The specialist then submits claims to the HMO, which matches the claim to the PCP's authorization and reimburses the specialist for services rendered to the member. The specialist may also have collected a portion of the charge from the member, i.e., the specialist's copayment. In turn, the HMO credits to the

---

1. The HMO's agreement with its providers prohibits billing the member for covered services, affording protection to the member from unnecessary charges. (HMO provider agreements also stipulate an arbitration process for disputed payments. These features are often duplicated in MBC provider agreements. See the MBC Sample Provider Agreements found in Appendix A.)

PCP's referral account the amount paid out in claims for specialty care. At the end of the member's contract year, the PCP shares in any surplus or deficit in the referral account. Some HMO systems withhold a portion of the PCP's monthly capitation payments to offset a potential deficit in this account. Also established is an upper limit to the PCP's risk concerning the referral account. The HMO assumes this extraordinary risk which is associated with the unforeseen costs of care for catastrophic illnesses. This risk-sharing system ultimately provides incentive for the PCP to avoid overuse of costly specialty care.[2]

As an example of how this payment system works, suppose Dr. Smith is paid $10 per member, per month (pm pm). Over the course of one year Smith collects $120 from the HMO for member Jones' primary care. He manages Mr. Jones' and his other patient's care well, so he receives an additional equivalent of $1 pm pm from the surplus of his referral account. His total annual compensation for Mr. Jones' care then is $120 plus $12, or $132. If Mr. Jones visited his PCP three times that year (the average number of physician encounters for HMO enrollees nationally in 1989 was 3.3), Dr. Smith was paid the equivalent of $132 ÷ 3 or $44 per office visit.

As stated earlier, in HMO systems, the PCP is the gatekeeper to health care. He decides when, what kind, and what level of care is needed, as well as its duration. He is the case manager coordinating and monitoring the overall delivery of care. His focus is to keep the member as healthy as possible and to return an ill member to health as quickly as possible. The financial incentives built into the system discourage the overprovision of medical services to the member (in contrast to traditional indemnity insurance, where reimbursement is based on the quantity of services delivered).

In addition to being care providers, PCPs often involve themselves in various committees within the HMO that help to oversee its clinical standards and operations. Depending on the HMO model, PCPs may see other non-HMO patients as well.

---

2. Aware that patients with prior serious illness may heavily utilize specialist referrals, some PCPs may decline to accept some new patients. Because of this, along with the general unpopularity of specialist refund accounts and withholds among providers, some HMOs are eliminating or modifying such systems.

OTHER KEY HMO FUNCTIONS

Aside from reliance on its PCPs for the coordination and management of care, HMOs attempt to contain costs through various alternative payment arrangements with hospital providers. Prominent among these are the use of per diems–a prearranged, negotiated fee per day of hospital care. By designating a limited number of hospitals as providers, and thus ensuring a volume of referrals for each participating hospital, HMOs are able to receive a per diem rate less than normally charged. Per diems may be negotiated along a schedule, so that if referral volume is lower than expected, the hospital's per diem charge increases.

Another common payment arrangement (mandated in several states) is the use of Diagnostic Related Groups (DRGs). Originally developed in the 1970s for Medicare purposes, this system pays for hospital days based on the respective diagnosis. A patient admitted with diagnosis "X," for example, usually requires five days of hospital care. The hospital is paid for the equivalent of five days of care regardless of the actual length of stay. DRGs represent a form of risk sharing between the HMO and the hospital. HMOs have revised and adapted the original Medicare DRGs for commercial purposes.

Some HMOs pursue discounted fees from hospitals, similar to per diems. Greater volume of patient referrals result in greater discounts from the hospital provider. Another innovative approach is called "bed leasing." An HMO may negotiate an arrangement with a hospital whereby it leases a bed(s). The HMO is assured of access to hospital care in this way, while the hospital is assured of a filled bed(s).

Utilization Management

Another key function of HMOs and other managed care entities is utilization management.[3] This term describes a variety of techniques and processes that help to ensure the appropriateness, neces-

---

3. An in-depth examination of utilization management is found in: *Controlling Cost and Changing Patient Care? The Role of Utilization Management*. Bradford H. Gray and Marilyn J. Field, editors. Institute of Medicine, National Academy Press, Washington, DC, 1989.

sity, and quality of care delivered to patients. These processes may be applied before, during, or after care has been delivered. Examples include preadmission certification, case management, concurrent review, peer review, and retrospective chart audits. Utilization management functions are staff intensive and highly specialized. (This topic will be more fully addressed in Chapter 6 concerning psychiatric and substance abuse utilization management processes.)

Originally associated with Medicare in the 1960s and then with HMOs, these technologies are now widely applied to many indemnity insurance products. This new "Utilization Management" industry, which did not even exist in the early 1980s, has been by and large a spin-off from the HMO field. These firms, the largest of which is Intracorp, a CIGNA company, perform various utilization management functions for the health care plans offered by employers and insurers. Functions include medical/surgical hospital admission precertification and concurrent review. These firms employ nurses and physicians and are typically not at financial risk for services they authorize. Hundreds of these firms operate today.

HMO MODELS

HMOs are usually structured around one of four common models, with some variations. These models are derived from how the HMO structures its panel of PCPs. These descriptions are aimed at giving overviews of how these different HMO models work. (Tables 2-3 and Figure 2-3 show the relative enrollments in these HMO models in recent years.)

Independent Practice Association (IPA) Model

IPAs are separate entities from HMOs. Typically they are representative organizations for physicians or other providers who sell their services through the IPA. IPAs may be extensive or very small, encompassing only a few practices. HMOs may choose to contract with several IPAs. Most IPA physicians continue to see non-HMO patients and carry on their own office-based practices.

HMOs pay their IPA physicians on a capitation basis. The IPA is

TABLE 2-3. Enrollment in the Four HMO Model Types Nationwide

	Plans	1990 Enrollment (000)	Plans	1989 Enrollment (000)	Plans	1988 Enrollment (000)
Group	77	10,350.0	85	9,844.8	85	8,775.4
IPA	371	16,961.1	386	15,428.0	407	15,138.8
Network	98	7,045.3	86	5,431.5	106	6,163.1
Staff	64	4,350.7	66	4,326.9	61	3,638.3
TOTAL OPERATING	610		623		659	
Developing	4		1		7	
Total U.S.	614	38,707.1	624	35,031.2	666	33,715.6

Source: *Marion Merrell Dow Managed Care Digest/HMO Edition,* 1991, p. 5.

paid a regular fixed amount, usually on a per member, per month (pm pm) basis. In return, the physician who is responsible for the patient's care must provide all necessary and contracted services.

IPAs may form partnerships with more than one HMO, while continuing to provide services to non-HMO patients. Alternatively, HMOs sometimes recruit physicians to form an IPA to serve their HMO only, ensuring an exclusive arrangement for that IPA.

IPA models are attractive to HMOs for several reasons. First, they are composed of well-known, community-based providers who usually have existing, successful practices. IPAs tend to be broad-based in terms of service delivery, creating better access for the HMO's members. These factors help in the marketing of the HMO to consumers, an important concern given increased competition. Also IPAs require less capital investment on the part of the HMO than do other models.

However, IPAs do have some drawbacks from the HMO's perspective. The independent nature of the physicians mean their practice patterns are more difficult to influence. Also the IPA represents, in effect, a bargaining unit for physicians–one that can obtain more favorable capitation payments from the HMO as well as other bonuses and inducements.

Staff Models

Staff model HMOs hire physicians as salaried employees. In order to receive covered medical services, members must utilize

FIGURE 2-3. IPAs Dominate HMO Industry in Enrollees

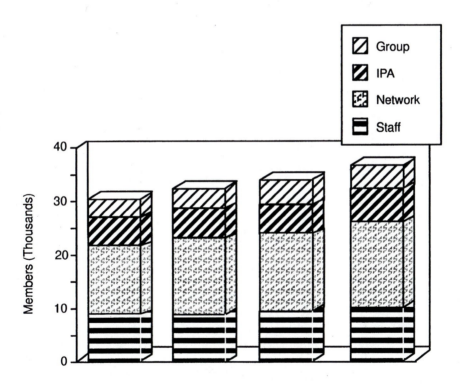

Source: *Marion Merrell Dow Managed Care Digest/HMO Edition,* 1991, p. 5.

these physicians as their PCPs. These providers practice in one or more clinic settings. In order to provide the necessary services to its members, staff model HMOs must hire a variety of physicians and specialists. Some contract out specialist and subspecialty services as well as hospital services. Cigna Health Plan in southern California and Group Health Cooperative in Seattle, Washington are examples of large staff model HMOs.

From the patient's perspective, staff model HMOs may seem restrictive. No community-based physicians can be accessed, only the HMO's staff physicians can deliver covered services to members. Some patients object to receiving care in a clinic setting. Such clinics may not be as conveniently located as other physician's offices and there may be more waiting for nonemergency services. Some patients, new to a staff model HMO, may complain at having to form a treatment relationship with a new physician since community practitioners are not involved in this model which is also called a "closed panel."

For the HMO, staff models are easiest to control of all the models with regard to practice patterns and service utilization. This is due in large part to the fact that the physicians are HMO employees and share a practice orientation compatible with the HMO's philosophy. HMO resources normally donated to utilization management may be allocated to other areas or passed along as savings to purchasers. Various economies of scale may also be obtained in such staff clinic settings. On the other hand, the salaries of such large numbers of physicians are a costly expense to HMOs and may negate other savings.

Group Models

Group model HMOs contract with large multispecialty physician groups to provide services to members. These physicians are employees or partners in the group. They share the expenses of their office or clinic operations. They are not employees of the HMO, but rather are compensated through capitation payments. These physicians usually serve non-HMO patients, or may contract with more than one HMO. This is sometimes referred to as an "independent" group model. One of the best known HMOs is the Kaiser Foundation Health Plan, which serves over 6.5 million members. It contracts with the Permanent Medical Groups for its physician services. This is said to be a "captive" group (i.e., dealing only with the one HMO's members and resembling a staff model).

Like staff model HMOs, group models give the HMO more control over practice patterns. They also limit members' choices, are "closed panels," and are open to criticisms regarding limited access and "clinic" atmospheres.

Network Models

HMOs sometimes choose to contract with several groups of physicians or independent practitioners to form a broad-based health care network. An HMO may have a panel of numerous family practice physicians, several internal medicine physicians, pediatricians, Ob-Gyns, etc. These systems are called network models. HMOs fund the physicians through capitation payments. The HMO may assist physicians in obtaining discounts from specialists, whom they must reimburse for services the network physician cannot provide. As with other models, if the network physicians provide an excessive number of procedures or make unneeded (and costly) specialist referrals, they will be at a financial loss concerning their HMO patients. Network model HMOs address some of the disadvantages of staff and group models by providing a large number of community-based physicians from which members may select for their primary health care.

INTERNAL ORGANIZATIONAL STRUCTURES

HMOs have boards of directors who have at least nominal responsibility for organizational and fiscal oversight and control. In reality, these boards may exert little influence over day-to-day operations. Boards have differing legal requirements concerning their composition and responsibilities, depending on state regulations.

The executive director or general manager is the key officer in most HMOs. This position provides day-to-day leadership and control over the HMO's operations. This is a CEO-type position which supervises the finances, Management Information System, marketing, and other functions. Individuals with educational backgrounds in business, finance, or health care administration are usually employed in these positions.

The other key position in an HMO is the medical director. This officer oversees the various medical management and utilization review components of the HMO. This is a complex and diversified position involving expertise in and knowledge of the current state of medical treatment as well as the ability to interact positively with a variety of constituencies. This may be a part-time position in small HMO operations.

Additionally, HMOs frequently have a marketing director, a financial director, and a provider relations director. Staff model HMOs may have a director for mental health/substance abuse services, since this function is provided by the HMO staff.

HMOs have departments that process claims, handle member relations, and provide utilization review. Various committees function within HMOs, often chaired by the medical director and frequently involving physicians from the HMO's panel of providers. Examples include a medical advisory committee that reviews which medical procedures should be authorized for coverage; a pharmacy committee that reviews which medications may be included in an approved formulary; a credentialing committee that reviews how new providers are selected; or a quality assurance committee that oversees the HMO's efforts to monitor the quality of care of its members. This last committee may also be the ultimate internal reviewer of member or provider complaints or grievances.

QUALITY ASSURANCE AND REGULATION

Like other American industries, HMOs and other managed care organizations have come to embrace the quality movement. This represents yet another influence of such systems of health care on the delivery of services to consumers. In years past the arbiter of quality was largely the physician, facility, or mental health provider operating in the context of the professional-patient relationship. Today most HMOs have departments staffed by professionals whose roles focus on the collection, trending, and analysis of data that is then cycled back into the HMO system to improve processes and, ultimately, care delivery. Quality assurance programs vary but common elements include reviews, audits, and studies concerning the utilization of services, consumer access to services (to primary care or specialist care), quality of services and quality benchmarking, consumer satisfaction with services, and provider credentialing. The HMO industry has become increasingly sophisticated in its ability to generate quality assurance information for the benefit of its providers, consumers, and customers. Critics of the industry say that such efforts are only in response to demands by customers and providers for better service, while defenders of the industry respond that such efforts produce services that are not only of high quality but are also cost-effective.

Quality assurance efforts by HMOs are mirrored in the managed care mental health care entities that contract with them. (See Chapter 5.) Such programs, the costs associated with them, and the burden they place upon individual practitioners may to some extent be influenced by the regulatory environment in which these businesses operate. Most area HMOs are highly regulated entities. State regulatory requirements vary, but respective departments of insurance bear degrees of oversight responsibility for the industry, as do other state-level regulatory groups. Such groups periodically audit HMOs financial, marketing, and service records and information to ensure conformity to state regulations. In staff model HMOs (as is the case with staff model mental health companies) various boards of the health professions oversee respective professional groups' practice.

The National Committee on Quality Assurance (NCQA), based in Washington, DC, is an increasingly influential non-profit organization that accredits health plans as a means of providing an evaluation of the HMO for purchasers, regulators, and consumers. NCQA's complex and ambitious accreditation standards focus on:

- Quality Improvement
- Utilization Management
- Provider Credentialing
- Member Rights and Responsibilities
- Preventive Health Services
- Medical Records

Its review of an HMO includes an extensive on-site survey by a team of physicians and administrators that may take several days and includes the review of enormous amounts of data as well as interviews of staff and providers. Its accreditation is rapidly becoming the industry's benchmark. Some states have legislated that such external reviews by independent third parties occur, while numerous multi-state employers have mandated NCQA accreditation for HMOs serving their work forces. Multi-state HMO chains such as Prudential, CIGNA, and U.S. Healthcare have responded by requiring NCQA accreditation by their HMOs. NCQA publishes its vigorous standards, which examine all functions of the HMO. These standards, which were jointly developed by employers, unions, and HMO staff, are demanding and encourage health plans to enhance their quality. The ultimate goal of this process will be not only to improve the quality of HMO services, but to better educate employers, unions, and consumers about important information needed for purchasing decisions. No comparable evaluation system exists in the traditional fee-for-service health care market. NCQA also publishes a period listing of America's HMOs and their accreditation status.

Another goal of this group is to standardize how HMOs specify, calculate, and report performance information, with the ultimate objective of giving purchasers and the consumer public easily understood "report cards" that can be used to compare health plans not just on the basis of price, but upon quality as well. A step toward this goal was taken in 1993 with the development of the Health Plan-Employer Data and Information Set or HEDIS. HEDIS includes 60 different measures that portray important comparative information about various HMOs. Such efforts will undoubtedly aid consumers in making better informed decisions about health care benefit purchases.

The Utilization Review Accreditation Commission (URAC)[4] also based in Washington, DC, was established with a focus of accrediting managed care organizations as a means of establishing consistent, fair, and effective Utilization Review (UR) processes. URAC's

---

4. Both URAC's and NCQA's addresses can be found in the Resource Section of this text.

voluntary accreditation process evaluates HMOs, PPOs, and managed care companies' UR processes against standards published by URAC. These standards have become an industry benchmark for UR processes. The standards focus on processes that cause minimal disruption to health care delivery while ensuring adequate and fair benefit denial decision appeal processes.

CURRENT TRENDS

The HMO industry continues to consolidate, while membership grows. Nationally, HMOs provided health care coverage to 19 percent of the population by 1994, according to the *Marion Managed Care Digest-HMO Edition*, 1994.[5] Five states–Massachusetts, California, Maryland, Minnesota, and Oregon–have 30 percent or more of their populations enrolled in HMOs, while another five have at least 25 percent of their citizens served through HMO health care systems. These statistics bear witness to the acceptance of HMOs by the employer community as mechanisms to provide care and contain costs. Regionally, HMOs have gained the greatest market share in the Pacific Coast area, including Arizona, in New England, and in the Mid-Atlantic region.

Most HMOs are owned by or affiliated with corporations. The corporate owners of HMOs often operate multiple HMOs in a variety of markets. Forty-six of these chains enrolled over 40 million of the 49 million HMO members in 1993. Based on 1993 enrollment the five largest HMO chains were the Blue Cross/Blue Shield system, Kaiser Foundation Health Plans, Prudential Prucare, the HMO Group, and CIGNA HealthCare.

Other trends in the HMO industry include growth in sales of the open-ended HMO option, a benefit design which offers members the choice at the point of service of using an HMO provider or

---

5. For the recent data concerning HMOs and PPOs contact the Marion Managed Care Digest which reports authoritatively about the managed care industry. Write to: Marion Merrell Dow, Inc., Managed Health Care Markets Department, 9300 Ward Parkway, Kansas City, MO, 64114 or call 1-800-3MARION.

obtaining care from a non-HMO provider utilizing out-of-network benefits. Increasingly, corporate-owned HMOs are likely to offer indemnity insurance products, PPOs, mental health carve-out arrangements, and Employee Assistance Program services, attractive options to large employers who wish to minimize the administrative burden of interacting with multiple health care service vendors. Due to competitive or regulatory pressures, nearly all HMOs offer mental health care benefits–a continuation of a trend in recent years. An indicator of more effective outpatient alternatives, the downward trend in hospital bed days per thousand members has continued in the 1990s, reaching 296 per 1,000 non-Medicare members (and excluding mental health/substance abuse bed days).

SUMMARY

HMOs are complex business structures performing the difficult tasks of both financing and delivering quality health care in a cost-effective way. While several basic systems models exist, no two HMOs are exactly alike.

After rapid growth in the 1970s and 1980s, HMO enrollment has slowed but still continues. During the 1980s, employers have increasingly accepted HMOs as a basic means of delivering health care services, while slowing the growth of health care costs. Physicians and other professionals have come to rely upon HMO affiliation as a practice maintenance strategy, while becoming increasingly adept at managing risk through capitated payment arrangements. Large corporations tend to dominate the industry, operating chains of HMOs in multiple sites while offering a range of products, which often include Managed Behavioral care services. This contraction of the number of HMOs in operation will continue in the 1990s with enrollment increases, in part due to new HMO products offering more choice to consumers. The field will likely continue to be dominated by a small number of large financial and insurance organizations that have made a commitment to the managed care field and have the resources and management expertise needed for growth and stability.

BIBLIOGRAPHY

Cigna. (1990, June). HMO enrollment at 34.7 million. *Employee Benefits News*, p. 5.

Joint Commission on Accreditation of Healthcare Organizations. (1989). *Managed Care Standards Manual*. Chicago, IL: Author.

Kongstvedt, P. R. (1989). Elements of management control structure. In P. R. Kongstvedt (Ed.), *The Managed Health Care Handbook* (pp. 19-23). Rockville, MD: Aspen Publications.

MacLeod, G. K. (1989). An overview of managed medical care. In P. R. Kongstvedt (Ed.), *The Managed Health Care Handbook* (pp. 3-10). Rockville, MD: Aspen Publications.

Marion Merrell Dow, Inc. (1994). *Marion Managed Care Digest/HMO Edition*. Kansas City, MO: (Company Publication).

Mercer, W. M., Inc. (1990). Integrated health plans: Managed care in the 90's. In *Driving Down Health Care Costs: Strategies And Solutions* (pp. 14.01-14.07). New York: Panel Publishers.

National Committee for Quality Assurance. (1994). *What is NCQA?* Washington, DC: Author

Reynolds, J. D. and Bischoff, R. N. (1991). *Health Insurance Answer Book* (3rd ed.). New York: Panel Publishers.

Utilization Review Accreditation Commission. (1994). *National Utilization Review Standards*. Washington, DC: Author

Wagnor, E. R. (1989). Types of managed care organizations. In P. R. Kongstvedt (Ed.), *The Managed Health Care Handbook* (pp. 11-18). Rockville, MD: Aspen Publications.

Chapter 3

Preferred Provider Organizations and Mental Health Point-of-Service Networks

Preferred Provider Organizations (PPOs) are entities through which insurance companies or employer groups purchase services for their subscribers or employees. PPOs are organizations, not actual providers. The providers who affiliate with a PPO may be physicians, dentists, hospitals, or nonphysician clinicians. The purchaser, on behalf of its members, negotiates discounted fee arrangements with the PPO in advance of service delivery. In exchange for this discount, employer groups or insurance companies provide incentives for clients to utilize the PPO providers. (See Figure 3-1.)

HOW PPOs ACHIEVE COST CONTAINMENT

The incentive for members to use PPO providers is achieved through benefit design. For example, the patient who chooses to use a non-PPO affiliated physician or hospital may have benefit coverage for only 70 percent of the charges versus 90 percent coverage for the PPO provider. Out-of-pocket costs to the consumer are higher when using these "out-of-network" providers or provider facilities. In this way, all medically necessary services will be covered and the consumer continues to exercise choice over which provider to use. At the same time, benefit design tends to drive service utilization toward the least costly provider (the PPO affiliate), while shifting more cost-sharing to the patient who chooses to go outside the PPO network for necessary services.

FIGURE 3-1. PPO Mechanisms

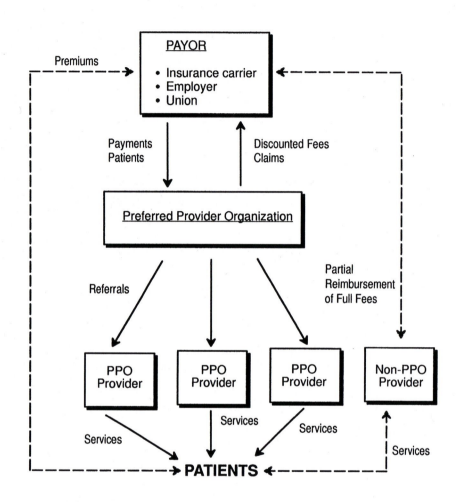

In PPO systems, benefit design drives patients to PPO providers, who have discounted their fees and agreed to utilization management procedures in return for increased patient volume. Patients may still choose non-PPO providers, but the PAYOR will reimburse a smaller share of charges, resulting in more cost-sharing by the patient.

PPO networks help to achieve further cost containment for the purchaser and consumer. This results from PPO affiliated providers having agreed to cooperate with the payor's utilization management procedures. More about this important feature in the next section of this book.

OTHER FEATURES

A variant of the PPO is the PPA, Preferred Provider Arrangement. This term implies a looser affiliation without an organization. A PPA actually refers only to a discounted fee arrangement between insurance carriers or other groups and a provider or providers. The term "PPO" refers to the organizing entity, but has become more generic over the years.

Another variant of the PPO is the Exclusive Provider Organization (EPO). In these arrangements, services are covered for reimbursement by a payor only if services are delivered by a designated provider, group of providers, or a designated facility. There is no coverage for services by out-of-network providers. Consumer choice in provider selection is severely restricted.

EPOs are utilized by employers or other payors who wish to obtain the greatest cost containment and have the least concern as to the consumer's choice. Due to their exclusive nature, EPOs can discount fees to a larger extent than most PPOs. The increased referral volume offsets the discounted fee structure. Thus EPOs can be lucrative arrangements for cost-effective providers. Like PPOs, Exclusive Provider Organizations participate in or provide other utilization management components. EPOs are more closely scrutinized for quality of service delivery since consumers cannot select an alternative provider if dissatisfied, and still retain needed coverage.

Although both are alternative health care delivery systems, PPOs differ from HMOs in important ways. HMOs take on financial risk for medical services. PPOs assume no risk, as risk remains with the union, employer, or insurance carrier. HMOs are highly regulated through federal and state statues; PPOs largely are not. Finally, HMOs are health care delivery systems. PPOs can be best described as organized brokers of health care services.

PROVIDER SELECTION

PPOs may be general, involving a range of health care providers, or they may be limited to hospitals or specialty areas such as dental, vision, or prescription services. (We will later examine mental health related PPOs or Networks.) PPOs can be organized by any of several groups, but focus on the selection of cost-effective treatment providers. Providers that have practice patterns inconsistent with this cost-effectiveness goal are still, at times, solicited for PPO membership. This is done in the hope that the utilization management functions will be able to modify such patterns. Such patterns are more easily discerned today by using Management Information Systems (MIS) to examine a provider's claim submission history.

Providers' documentation of credentials are collected and other administrative data are also maintained by the PPO. Claim submissions are sometimes audited. These steps help to assure quality for consumers and discourage fraudulent practices by providers in the PPO.

DISCUSSION AND TRENDS

PPOs have flourished in recent years as the market pursues the goals of controlling health care costs while providing consumer choice. They have become attractive options for employers seeking an entry-level managed behavioral care choice for their workforces. The financial viability of America's PPOs is difficult to ascertain: Some are subsidized by parent organizations; others operate as loss leaders, in effect; incomplete financial reporting confounds other estimations.

Corporate PPO chains will likely continue to develop in coming years. (Sixty percent of PPO members were covered through the 35 largest PPO corporations in 1989, according to the *Marion Managed Care Digest*—see Table 3-1). Another trend is toward the offering of EPO features, especially by PPOs owned by employers and HMOs. PPOs are likely to increase their offering of discounted dental care, chiropractic care, and workers compensation as well as mental health services in the future. PPOs are more likely to focus on the recruitment of cost-effective providers as they become

TABLE 3-1. Thirty-Five Largest PPO Chains in 1989

CORPORATE NAME/HEADQUARTERS	No. of Plans	Covered Employees
Blue Cross and Blue Shield Assn./Chicago, IL	56	6,736,816
Columbia American Corp./Phoenix, AZ	1	1,449,800
Health Care Compare Corp./Downers Grove, IL	1	900,000
Metropolitan Life Insurance Co./Westport, CT	59	754,959
Occupational-Urgent Care/Sacramento, CA	1	720,000
San Diego Comm. HC Alliance/San Diego, CA	1	625,000
Beech Street PPO/Irvine, CA	1	592,878
Private HealthCare Systems Ltd./Lexington, MA	7	576,000
Prudential Insurance Co./Roseland, NJ	2	535,149
Aetna Life & Casualty Ins. Co./Hartford, CT	4	519,049
Travelers Insurance/Hartford, CT	51	461,235
Amer. General Group Ins. Corp./Dallas, TX	3	389,032
Admar Corp./Orange, CA	7	365,379
Preferred Health Network Inc./Monterey, CA	2	355,496
Transport Life Insurance Co./Fort Worth, TX	1	283,000
August Intl. Corp./Orange, CA	1	260,000
Pacific Health Alliance/San Mateo, CA	1	226,118
PPO Alliance/Irvine, CA	1	210,000
Equicor-Equitable HCA Corp./Nashville, TN	28	190,011
Metrocare National Inc./Portland, OR	7	164,995
CIGNA-Connecticut General/Bloomfield, CT	31	163,000
The Hartford/Hartford, CT	3	156,286
Capp Care Inc./Fountain Valley, CA	90	150,000
Health Risk Management/Minneapolis, MN	1	143,500
Mass. Mutual Life Ins. Co./Springfield, MA	27	141,629
Intergroup Services Corp./Radnor, PA	1	130,000
Interplan Corp./Stockton, CA	1	120,000
Sisters of Providence/Seattle, WA	2	116,955
General American Life Ins. Co./St. Louis, MO	1	108,082
Medical Control Acquisition Corp./Dallas, TX	1	103,000
Self-Labor Trust Fund/Newark, NJ	1	100,000
Humana Health Care Plans/Louisville, KY	20	97,005
New York Life Insurance Co./New York, NY	1	80,000
United Northwest Services/Spokane, WA	1	75,000
John Hancock/Boston, MA	5	71,362
TOTAL	**421**	**18,070,736**

Source: *Marion Merrell Dow Managed Care Digest/PPO Edition*, 1990, p. 8.

increasingly aware of practice patterns through better management information systems and technologies. Owners of PPOs will likely confront practitioner opposition to exclusion from networks and will also continue to oppose increased regulation of the industry.

POINT-OF-SERVICE NETWORKS

An emerging trend in employer-sponsored health care benefits is a variant of the PPO, the Point-of-Service (POS) network. According to some, POS networks unite the best features of traditional indemnity insurance with the HMO philosophy. POS networks offer a choice to their members who may, *at the point of service,* choose to utilize a network provider or a non-network provider. By choosing the network provider the consumer enjoys richer benefits, lower out-of-pocket expenses, and reduced paperwork such as completing claim forms. The health care plan still provides coverage for non-network services, but with increased cost-sharing, reduced benefits, etc. Many large employers have come to view these POS network plans as a palatable first step into the managed care real— one that preserves choice and yet through cost-sharing helps employees become more aware of the actual cost of health care. Table 3-2 illustrates a sample benefit summary associated with a POS network.

Though not affording absolute reductions in health care costs to employers, POS networks are often able to slow rising costs and help employers better predict costs. This is due to the inherent qualities of a coordinated network of providers working together to manage patient care. Case management helps to reduce the duplication of services and discounted fee arrangements negotiated by the POS managers with network providers also help to reduce cost increases to purchasers. Quality management programs are used to evaluate outcomes and monitor the care delivered.

Employers increasingly view the delivery of quality mental health services to their workforces as an important but costly endeavor. Noting that as few as five percent of their employees claims (those with mental health or substance abuse diagnoses) often account for as much as 25 percent of the company's health care expenditures, large self-insured employers are turning to this variant of the POS

TABLE 3-2. Sample POS Network Benefits: Medical/Surgical

In-Network Benefits	Out-of-Network Benefits
• Most services covered 100% after small co-payment	• Most services covered at 80% level
• No deductible	• Deductible = $300 for an individual, $600 for a family per year
• Out of pocket maximums $500/$1,000	• Out of pocket maximums $3,000/$6,000
• Preventive services available	• No preventative service available
• No claims forms to file	• Participant must file claims forms
• Pre-certification is automatic, i.e., provided by the network and is transparent to the participant	• Participant is responsible for contacting pre-certification entity

network as a means of delivering mental health services to their workforces. Managed Behavioral Care firms, eager to expand their market beyond HMOs, have quickly responded by organizing and managing networks of mental health and substance abuse providers and facilities to serve the "employer market."

MBC network managers provide case management, utilization reviews, and other services discussed elsewhere in this book, that help to control costs and ensure quality care. These networks may be offered in conjunction with employer-sponsored Employee Assistance Programs, which are sometimes also delivered by the MBC firm. Some employers design such services to function as the assessment entity while the network of mental health providers offer treatment services. Network managers screen, accredit, train, and monitor the performance of network-affiliated providers.

For consumers, incentives are structured into these benefit designs that motivate them to utilize network providers. As with POS networks, features such as enriched benefits, reduced out-of-pocket expenses, and little or no paperwork achieve this end. Many mental health provider network benefit plans provide for coverage even if the employee chooses to select a non-network provider for care. (See Table 3-3.)

These systems also offer convenience, since the employee need only dial a toll-free telephone number to access either emergency or routine care through the network. Eligibility for coverage of needed mental health services may be accomplished quickly at this juncture. The MBC staff then monitor and manage both the financial (i.e., paying the provider's claims or bills) and clinical resources needed to address the patient's needs. In mature, smoothly functioning networks, activities such as concurrent reviews are conducted on a collegial basis between the clinicians who manage the network and the clinicians who provide the care. In new or overly inclusive networks, this may not be the case however. In these scenarios, providers, seeking referrals, may join a network only to find that

TABLE 3-3. Sample POS Network Benefits: Mental/Substance Abuse

	In-Network	Out-of-Network
Deductible	$0	$300/600
Out-of-Pocket Maximums	$500/1,000	$3,000/6,000
Lifetime Maximums	$500,000	$50,000
Hospital Confinement Limits	None (Length of care is based on medical necessity)	30 day/year 2 substance abuse confinements per lifetime
Inpatient Coverage per Admission	100% after $100	80% after the deductible
Outpatient Coverage per Office Visit	100% after $10 100% after $5 (group therapy)	50% after the deductible

they do not have the skills, clinical orientation, or efficiency in practice to be a successful network provider in a MBC system. This may lead to disagreements and complaints and even the involvement of the patient in the dispute. (Refer to Chapter 5 for a full discussion of MBC core functions.)

These mental health provider networks, developed to serve widespread employee populations along with managed care systems serving growing HMO populations, represent the evolving trend in the mental health care delivery system in the 1990s. As their prevalence increases the implications for mental health clinicians and facilities are enlarged. A thorough understanding of the clinical and administrative dynamics and processes of these MBC systems is essential for professionals serving America's mental health needs.

ANY WILLING PROVIDER STATUTES

Recent legislative developments that impacted PPO products, whether medical/surgical or mental health, are amendments or subsections of state laws that govern PPOs commonly referred to as Any Willing Provider statutes. These statutes have been cited by professionals in the health care field as the basis for entry into PPO networks. Essentially they mandate that any willing, qualified facility, physician, or other practitioner who will accept the discounted fee-for-service arrangement inherent in PPO systems must be included as a preferred provider. In states that specifically include licensed mental health professionals, such providers have successfully used the statute as a basis for inclusion in mental health PPO networks.

The overall effect of such statutes has been to modify the character of Preferred Provider Organizations, broadening the number of providers eligible for reimbursement for services offered to PPO members and, according to the insurance industry, increase the cost of services to consumers since the expense of credentialing additional providers inflates the price of the product. That mental health professionals have used these statutes to gain entry to mental health PPOs–in effect to discount their fees in return for exposure to prospective PPO clients—is testimony to the influence of managed care systems in today's mental health care market.

BIBLIOGRAPHY

Cigna. (1990, November). Preserving products attractive to customers. *Managing Integration,* pp. 1-3.

Marion Merrell Dow, Inc. (1990). *Marion Managed Care Digest-PPO Edition.* Kansas City, MO: Author.

Reynolds, J. D. and Bischoff, R. N. (1991). *Health Insurance Answer Book* (3rd ed.). New York: Panel Publishers.

Wagnor, E. R. (1989). Types of managed health care organizations. In P. R. Kongstvedt (Ed.), *The Managed Health Care Handbook,* (pp. 11-18). Rockville, MD: Aspen Publishers.

Chapter 4

Employee Assistance Programs and Managed Care

Employee Assistance Program (EAP) refers to employer-sponsored counseling and intervention services aimed at assisting employees with substance abuse, mental health, legal, financial, family, or other problems that impact worker productivity or safety. Estimates vary, but there may be well over twenty thousand separate EAPs today, with the majority provided by vendor organizations. Increasingly, an EAP product has become a mainstay of MBC companies, offered along side or integrated with Point-of-Service products for the employer market and exclusive provider products for the HMO market. Some employers have structured their EAP services as a mandatory access point to mental health and substance abuse treatment services. Others have purchased EAP designs that feature short-term counseling aspects, described later in this chapter.

Thousands of counseling professionals are employed directly or indirectly in the EAP field. Some practice on-site at employer locations providing counseling, consultation, and training services. Others are EAP professionals who are employed for managed care vendor companies. Still others are members of group practices who provide EAP services as a part of their referral relationship with managed care companies who offer EAP products to employers. A nationally recognized credential, the Certified Employee Assistance Professional (CEAP) is offered to counseling professionals interested in demonstrating their knowledge and expertise in the EAP field by the EAP Association, a group based in Arlington, Virginia. This group also publishes a code of professional conduct for professionals in the EAP field and organizes annual continuing professional education conferences.

Despite some calls from within the EAP field, states have been reluctant to establish the machinery to license or otherwise regulate the practice of therapists who provide EAP services. Many such professionals drawn from the fields of clinical social work, clinical counseling, or psychology, are licensed in their respective discipline. (See EAP Staffing section of this chapter.)

External Programs is a generic term referring to various programs developed and sold by Managed Care companies to employers, groups of employers, unions, or associations. Counseling services may be provided to employees on site or in off-site counseling settings. Most programs today are of their type. Managed care companies may offer this service through salaried staff or through contractual arrangements with affiliated providers who have EAP skills and expertise.

Historically, EAPs have had dual purposes: aiding the individual to overcome personal problems that affect workplace performance and assisting the employer to have a healthier, more productive labor force. Many employers are adding another dimension to their EAPs' tasks, that of helping to manage mental health care benefits. This challenge offers EAPs new opportunities as well as threats. It promises to transform traditional EAPs.

"This is a crucial time for the EAP field," says Dr. Dale Masi, president of Masi Research Consultants in Washington, DC and a professor of social work at the University of Maryland (Personal communication, 1990). Masi, one of the pioneers in the EAP work field, believes these programs are in danger of being swept away as MBC systems take over many functions once associated with EAPs. "It's up to EAPs themselves to respond to this challenge and find their future identity," Masi says. She believes this will involve EAP professionals in more managed care functions.

EAPs have always had as part of their function the assessment (role induction and diagnosis) of MH/SA problems and referral (determination of the most appropriate treatment resource). EAPs have also provided monitoring and follow-up (case management) for their clients' progress. These are key managed care tasks as well, although many in the EAP field have been slow to recognize the similarity to MBC systems. Many EAP professionals have been averse to wearing any sort of managed care label, and instead have opposed and resisted managed care technology, viewing managed care as an intrusion and an impediment.

Understanding that many EAP tasks are managed care functions is important. A core philosophy in the managed care arena is that an accurate diagnosis leads to proper treatment. An independent EAP (or Managed Care) assessor who is not affiliated with any treatment facility or group may eliminate any economic incentive to refer to a particular provider or institution. Referral to an appropriate level of care may be based solely on clinical presentation. Contrast this with some facilities which, for example, provide "free assessments" but who usually refer assessed patients to their own services. These assessments then become a community relations vehicle and a means of role induction for the prospective patient.

Another example of economic incentives biasing accurate assessment of patient needs is the EAP marketed by some hospitals. While offered at a substantial discount, many employers have found they are not such a bargain after all, since these EAP counselors may inappropriately refer employees to their hospital's inpatient setting when the patient could have been equally well served on an outpatient basis. Thus an accurate diagnosis established by EAP professionals, as within managed care systems, can lead to patient referral to an appropriate level of care and treatment setting, while avoiding referrals based on economic incentives.

Finally, properly qualified EAP staff may provide the case management services offered by MBC specialty programs. These case managers both monitor the clinical services provided and authorize benefits to pay for the cost of services.

The evolution of MBC systems has witnessed many of these EAP related functions, as well as others assumed by the staff of the MBC organization or by other providers. Employers are reexamining what their EAPs are achieving, at what cost, and how they can be integrated with MBC functions or organizations. Some think that EAP programs and staff will fail to respond to MBC and will largely disappear as a separate entity in the coming years, unless they integrate managed care philosophies and functions. How they can achieve this while retaining their valuable qualities of service and advocacy in the business environment of the 1990s represents EAP's greatest challenge.

BACKGROUND AND DEVELOPMENT

EAPs have their origin in early twentieth century employer-sponsored counseling services. Staffed with nonprofessionals, these early efforts were inspired by the Temperance movement. They aimed at helping employees with alcohol abuse and its resulting family problems. The first such program was established in 1917 by Macy's Department Store in New York City. The field of occupational social work traces its origin to these early efforts by employers to intervene with troubled workers. Such programs were boosted by the Alcoholics Anonymous movement in the 1930s and particularly by World War II. During the War, worker productivity and safety were important to national security and more employers instituted these programs. They were then called Occupational Alcoholism Programs (OAPs), a term that persisted into the 1970s. One of the most prominent was that of Kaiser Shipbuilding, one of the companies owned by industrialist Henry Kaiser, the pioneer of Health Maintenance Organizations. Allis-Chalmers, Consolidated Edison, Illinois Bell, and Kodak also established these programs. Union involvement in EAPs dates to this era. After the War, interest declined and during the prosperous 1950s fewer than fifty programs functioned nationwide.

The EAP movement became reenergized in the late 1970s with America's new recognition that substance abuse and psychiatric problems were widespread and were creating much human suffering as well as affecting our productivity and national competitiveness. OAPs changed into EAPs, the name change reflecting the new "broad brush" approach. Their focus expanded to include identifying and assisting workers with problems other than alcohol abuse. The military recognized the need for such services in the 1970s as well, and the U.S. Navy's EAP became a prototype. America's heightened consciousness of substance abuse problems and the enactment of the Drug Free Workplace Act in the late 1980s added further momentum to EAP development.

Ironically EAPs did not take advantage of an opportunity in the 1980s to supplant the managed care industry. Had the EAP field better focused its energy and resources on the management of both the clinical and financial resources needed for the care of employees, the managed care industry may not have mushroomed in the late 1980s. Inflexible views about the role of the EAP, lack of identity as a profession, inadequate training, and other issues prevented the EAP community from assuming the role played by managed care systems. In fact, some employers came to question whether or not their EAPs' referral patterns were actually escalating health care costs needlessly.

Today there are well over twenty thousand EAPs, large and small, most of which have been implemented in the last ten years. Most all the Fortune 500 companies have such programs, as do many governmental bodies, some unions, and large numbers of small to medium-sized employers.

HOW EAPs WORK

The central task of an EAP is the early detection, assessment, and amelioration of worker problems that affect productivity. Toward this goal, EAPs have traditionally had the following basic components, which are also described in Figure 4-1.

- *Consultation/Policy Development.* EAP staff are technical support to human relations and other managers in developing policies concerning substance use/abuse, as well as other worker behavioral problems and issues.
- *Training.* EAPs provide information to front line supervisors, managers, and union personnel about how to identity, document, and refer troubled workers to the EAP.
- *Prevention and Awareness Activities.* EAPs aim to publicize their services to employees, thereby attracting voluntary referrals, or helping employees prevent problems.
- *Assessment and Referral.* EAP staff interview troubled employees and refer them to treatment or other resources. They provide follow-up monitoring of the case until the problem is resolved. This may be coordinated with the company's supervisors or managers.
- *Statistical Reporting.* EAPs collect and report various aggregate data to the employer about the utilization of services.

Referrals to EAP counselors may be voluntary, that is, initiated by the worker or dependent without any coercion from the company.

FIGURE 4-1. Traditional Components of EAPs

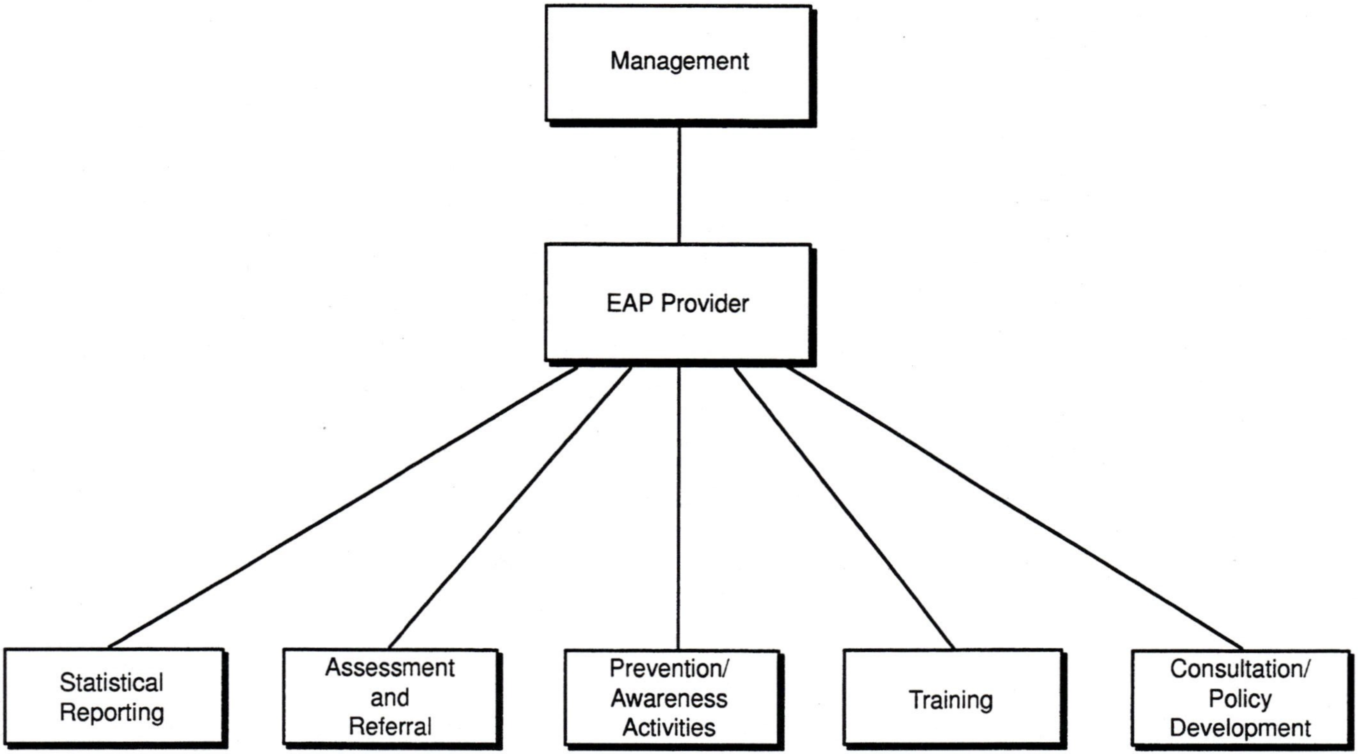

Alternatively, a supervisor may identify a deficit in work performance and suggest or mandate EAP use as a means of addressing the job performance difficulty. Positive results from drug screens may also result in mandatory EAP referrals. These cases, called supervisory or mandatory referrals, involve job jeopardy and its obvious legal ramifications. They require close coordination between EAP staff, the employer, and treatment resources. Confidentiality is stressed in either case, and information reported to supervisors is limited to essentials and provided within the normal bounds of disclosure processes. Figures 4-2 and 4-3 show the client flow in EAPs.

For our discussion, the key aspect of traditional EAP services is that EAP staff assess when and what type of treatment service is needed and select an appropriate treatment resource or provider.

BASIC DELIVERY SYSTEMS

The above EAP functions can be carried out in one of several delivery systems. Here are some of the most common ones.

Consortium

Several employers join together to develop a common EAP entity for their respective employees. Costs are shared. This arrangement often makes EAP services available to small employee groups that otherwise would not have such a program. Industrial or office parks are typical settings for consortiums. EAP staff are directly or indirectly employees of the consortium.

Network

Employers utilize a centralized EAP staff, which arranges training, consultation, and local assessment and referral services through a network of contractors or "affiliates." Access to initial telephonic screening is provided by 800 numbers prior to referral for further assessment. This is a type of external program. Employers with widely dispersed employee populations often utilize such models. These programs are sometimes criticized as impersonal or detached due to a perception of overreliance on telephonic screening and intake services.

FIGURE 4-2. Voluntary Referral Flow Chart

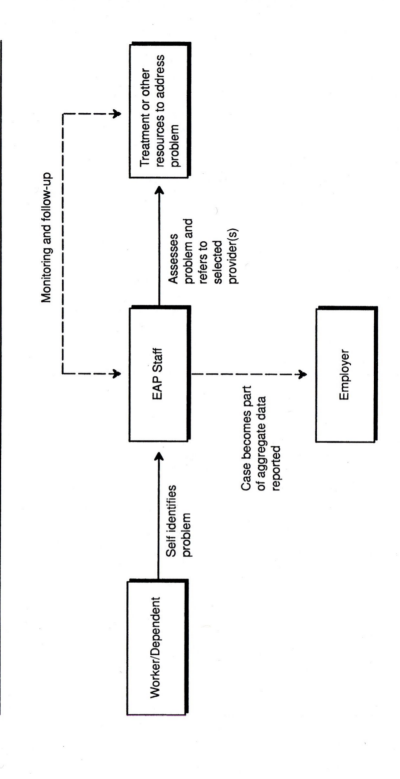

FIGURE 4-3. Supervisory or Mandatory Referral Flow Chart

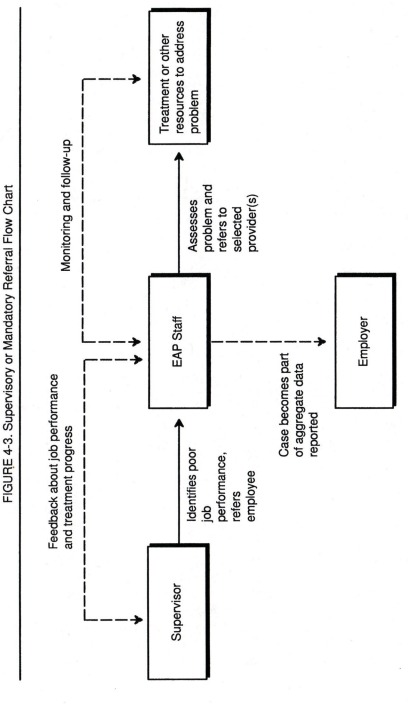

Monitoring and follow-up

Treatment or other resources to address problem

Assesses problem and refers to selected provider(s)

EAP Staff

Feedback about job performance and treatment progress

Identifies poor job performance, refers employee

Case becomes part of aggregate data reported

Employer

Supervisor

In-House or Internal Program

Employers hire EAP staff that usually function out of the company's medical department. In essence, the company "builds" its own program, usually providing assessment and referral services on site. Staff are extremely familiar with the company and its workforce. These programs must work to overcome the negative impact on utilization frequently brought about by worker distrust based on perceptions that the staff are too closely associated with company management. (Unions may "build" similar programs for their members in one or more workplaces and face analogous distrust by management.)

External Programs

A generic term referring to various programs developed by EAP firms and sold to companies or other employers. Services may be provided on or off the work site. Most programs today are of this type.

EAP STAFFING

A general trend in the field has been one of increasing professionalization. With its alcoholism-specific focus, the early OAPs and EAPs often utilized recovering employees, transferred from their original positions to work in or help develop the service. These individuals, trained in counseling essentials, were basically peer counselors—employees who had achieved sobriety, were involved in the self-help community, and could easily relate to those likely to use the EAP.

With the advent of broad-brush EAPs in the 1970s and 1980s, staffing needs shifted. Individuals with broader counseling and assessment skills were required. Clinical social work, with its history of interest in services delivered in occupational settings, has been heavily drawn upon for EAP staffing needs. Psychologists, substance abuse counselors, and psychiatric nurses are also well-represented in EAP positions. Superior salaries and good working conditions have made EAP staff positions attractive to many (Bennet, Blum, and Roman, 1989). The number of professionals employed directly or indirectly in the field is not known, but may range into the tens of thousands.

In the late 1980s, the Employee Assistance Professionals Association (formerly ALMACA), which represents several thousand members, initiated the Certified Employee Assistance Professional (CEAP) credential. This credential does not have an educational standard, but instead it is awarded to individuals with EAP work experience who pass a competency-based test. Presently there are over 2500 holders of the CEAP credential.

There are no professional degree programs in "EAP." Numerous workshops and seminars offer EAP training and CEU credits. The School of Social Work at the University of Maryland offers a specialization EAP work for its MSW students. But it is unlikely that academia will soon start formal degree programs in this field. According to Dale Masi, a social worker who founded the University of Maryland's EAP specialization tract, many schools are waiting to see what the future holds for EAP, particularly whether or not its functions will be integrated into managed care systems, causing EAP to be lost as a potential field of study in and of itself.

DO EAPs CREATE A RETURN ON INVESTMENT?

There has always been discussion about the extent of savings to employers achieved through their EAPs. Cost savings can be measured by evaluating data from several areas. Some areas lend themselves to quantification much more easily than others, while changes in some categories of data cannot be easily attributed to effective EAPs.

Data pertaining to medical claims costs (employee/family) and turnover rate due to MH/SA problems are easy to quantify and relate to EAP effectiveness. This is not the case, however, for data pertaining to overall workforce turnover, absenteeism, sick days, workforce morale, grievances, and on-the-job accidents.

Some internal EAPs have produced excellent studies of their cost savings to employers. McDonnell Douglas Corporation, disappointed with its EAP's performance, restructured the program in 1985. It asked its consulting firm, Alexander and Alexander, to evaluate the financial offset of the revitalized program. Over a four year study period, Alexander and Alexander reported substantial savings through the EAP, as much as a 35 percent reduction in medical claims costs (McDonnell Douglas Corporation Employee Assistance Program Financial Offset Study 1985-1988).

Most employers and EAP providers have not produced studies such as this. However there is general agreement among employers that EAPs are valuable tools that serve many purposes. Many employers feel EAPs help avoid the unnecessary litigation of unlawful discharge suits brought about by dissatisfied former employees, terminated for job difficulties related to personal problems. Further, EAPs are increasingly perceived as yet another important mechanism available to management to develop and maintain a healthy workforce. They are also viewed as a key employee benefit.

FUTURE TRENDS

Like all other aspects of clinical practice, the development of managed care organizations presents both challenges and opportunities to EAPs. It is likely that EAPs will continue their evolutionary course, incorporating new and expanding upon existing managed care functions. An alternative scenario is that MBC will incorporate EAP functions into existing managed care technologies and systems, effectively eliminating the EAP field as an independent and separate entity.

How have professionals within the EAP field responded to MBC? Most have hardly welcomed it. Many EAP professionals, long accustomed to making decisions about which treatment resources to utilize, find this role negated or preempted by MBC and have reacted angrily against managed care systems, often under the rubric of client advocacy. Many have expressed valid concerns about the operations and philosophy of some MBC systems. Others have encouraged colleagues to take up the mantle of managed care and extend their scope of practice into this new practice area.

For example, Lee Wenzel, a consultant for Managed Care Systems in Eden Prairie, Minnesota, encourages EAP professionals to take an aggressive course in building on their case management expertise and expanding the role into both clinical and financial management of services. Wenzel also believes EAPs can take over administrative duties provided by MBC or Third-Party Payors (TPAs). These tasks include eligibility (for benefits) determination, verification of diagnosis, and even claims adjudication and payment. Wenzel states that "EAPs are still one of the best examples of managed care, if only we knew it and believed it. . . . We need to cherish our heritage and grow from it" (Wenzel, 1990).

These views have been recently echoed by the field's professional organization, EAPA (see Dolan, "Development of MBC Services is an EAP's Best Bet for Longevity," July, 1990, *EAPA Exchange*). While a major focus of this organization in the last decade has been the ongoing task of legitimization and professionalization of the field, it has addressed the MBC issue in ways similar to other professional associations. Task forces have been formed to study the matter. Continuing education activities have been offered on the topic. Some groups have even made efforts to develop treatment standards that would guide referral and level of care decisions. Undoubtedly MBC will continue to be an issue vital to EAPA.

Meanwhile, how are employers reassessing their EAPs and the need for them? Table 4-1 is a list of questions that benefit managers, human resource staff, benefit consultants, and others may find useful concerning how to evaluate the capacity of EAPs to integrate MBC functions.

TABLE 4-1. Questions for Benefit Managers, Benefit Consultants, and EAP Administrators to Consider Concerning Adding MBC Components to EAPs

---

Concerning Clinical Service Delivery

- What clinical services are presently being delivered through the EAP?
- How does the organization wish to expand clinical services?
- What are the costs associated with expanded services, i.e., staffing, offices, etc.?
- Which services should be added? Extended Treatment Component? Concurrent Review? Precertification? A Provider Network? After Hours Crisis Intervention?

Concerning Staff and Program

- What are the staff's credentials and training?
- Can existing staff perform increased clinical services?
- Is more training needed for EAP staff? At what cost?
- Will EAP staff need more clinical supervision with additional clinical duties? At what cost?
- Does the program provide 24-hour access?
- How can its information system accommodate added functions?
- Can the program function as a TPA?
- What is the EAP staff's level of sophistication concerning managed care technology?

- Can the staff provide meaningful consultation to the organization about MBC technology and implementation?

Concerning the Referral Network

- How formalized is the EAP's referral network?
- Are discounted fee arrangements involved?
- Is the existing network cooperative with utilization management procedures?

Regarding Referral Patterns

- What is the referral pattern of the EAP?
  −use of outpatient resources?
  −use of inpatient resources?
- Is inpatient care being overutilized by the EAP? If so, why?
- Does the staff seem to overutilize one particular provider or institution? Why?
- Does the EAP staff accept renumeration from referral resources or individuals?

Regarding Staff

- What is the level of training of existing staff?
- Are existing staff qualified and credentialed to treatment services?
- Would additional professional supervision be required if staff perform treatment services?

General

- Has the EAP been evaluated by an independent third party with appropriate resources and sophistication concerning both EAP and MBC systems?
- Does the organization presently understand the MH/SA benefit utilization and claims costs?
- Can benefits be redesigned to support an EAP with managed care aspects?
- There is general agreement that EAPs are important components of the overall benefit/human resource mix and that they save money. Can the existing EAP be retooled and redesigned to include MBC functions, thus increasing savings, eliminating duplications, and improving client service?

EAP RETOOLING

With the dwindling skilled workforce in the 1990s, employers have increasingly turned to Employee Assistance Professionals for input about and management of various employer-sponsored services aimed at promoting and maintaining a healthy, stable workforce. EAP staff have found themselves developing, providing, or consulting about the purchasing of child care, elder care, health promotion, worker education, and legal assistance services. These programs and functions may become customary components of future EAP models of service delivery. But employers will also look to EAPs for help in meeting the twin goals of providing for their employees' mental and emotional health needs while containing or restraining the rising cost associated with providing these treatment services.

Employee Assistance Professionals have responded by developing an EAP service featuring a short-term counseling component. One to five or one to eight visit models are common in this type of EAP model. The length of the treatment benefit is based on current awareness that mental health therapy is inherently brief and that modern treatment approaches stress time-sensitive interventions and rapid problem resolution. Only cases requiring extensive treatment (such as medication, structural outpatient substance abuse programs), specialized services, or inpatient stabilization would be referred to outside providers or facilities. Short-term counseling EAP models challenge practitioners to become skilled in solution-oriented therapy and in crisis intervention skills.

Employee Assistance Programs offering expanded managed care functions, all through one vendor, are of interest to many employers. These EAPs provide easy access to employees, referral to a credentialed, contracted, provider network, and the availability of utilization management specialists.

The short-term counseling model EAP is attractive to employees who can receive this counseling at no out-of-pocket expense. They can continue with their initial counselor avoiding a disruptive referral to a new therapist. They will view this service as another logical step in the evolving process whereby the institution of the "workplace" facilitates access for its valuable employees to diverse employer-sponsored health, educational, and social services—once the domain of other institutions in American life.

To the employer, this model offers the flexibility of structuring these important counseling sessions along the lines it desires concerning sites and locations. The counselors provide the therapy work for the employer, in contrast to private practitioners over whose practice orientations employers have much less control. Instead, these counselors will work toward returning the employee to his or her normal level of functioning as soon as possible, having no incentive to "overtreat" or to overutilize costly inpatient resources. Importantly, employers using this short-term counseling model EAP will be able to reduce expensive health care benefits, aware that there will be no loss of service availability to employees who will access mental health services through their EAP counselors. Employers who will utilize this model EAP must be careful to ensure adequate levels of staff training, clinical supervision, and psychiatrist involvement so as to avoid shortcomings in client care. Employers should evaluate the treatment outcomes achieved by their staff and closely monitor client satisfaction.

To EAP professionals, this model represents an opportunity to expand their traditional professional role, to the betterment of both the employee and the employer. EAP staff utilizing this model must become skilled in the "brief" or solution-focused therapy techniques.[1] They must also look to researchers to inform them as to which conditions are most amenable to treatment within the confines of the program and to answer other questions related to client service and treatment outcomes.

Figure 4-4 depicts a typical managed care company's product line, indicating how EAP services may stand alone or be integrated into other managed care facilities.

Table 4-2 describes many of the needs and advantages employer customers have in relation to EAPs and their integration with managed care functions. Employers are often attracted to the simplicity of using only one vendor to provide both EAP and managed care services, thus reducing administrative burdens.

---

1. Most courses of therapy in the United States are delivered in a few sessions. Developments in the area of time-sensitive therapies will help counselors achieve even more rapid results. See Pekarik, G. and Wierzbicki, M. "The Relationship Between Clients' Expected and Actual Treatment Duration." *Psychotherapy*, Vol. 23, No. 4, 1986, pp. 532-534; Koss, M. P. "Length of psychotherapy for clients seen in private practice." *Journal of Consulting and Clinical Psychology*, Vol. 47, 1979, pp. 210-212; and NIMH, "Provisional data on federally funded community mental health centers, 1978-79." Report prepared by the Survey and Reports Branch, Division of Biometry and Epidemiology, Washington, DC: U.S. Government Printing Office.

FIGURE 4-4

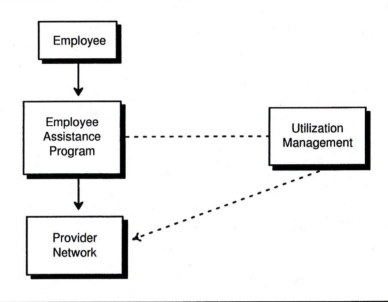

TABLE 4-2. Traditional EAP Model Contrasted with Enhanced EAPs with MBC Components

A). **Traditional EAP Model**

Direct Client Services

a. Self/Supervisor identify client
b. EAP staff assess client
   (1-3 visits)
c. EAP staff refers client for
   treatment to informal network
d. EAP Staff provided follow-up and
   monitoring of case; coordinates
   with supervisor as needed
e. Case Closure

Indirect Services

a. Policy Development
b. Consultation Statistical
   Reporting
c. Training

B). <u>Enhanced EAP - Model One</u>, A Managed Care EAP with a Network

<u>Direct Client Services</u>   <u>Indirect Services</u>

a. Self/Supervisor/Others identify
   client
b. EAP staff verify eligibility
c. EAP staff assess client
d. EAP staff educate client
   about benefits
e. EAP staff refer to a Participating
   Network Provider (formal
   arrangement with provider may
   include acceptance of discounted
   fees)
f. Benefit Design incents clients to use
   network provider. Out-of-network
   providers selection is still a covered
   benefit. Incentives to the client to use
   in-network providers may include
   —lower or no copayment
   —no claim forms to complete
   —richer benefits with in-network
     provider
   —broader selection of providers
g. EAP staff provide follow-up and
   monitoring, coordination with
   supervisor if needed
h. Case closure

a. Policy Development

b. Consultation/Statistical Reporting
c. Training
d. Awareness Activities

C). <u>Enhanced EAP - Model Two</u>, A Managed Care EAP with an Extended Treatment Component, Plus Network

<u>Direct Client Services</u>   <u>Indirect Services</u>

a. Self/Supervisor/Others identify
   client
b. EAP staff verify eligibility
c. EAP staff assess client
d. EAP staff educate client
   about benefits

a. Policy Development

b. Consultation/Statistical Reporting
c. Training
d. Awareness Activities

e. EAP Staff Clinicians Provide Direct Treatment Services to an eight-visit limit. If the need exists for further services after the eighth visit, the client is referred into the Network.*

f. Benefit Design encourages the client to use the EAP clinician, i.e., at no cost to the employee as these services have been pre-paid by the employer.

* This model is in part based on data indicating that most episodes of psychotherapy or counseling provided by recognized practitioners in the United States is of a short-term nature and that short-term counseling is preferred by most individuals. For example, studies have shown that over 70% of consumers expect therapy to last ten or less visits, while the modal number of visits to therapists in the U.S.A. is one. Studies show that close to half of private practice patients are seen four times or less and nearly 3/4 terminate by the tenth visit. This EAP Model provides counseling services at no cost to the client, in durations that most consumers seem to want, as well as the duration that office-based practitioners can provide efficaciously to most clients. (See: National Institute of Mental Health. [1981]. Provisional data on federally funded community mental health centers, 1978-1979. Report prepared by the Survey and Reports Branch, Division of Biometry and Epidemiology. Washington, DC: U.S. Government Printing Office; Pekarik, G. [1983]. Follow-up adjustment of outpatients dropouts. American Journal of Orthopsychiatry, 23, 532-534; and Taube, C.A., Burnes, B.J., and Kessler, L. (1984). Patients of psychiatrists and psychologists in office-based practice: 1980. American Psychologist, 39, 1435-1447.)

D). **Enhanced EAP - Model Two**, A Managed Care EAP with Concurrent Review Functions

Direct Client Services

a. Self/Supervisor/other identity
b. EAP staff verifies eligibility
c. EAP staff assess client
d. All clients must be assessed by EAP staff in order to access benefits
e. EAP staff educated client about benefits

Indirect Services

a. Policy Development
b. Consultation/Statistical Reporting
c. Training
d. Awareness Activities

  f. EAP staff refer client to
   in-network provider. This is a
   formal provider network. (Client
   may opt for out-of-network
   provider with inherent
   disincentives.)
  g. EAP staff authorize treatment–
   forwards authorization to
   provider and claims payment
   function.
  h. EAP staff pre-certify admissions
   on a 24-hour basis.
  i. EAP staff provide concurrent
   review of hospital admissions
   and of outpatient care.
  j. Benefit Design encourages the
   client to use the EAP Network
   Provider.
  k. Claims function pays providers
   based on EAP authorization.
   (Out-of-Network benefits claims
   payment may be made through
   this operation as well.)
  l. EAP staff monitor treatment,
   provide follow-up, coordinate
   with supervisor, if needed.
  m. Case closure.

BIBLIOGRAPHY

Beiheh, J. K. and Earle, R. H. (1990). *Successful Private Practice in the 1990s.* New York: Brunner/Mazel Publishers.

Bennet, N., Blum, T., and Roman, P. (1989, March). EAP salary data: Selected results from a national survey. *ALMACAN,* pp. 34-36.

Bureau of National Affairs, Inc. (1987). *EAP: Benefits, Problems, and Prospects.* Rockville, MD: Author.

Employee Assistance Professional Association. (1990, October). Standards for employee assistance programs. *EAPA Exchange,* [Special section], pp. B-E.

Hickox, R. F. (1990, August). At McDonnell Douglas . . . EAP does it again. *Employee Benefit News,* p. 1, 48-49.

Masi, D. (1990, November). Personal Communication.

McDonnell Douglas Corporation Employee Assistance Program Financial Offset

Study 1985-1988. D. C. Smith, Director, EAP, McDonnell Douglas Corporation, Personal Communication, Sept. 1990.

Nye, S. G. (1990). *Employee Assistance Law Answer Book.* New York: Panel Publishers.

Smollen, E. (1990, November). Certification update. *Employee Assistance,* pp. 35-36.

Staff. (1989, August). McDonnell Douglas Corporation's EAP produces hard data. *ALMACAN,* pp. 18-26.

Walker, P. L. (1990, August). EAP education. *Employee Assistance,* pp. 28-30.

Wenzel, L. (1990, July). Let's take credit for being the good case managers that we are. *EAPA Exchange,* p. 16.

Wrich, J. T. (1980). *The Employee Assistance Program.* Center City, MN: Hazelden.

Chapter 5

Managed Behavioral Care Systems

In recent years the technologies used in the alternative health care delivery systems described earlier have made their impact on mental health and substance abuse (MH/SA) treatment. Increased sophistication on the part of employers and insurance carriers, spiralling MH/SA benefit costs, better information gathering, and new treatment approaches have created the dynamics which are profoundly changing practice patterns in mental health. The result has been a wide range of evolving mental health and substance abuse treatment delivery systems and benefit designs.

This chapter will discuss the generic types of products that managed care companies sell and administer on the behalf of three markets: businesses or unions, HMOs or insurance, and public sector entities such as Medicaid, governmental units, or community mental health systems. The technologies of managed care will also be discussed as they are rapidly infiltrating all levels of behavioral health care delivery in the United States. For both students and practitioners an understanding of these systems is vital. Importantly, clinicians who serve mental health and substance abuse patients today must relate to these systems in one of three ways: as a provider of services, as an employee of these systems, or as an operator of these systems.

UNDERSTANDING MANAGED CARE PRODUCT LINES

Mental health care companies have attempted to standardize delivery systems into "off the shelf" products in order to ease administration and reduce the costs associated with customization. Actual benefit levels, limits, and consumer cost-sharing mechanisms such as copayments and deductibles may still be chosen by the customer (the employer, union, HMO, etc.), as such cost-sharing devices may impact cost and utilization.

Figure 5-1 describes a typical product line of managed care delivery systems. It is arranged to show how the degree of consumer choice of treatment provider affects costs. Employee Assistance Programs may be coupled with any or all of the products and EAPs themselves and may offer multiple products or delivery designs. Preferred Provider Organizations delivery systems deliver savings through discounted fee arrangements, and services are not case managed. Point-of-Service (POS) products, as discussed earlier, allow consumers to access a referral easily through a dedicated toll free telephone number and receive services through clinicians affiliated with the provider network or with other clinicians but at greater cost or with diminished benefits. Exclusive Provider Organization (EPO) products direct patients to practice groups or networks of clinicians who offer all needed clinical services. EPO products may or may not include any out-of-network benefit coverage. These delivery systems, in contrast to PPOs and POS products, are frequently funded through capitated, at-risk arrangements between the customer and managed care company, or between the customer and practice group. Their ability to direct care (gatekeeping) to limited groups of clinicians or facilities, aggressive case management, and a wide use of alternatives to expensive inpatient care results in lower costs to consumers and customers.

Understanding these generic products helps clinicians practice in roles best suited to their skills, experiences, and preferences. Some clinicians or group practices may be contracted with managed care companies to provide services to patients with any of these benefits. Other clinicians with an interest and knowledge of occupational clinical practice may best be suited for the delivery of EAP services. Clinicians skilled in crisis intervention or who offer services that provide alternatives to hospital-based care may best be suited as providers in EPO systems.

VALUES AND BELIEFS ASSOCIATED WITH MBC

All industries reflect certain values in their day-to-day operations. This is true in the MBC field as well. Their values impact

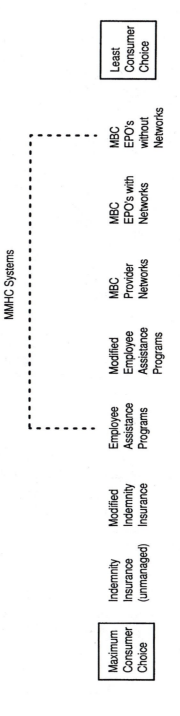

FIGURE 5-1. MBC Systems and Consumer Choice of Treatment and Treatment Provider

73

both the clinical and administrative aspects of their activities. MBC values are probably shared by a large proportion of practitioners and administrators today. Others view MBC's philosophies as an unpalatable departure from traditional themes long found in the health care field.

MBC bases much of its structure on the belief that most people can "get better" (recover, overcome their presenting problem, find a solution, etc.) and that they want to improve as quickly as possible. As a result, those in the MBC field view themselves as advocates for clients since they see MBC as an avenue to help consumers achieve this goal of rapid change and improvement. Also, MBC systems tend to focus on clinical technologies that help people achieve this goal of returning to their normal status or highest level of functioning as quickly as possible. Related to this belief is the notion that most consumers want help with specific, not global, problems and that treatment can be intermittent since specific problems needing professional attention may come and go over the course of a lifetime. Clinicians who hold this belief view themselves, in effect, as providing needed "tune ups," not full engine overhauls.

A belief in the importance of efficiency is inherent in MBC. While critics have said that MBC's quest for efficiency sometimes overlooks client care, clinicians in these systems believe that a lack of efficiency in many aspects of traditional mental health delivery systems escalates costs to consumers unnecessarily. When taken to the last degree, this escalation endangers mental health and substance abuse treatment benefits for many Americans.

Another belief common to MBC is that treatment is best delivered in the least restrictive and most normal setting possible. Outpatient treatment is stressed. MBC clinicians believe that most consumers prefer this orientation and desire treatment that is the least invasive and least disruptive possible. Related to this is the belief that hospital resources for MBC clients are needed for stabilization of acute crisis, and that the primary treatment should be provided on an outpatient basis when the client's condition permits. MBC clinicians point out that while this belief is prevalent in other health care fields, mental health practitioners and institutions have been slow to embrace the idea.

Unlike some indemnity insurance plans that reimbursable provider status to one or two professions, many MBC managers believe a range of providers is desirable. They believe this gives their clients greater choice, better access in some areas, and increased treatment options. This value is frequently operationalized through staffs and provider networks that feature not only psychiatrists and psychologists, but also clinical social workers, professional counselors, marriage and family therapists, clinical nurse specialists, and substance abuse counselors.

MBC stresses the belief that adequate clinical case management improves the continuity of care. These systems designate a "case manager" who has responsibility for the overall coordination (both clinical and financial aspects) of the client's care throughout a treatment episode. Clinicians in MBC believe this case management function greatly assists the client in transversing various treatment pitfalls and reduces the likelihood of wasting treatment resources through ineffectiveness, inefficiency, or duplication.

While focusing on such "micro" management of care and resources, MBC systems also value the "macro" management of the resources needed to provide care for large populations of patients, a different perspective than that normally taken in everyday practice. They attempt to achieve economies of scale, obtain favorable pricing and charge arrangements, and in other ways manage resources so as to obtain optimum, if not maximum, care for each member.

Finally, MBC's philosophy is that much care delivered to consumers today is unnecessary; much other care is ineffective. More care does not necessarily mean better care. MBC views these factors as weighing heavily in the escalating costs of mental health and substance abuse care. It operates with the belief that these escalating costs, unless checked, will force employers to reduce or eliminate MH/SA benefits from their health care benefit plans entirely. They believe that MBC, with its emphasis on accountability and structure, can ensure necessary and cost-effective care for its members. The rapid growth of MBC in recent years has been an endorsement of this belief by the ultimate major purchasers of mental health care: employers.

ELEMENTS OF MBC SYSTEMS

Managed Behavioral Care systems have four core elements and a range of secondary elements. The components can be delivered to HMO or Employer customers either by specialty, MBC firms, or by Employee Assistance Program (EAP) firms. Core elements include:

- Gatekeeping
- Provider Network Development
- Utilization Management[1]
- Clinical Case Management

Secondary elements or functions of these systems include:

- Benefits Design or Re-design
- Eligibility Verification
- Benefits Interpretation
- Emergency Intervention and Access
- Evaluation
- Employee Assistance Functions (training, awareness and education activities)
- Quality Assurance
- Claims Processing and Adjudication

(See Figures 5-2, 5-3, and 5-4.)

This chapter explores how the functions of these various aspects of MBC systems work, how patients are served, and how providers are utilized. MBC is a growth industry and an emerging field of practice for mental health clinicians and administrators. The reader will find that often MBC systems parallel the HMO models described in Chapter 2, yet many variations exist. No one "model" prevails. A familiarity with these core functions provides a basis for understanding the mechanics of this industry.

Gatekeeping

In medical HMOs the Primary Care Physician (PCP) serves as the gatekeeper to all of the system's services such as specialty care,

---

1. Discussed in Chapter 6.

FIGURE 5-2. Managed Behavioral Care Core Functions

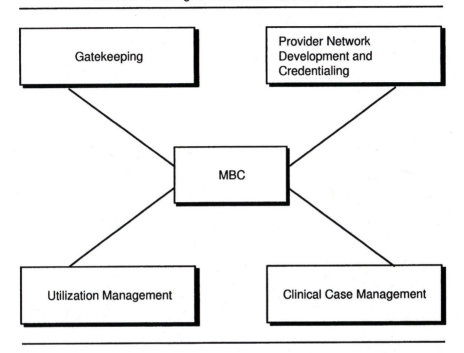

testing, or inpatient treatment. MBC clinicians serve this gatekeeping function concerning mental health and substance abuse services.

The gatekeeper's objectives are twofold: assessment and treatment planning. First, the client's presenting problem is assessed and a diagnostic impression is reached. Second, the type, level, and intensity of treatment, and the provider type are matched to the presenting problem. This treatment plan and designated provider or facility are then authorized for coverage through the client's benefit plan. This task requires substantial skill, experience, and expertise. A thorough knowledge of available community resources is also invaluable. These clinical decisions are often made in multidisciplinary team meetings. The input from clinicians of different professional training and backgrounds strengthens these decisions.

FIGURE 5-3. Secondary Managed Behavioral Care Functions

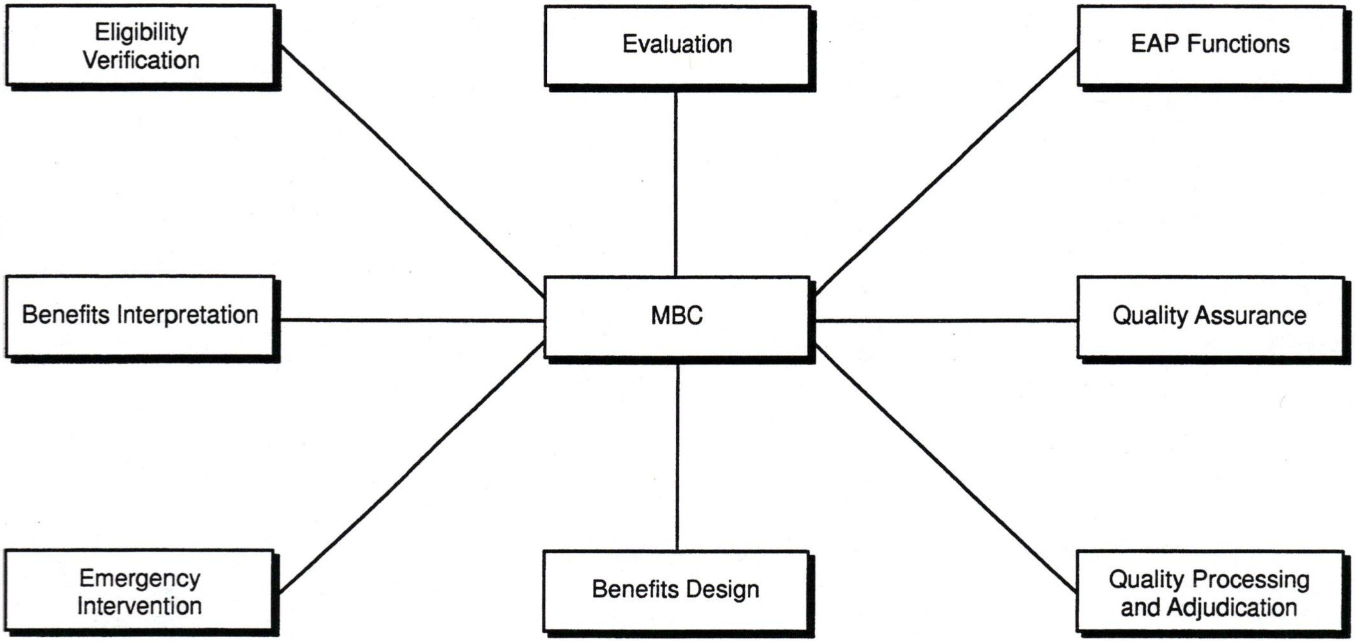

EAP Functions

Quality Assurance

Quality Processing and Adjudication

Evaluation

MBC

Benefits Design

Eligibility Verification

Benefits Interpretation

Emergency Intervention

FIGURE 5-4. MBC Client Flow Chart

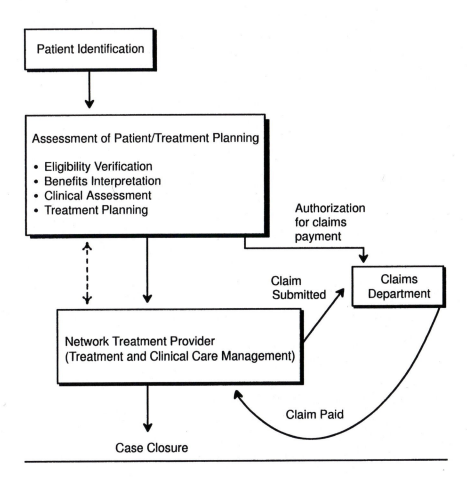

If conducted improperly, this gatekeeping function can have negative consequences for both the client and the MBC organization. For example, if, due to a diagnostic error, the recommended treatment is not the most effective one available, or if it is not delivered as intensively as needed, the client may not improve. The client may present again at a later time in a deteriorated condition, requiring more intensive (and expensive) care. The result is that the client has not been well served toward his or her goal of improvement, while the MBC firm has incurred more costs than would have been necessary had care been effective initially.

This gatekeeping function may be provided by a MBC firm's employees or by contracted providers. It is usually conducted by nonphysician clinicians in consultation with a psychiatrist. A more intensive assessment utilizing medical personnel is frequently provided to substance abuse or other clients presenting with medical complications. In some HMO systems, a referral to the MBC staff for assessment and treatment occurs only after a PCP has assessed the client, ruling out purely medical etiologies.

Gatekeeping is a key aspect of MBC systems and helps to reduce unnecessary and costly care. Its greatest impact concerns unnecessary hospital care, the most costly segment of mental health and substance abuse treatment. The gatekeeping function requires, in effect, clinical assessment before hospitalization. This function (along with Preadmission Certification, discussed later) eliminates or reduces the consumer's choice of and ability to select costly inpatient treatment modalities, without assessment by nonhospital affiliated clinicians.[2]

Provider Networks

After assessment and treatment planning, MBC clients are directed toward providers who are affiliated with the MBC firm. This is said to be the MBC firm's provider network. Care is then authorized for reimbursement to the providers who are members of the network. Provider network members are recruited, or selected for inclusion, based on several factors. These include clinical skills and services, geographical considerations, cost-effective practice patterns, congruent values with MBC systems, and willingness to comply with utilization review processes. Providers are "credentialed" by the MBC firm as a quality assurance measure. This process may entail the submission by the provider of documentation of a profes-

---

2. This gatekeeping function, especially vis-à-vis hospitalization, is also exemplified by many Community Mental Health Centers (CMHCs).

sional license, educational background, DEA registration (where appropriate), adequate malpractice insurance coverage, the absence of misconduct or ethical violations, and the adequacy of emergency access for referred clients. MBC groups confirm such documentation with licensure boards and other entities when appropriate. Credentials of providers are periodically reviewed and updated. MBC staff usually interview potential providers to assess clinical skills and to orient them to the system.

Providers sign agreements with MBC firms that contain various stipulations about service and reimbursement arrangements. A schedule of allowable fee maximums is agreed upon for the services the provider will render to MBC clients. Like HMO-PCP agreements, these arrangements prohibit the provider from billing the client inappropriately, prescribe mechanisms for the resolution of disputes, discuss the confidentiality of client information, and indicate what type of services the provider will deliver. Examples of provider credentialing materials and a sample provider agreement are found in Appendix A.

MBC firms further their goals of providing cost-effective, quality care through the utilization of provider networks. Cost savings are achieved through recruiting effective and efficient service providers, while obtaining a discounted fee arrangement (a reduction of 15 percent or more of usual charges is often obtained). At the same time their credentialing and screening process ensures that quality services will be offered to their clients.

To providers, affiliation has some drawbacks and several advantages. An obvious drawback is the discounted fee requested by the MBC entity. In addition, the credentialing and utilization review processes may present additional paperwork and be time consuming tasks. (Obviously those providers or facilities who are not philosophically attuned to MBC or whose treatment preferences are not compatible with MBC's authorization patterns will find network affiliation difficult or problematic.) However, membership in one or more MBC networks can ensure a steady source of referrals. In communities with an overabundance of facilities or individual providers, such an affiliation may be crucial and may be an important means of developing a successful practice. (See Chapter 8 for more discussion of this issue.)

Networks may be as large or as small as the MBC requires in order to serve its members. Networks may include only such facilities as hospitals or detoxification centers, or they may include only individual outpatient practitioners; often they include both. In determining the size and composition of their networks, MBCs consider factors such as their member population's utilization of services history (which can be analyzed by examining past claim submission data), the geographical distribution of members, the quality of service delivery and practice patterns of the community of providers, and customer input concerning the provider network. A large consideration on the part of MBC is the cost-effectiveness of a provider network applicant's practice. Firms have successfully resisted efforts by groups of providers for automatic inclusion in such networks. Obviously, if all providers or all hospitals in a given community were network members, any cost-effective practice on the part of some would be offset by the lack of such practice on the part of others, thus negating an important MBC objective.

The way in which networks are utilized varies. In some arrangements, an MBC client is assessed by a staff clinician of the firm. Treatment is then authorized to be conducted at the office of a network provider. In other arrangements, the client may seek assessment with any MBC network provider. The provider then communicates the assessment information to the MBC staff, who authorize further care with the provider. Still other arrangements include specially designated network providers who provide assessment only, while treatment services are offered through other providers. Although this procedure may inconvenience the client (who must see both an assessment clinician and a treatment clinician), it removes any incentive for the assessor to recommend treatment that would benefit the assessor's practice. By modifying these assessment and treatment provision arrangements, MBC firms may share gatekeeping responsibilities with network providers.

The proportion of treatment services delivered by the network versus the MBC staff may vary as well. In some instances the MBC firm functions only as a developer and manager of a MH/SA preferred provider organization, providing little or no treatment services.

For example, the ACME FLANGE Company is a large self-insured employer with factory operations in three cities and a small sales force scattered about the nation. ACME's benefit manager, working with his benefit consultant, decides that ACME will take steps to control the cost of its MH/SA claims, after it is realized that these claims are inordinately costly in relation to all health care claims submitted by ACME's employees. One strategy ACME will use, they decide, is to employ a MBC firm to develop and administer a network of cost-effective providers and facilities for their employees in various locations. They select a firm that already has networks of providers in two of the three cities and most of the locations of their sales force. The firm is quickly able to recruit and credential a network in the third city. ACME wishes its employees to have immediate access to these providers, so the gatekeeping function is also delegated to the respective provider selected by the employee, and is essentially deemphasized. ACME purchases the MBC's network, i.e., its ability to develop and administer a network of cost-effective service providers. The firm receives an administrative fee from ACME. Its providers receive more referrals. ACME receives quality services for its employees while enjoying the cost savings associated with their discounted fees and cost-effective practice patterns. In this example ACME continues to be at risk financially for the cost of services and continues to utilize a third party administrator (TPA) to process and pay claims.

In other scenarios, an MBC firm might utilize network providers minimally. MBC entities may utilize their own staff to provide most services. When an MBC firm assumes the risk for the services of HMO members, it may wish to control costs by having a limited provider network and instead employ staff to provide most of the services its members require. It becomes the exclusive provider network for MH/SA care to the HMO's members. In this scenario, the MBC firm might utilize a network only for specialized services or inpatient care. To a large extent, the MBC firm has internalized its network, employing practitioners directly. These configurations have many of the advantages and disadvantages of administration that are inherent to staff model medical/surgical HMOs.

How the MBC firm utilizes its network may also change with time as its relationship to its accounts (customers) changes. Returning to the ACME FLANGE Company example, after one year's experience with the arrangement described, ACME reevaluates its benefits for mental health and substance abuse treatment in light of continuing cost increases in its health care claims and its sagging profits. In reviewing the MBC network's performance it finds that most of its employees are using its members as opposed to other providers. However, it finds that employees are often selecting the most costly providers for services that could be as effectively delivered by other professionals.

In view of this development, ACME asks the MBC to increase its gatekeeping function, focusing on matching the treatment need with the least costly provider who can appropriately deliver necessary services. The MBC firm responds by designating its staff clinicians in one city and selected network assessment providers in the other locations to serve as gatekeepers to the system. The gatekeepers are able to direct referrals to network providers on a more cost-effective basis, better matching the level of treatment need with level of provider. (In actual operation this might mean that psychologists, licensed clinical social workers, professional counselors, or marriage and family therapists would be authorized to perform more counseling services, while psychiatrists in the network would be authorized for therapy services that only they are skilled in and qualified to provide.)

Through the MBC firm's services, ACME is able to gain more control of its costs at the expense of some choice on the part of its employees. ACME's management had exercised this choice in advance, by purchasing this gatekeeping function through the MBC firm.

Clinical Case Management

This term refers to the assortment of activities concerning the coordination and monitoring of client services throughout the treatment episode. The development of this function in MBC systems parallels that of the PCP who is medical case manager in HMOs. It also reflects the belief on the part of MBCs that treatment resources are misused in the absence of clinical oversight. This function in MBC arrangements is the key to the management of care.

Important aspects of the clinical case manager function include:

- coordination of care with treatment providers;
- coordination of care with PCPs and other medical services;
- referral to available community resources for additional services not included in the client's benefits (examples include self-help or support group referrals);
- benefit interpretation.

The clinical case manager may be the treatment provider (as in the case of staff model operations) or may be the MBC staff member who consults with the treatment provider and performs concurrent review functions. (See Chapter 6 for a discussion of this and other utilization review functions in MBC systems.) In either situation, the clinical case manager is the point of interface between the client and available treatment resources. (See Table 5-1.)

Additional Functions

Several additional functions are available through MBC firms. Some may be viewed as add-ons to essential components. Essential components include eligibility verification and benefits interpretation. These are straightforward tasks. When a client accesses services, his name is verified as an active, eligible member of the benefit or group health plan. Rosters of members are kept current according to changes in employee groups or health care plan membership. This is a clerical function, while interpretation of benefits is an important clinical function involving the case manager. In each case benefits must be interpreted as they pertain to the client's assessment. Excluded conditions and benefit limitations must be considered in this task. MBC must be judicious concerning benefit interpretation, providing only the services previously contracted for with the customer. A common abuse of benefit interpretation can occur in the unmanaged practice environment when the clinician interprets benefits to cover services he or she is accustomed to providing, such as long-term psychotherapy aimed at characterological change or marriage counseling, even though neither is actually a covered benefit.

Another essential aspect of MBC is emergency intervention. MBC administrators realize that psychiatric crises occur at all hours, so their systems must be organized to offer accessible crisis

TABLE 5-1. Steps in the MBC Clinical Case Management Process

Case Identification
- Self-initiated
- Family, physician, employer initiated

Assessment of Patient
- Benefit eligibility determination
- Benefits interpretation
- Clinical assessment
- Diagnosis established

Treatment Plan Development
- Type of treatment determined
- Setting for treatment determined
- Intensity of treatment determined
- Duration of treatment estimated
- Providers of treatment determined
- Patient (and family/employers) agrees to treatment plan

Treatment Plan Implementation/Monitoring
- Arrangements made with provider for service delivery
- Transfer of patient coordinated
- Reimbursement arrangements coordinated
- Authorization written for claims payment
- Treatment progress monitored, treatment plan modified as needed

---

counseling at all times. Prompt intervention also can diffuse many crises and thereby prevent a costly hospitalization.

Benefits design consultation is also offered by MBC entities. In the example of ACME, benefits were changed to encourage the utilization of outpatient care and the designated provider network. Prior to the introduction of managed care, ACME's benefits paid 100 percent of the employee's inpatient claims, while only paying 50 percent of outpatient claims. ACME's MBC firm recommended changes resulting in a structure featuring employee cost-sharing, and incenting the employee to use ACME's network. Table 5-2 shows how ACME's new benefit design works, providing coverage for employees who use the network providers as well as for those who do not.

Some large MBC entities may also process, adjudicate, and pay

TABLE 5-2. ACME Benefits

In-Network Benefits		Out-of-Network Benefits
Mental Health		
Outpatient		
up to 20 visits per year	$10 copayment (individual Tx) $ 5 copayment (group Tx)	70% coverage of charges after meeting $250 deductible
Inpatient		
up to 30 days per year; 2-1 conversion to partial hospitalization days	20% copayment	70% coverage of charges after meeting $500 deductible
Substance Abuse		
Outpatient		
up to 20 visits per year; unlimited group treatment	$ 5 copayment (group Tx) $10 copayment (individual Tx)	70% coverage of charges after meeting $250 deductible
Inpatient		
up to 30 days per year; 2-1 conversion to partial hospitalization days	20% copayment	70% coverage of charges after meeting $500 deductible

claims as well as provide evaluation or outcome studies about treatment. Some firms regularly survey their clients concerning clinical services provided by their staff or network providers and facilities, utilizing this data in management decision making.

MBC firms also have various quality assurance features, some of which may interface with those of their HMO customers. These include peer reviews, random chart audits, examination or audits of readmissions to hospitals within a prescribed period (thirty days for example), examination or audits of reapplications for outpatient care, credentialing and updating of provider credentials, and compliance with state regulatory agencies. Many MBC firms, especially those who provide direct treatment services, may be licensed and regulated for mental health and substance abuse services by state regulatory entities. Licensure of individual practitioners employed directly by the MBC firm is yet another level of quality assurance.

Finally, with convergence of MBC and EAP functions, many firms are able to offer the supervisory training, employee education, and other components of traditional EAPs, rounding out the constellation of services available to employer accounts.

Internal Organization and Staffing Patterns

MBC systems that provide assessment and treatment services directly to clients (as opposed to those that only manage benefits) are often clinically organized to resemble other large counseling concerns, such as group practices, private clinics, or community mental health centers. Their internal operations tend to be focused on the provision of services to acute clients and on helping all clients improve on a timely basis. Many offer intensive outpatient substance abuse programs, partial hospitalization, crisis intervention teams, and ambulatory detoxification. Group therapy programs are used as well.

Some administrative organizational structures may be centralized while others are retained on local levels. For example, a large MBC company may have one centralized customer service department, responding to member inquiries or provider questions, while each local office may carry out some customer service functions. Management information systems, tracking service utilization data, and generating summary reports may be best done on a centralized basis, as may claims processing.

Staff positions within these systems parallel those in other counseling settings. Administrative titles include "Executive Director" or "Network Manager." Psychiatrists in such systems hold positions such as "Medical Director" or "Consultant." They provide direct services and supervision of clinical and utilization review processes. Clinical directors are often senior clinicians with responsibility for overall staff services and training. MBC entities may also have staff positions relating to the coordination of quality assurance activities and substance abuse treatment services.

In a 1988 report concerning 1986 surveys of HMOs, Shadle and Christianson found wide variation in the ratio of MBC staff to members (commonly expressed as a Full Time Equivalent [FTE] per ten thousand-member ratio). These variations are due in large part to the assortment of MBC arrangements and benefit structures. Given this, a range of one to two FTEs per ten thousand members for nonphysician staff is common in the industry.

What types of mental health clinicians are best suited for the growing employment opportunities in MBC? First, a great deal of clinical skill and experience is required of clinicians in these challenging systems. Clinicians must be licensed or certified for independent practice and have a thorough knowledge of current clinical practices. Especially important is a familiarity with brief, solution-focused treatment techniques. (See Chapter 8.)

Some MBC managers view clinical values as equally important in these settings. "Clinicians from all mental health fields can work well in managed care settings if their values are congruent with managed care practice," says Dr. John Bistline, chairman of the American Mental Health Counselor's Association's Special Interest Network on Managed Care (Personal communication, 1990). Bistline, a supervisor in MBC systems for five years, believes that MBC staff who are interested in seeing their clients change quickly, while utilizing the least invasive treatment interventions appropriate, are most successful in these settings.

"The recruitment of staff for MBC practice is challenging especially concerning psychiatrists," according to Demetrios Julius, MD, a consultant to MCC Companies and to Masi Research Associates, an EAP evaluation firm (personal communication, 1990). Julius, who has been involved in managed health care since the 1970s, advises that a special combination of skills and interests is required.

First, the psychiatrist must have excellent clinical skills and be abreast of current treatment methodologies and research issues. He must be interested in working as part of a multidisciplinary team. Familiarity with the strengths and limitations of other mental health professionals is important as is the case with other community-oriented psychiatry settings. He also must be philosophically attuned to managed care values, as well as aware of emerging managed care technologies. Finally, the psychiatrist must be comfortable with the evaluative and peer review nature inherent to these settings. Individuals who combine all these characteristics find Managed Behavioral care to be a good fit and a challenging opportunity (Julius, Personal communication, 1990).

KEY ADMINISTRATIVE ASPECTS OF MBC SYSTEMS

MBC firms are constructed in a variety of configurations. A description of all the types is beyond the scope of this book, but certain elements, embodied in almost all such organizations, are relevant to this context. Therefore, this chapter will focus on these aspects:

- Contracts between MBC firms and their customers
- How MBC firms are financed
- How MBC firms measure and use service utilization data

Bear in mind that some MBC entities also pay claims, develop and administer provider networks only, or provide only employee assistance programming. Also EAPs are increasingly making transitions into MBC functions. These issues are addressed elsewhere within this book.

This chapter will enable the reader to understand the essentials and speak the language of MBC utilization data, which measures clinical services in nontraditional ways. We will also explore how utilization projections or estimates, along with the type of services the MBC is contracted to provide or purchase, derives what it charges to its customers (HMOs or employers). We will examine the pitfalls of this "capitation" funding system which has sometimes resulted in the failure of MBC organizations, with resultant disruption in patient services and providers' practices.

MBC Contracts: Key Components

MBC firms contract with HMOs, insurance carriers, employers, groups of employers, or unions. Like other businesses, these firms are bound by the terms of their agreements; they deliver no more or no fewer services than specified in their agreement. Like any other business they attempt to deliver their services and make a profit. Given the enormous growth of managed care in recent years, these firms have generally been able to do so, while reducing or slowing the cost for MH/SA claims to their customers. Both the firms and their customers relate this accomplishment to MBC's ability to reduce the use of unnecessary, inefficient, or ineffective care while achieving acceptable levels of customer satisfaction.

Service Standards

Contracts between the MBC firm and the customer have several important specifications that influence the nature of the service delivery systems. For example, the contract may specify the following various service standards which affect the ultimate configuration of the MBC operation.

Access Parameters. MBC contracts specify that initial assessment and diagnostic services will be available to all members. These include provisions for emergency services to clients, twenty-four-hour availability of staff, the availability of routine initial assessments, and geographic service issues such as a standard for reasonable client drive time to a clinic or provider.

Provider Parameters. The customer may specify in the contract how the provider credentialing process will be implemented and monitored, what types of providers may be credentialed, etc.

Quality Assurance Parameters. The customer may specify various functions related to quality oversight including peer review, clinical chart audits, complaint and grievance policies, and appeal procedures.

Utilization Data Reporting. This includes provisions for the type and timing of statistical reports. For example, an HMO which employs a MBC firm to manage its members' MH/SA benefits might specify that the firm will report utilization of services data (i.e., units of services delivered by employer account. In this way the HMO can monitor, account by account, the total amount of both medical and mental health services delivered to each of its employer groups).

Out-of-Service-Area Emergencies. The MBC firm and the customer specify how they will manage the care of a member or employee who has a need for treatment while traveling or working outside the normal service area. The financial obligation for the care is also specified.

Benefit Descriptions and Limits. A maximum number of therapy visits and hospital days available are specified. Benefit limits may be described in dollar maximum per year. Benefits may also be limited on a "per lifetime" basis. (Table 5-3 gives an example of typical benefit limits.) Benefit descriptions in MBC contracts specify that only medically necessary services and/or preauthorized services are covered under the plan or system. Protocols for the coverage of emergency presentations or admissions may also be described.

Copayment or Coinsurance Levels. Copayments by the client are an important contractual provision for MBC systems. Copayments are widely perceived as a means of cost-sharing and of deterring inappropriate utilization of specialist's services. For example, a HMO may establish a copayment for basic health care (Primary Care Physician visits) at a level of $5 per visit. However, a specialist copayment to the MBC staff or providers might be $10 or $25 per visit.

Disenrollment Policies. Contracts provide for a process by which a member may be expelled from the MBC system. Examples include members who refuse to pay necessary copayments, who refuse reasonable treatment plans, or who are abusive to the staff or network providers.

Exclusions

A key aspect of the contract by which MBC firms operate concerns "exclusions." These are services that the customer has not purchased from the MBC entity. They are not a "covered benefit" under the health care schema.

Court-Ordered Treatment. Provisions specify that simply because treatment, or treatment with a particular individual or institutional provider, is ordered by a court it will not necessarily be covered by the MBC system for reimbursement purposes. MBC systems may cover such treatment if it is assessed by the system as being necessary. A common occurrence in this area involves a court which, in effect, sentences a member to thirty days in a hospital for treatment for a substance abuse related offense. The hospitalization

TABLE 5-3. Benefit Description and Limits

MENTAL HEALTH

Outpatient Therapy	20 visits per calendar year
Partial Hospitalization	2 - 1 equivalency to inpatient day maximum
Inpatient Hospitalization	30 days per calendar year

SUBSTANCE ABUSE

Outpatient Therapy	50 visits per year, limited to structured treatment program
Partial Hospitalization	2 - 1 equivalency to inpatient day maximum
Inpatient Hospitalization	30 days per calendar year, limited to 60 days per lifetime

would not be covered by the MBC firm unless it assessed the hospital care, and its length, as the necessary level of treatment for the client.

Treatment for Disorders Not Shown to Be Amenable to Short-Term Interventions. Since a philosophy of MBC firms is that treatment should be directed at returning the client to his normal level of functioning, their contracts use this clause to exclude the long-term therapy that may, or may not, be successful at altering basic personality or characterological features. MBC firms usually serve this population with crisis intervention and other services aimed at stabilization only, not characterological change. This exclusion operates in cases of stable personality disordered clients not in an acute crisis at or near their normal level of functioning. Services for this population would include crisis intervention and stabilization, but not the extensive long-term therapy sometimes provided to this client population.

Experimental Therapies. Provisions are made for the exclusion of untried or unproven treatments (as determined by the HMO's, insurance carrier's, or MBC firm's medical directors or reviewers). Examples may include vitamin or nutritional therapies, experimental drug therapies, etc.

Treatment for Disorders Classified on V Code Diagnoses in the DSM-III-R. Marital therapy is usually excluded through this clause.

Table 5-4 summarizes the key features of MBC contracts that impact clinical services.

Financing

MBC systems can be funded in several ways. The most common funding mechanism, capitation, will be discussed here as it applies to an HMO population. Employers may also purchase MBC services through capitation arrangements.

Just as HMO members pay a fixed fee and in turn receive all their health care services, MBC firms are often funded through a similar mechanism. Arriving at this "price" for a contract is a vitally important process.

The MBC group will carefully study the demographics and uti-

TABLE 5-4. MBC Contracts: Key Components

Service Standards
- Access Parameters
- Provider Parameters
- Quality Assurance Parameters
- Utilization Data Reporting
- Out-of-Service-Area Emergencies
- Benefit Descriptions and Limits
- Copayment or Coinsurance Levels
- Disenrollment Policies

Exclusions
- Court-Ordered Treatment
- Treatment for Disorders Not Shown to Be Amenable to Short-Term Interventions
- Experimental Therapies
- Treatment for Disorders Classified on V Code Diagnoses in the DSM-III-R

lization of services history of any prospective group of members (HMO members, employee population, etc.). Large MBC firms employ specialists in this process. An MBC organization will carefully study the benefit schedule that the prospective customer desires, as well as proposed exclusions to the benefit plan. It also will evaluate its own history of managing such benefits.

Other factors important in formulating a capitation figure include local cost considerations, such as hospital costs; provider availability, quality, and familiarity with managed care systems; and other market-specific factors.

A capitation rate[3] or cap. rate will then be proposed and negotiated between the MBC firm and its customer. This number, multiplied by the current number of members, will be paid to the MBC firm each month. From this revenue, plus possible copayment revenue, the MBC firm must finance all aspects of its operation.

In this scenario, the MBC firm is then fully at risk for the cost of all clinical services needed by its members. The financial risk for mental health care has been transferred from the HMO or self-insured employer to the MBC entity. Figure 5-5 and Table 5-5 show examples of how capitation funds a MBC system in which the respective parties have agreed upon a $4 pm pm.[4]

This type of funding system is found in a modified form in Employee Assistant Program (EAP) services. EAPs traditionally have not been financially at risk for all clinical services, and therefore their charges have been considerably less than MBC groups. As EAPs evolve toward providing more MBC functions, this will change. (See Chapter 4 for a discussion of EAPs and how they may change in the future as a response to MBC systems.)

In providing their products, EAPs are typically funded on a "per

---

3. Capitation is paid each month and is based on the number of actual enrollees in the plan that month. Since plan membership varies from month to month, the capitation revenue may vary correspondingly. Capitation is said to be a "per member, per month" (pm pm) figure.

---

4. Actual capitation rates vary widely depending on the above factors. A range of $1.00 to $5.00 pm pm is common. This contrasts with MBC's forerunner, Employee Assistance Programs which are often priced at $1.25 to $2.50 per employee, per month (pe pm).

employee, per year" (pe py) basis. For example, to serve an employer account of one thousand employees the EAP firm might charge $15 pe py or $15,000 annually.

These capitated funding arrangements offer a simplified payment system, but one that is also filled with pitfalls, especially for MBC groups and their members. Many such organizations, particularly those that are smaller or poorly managed, have learned this painful lesson and have failed. There are several ways this can occur. Some common scenarios follow.

Apple MBC contracts with Bob's HMO (an IPA model), which has a membership of fifty thousand, at a cap. rate of $4 pm pm, or $200,000 per month. Administrative and clinical staff are hired, a network of providers is established, and two offices are leased, since the HMO serves a widely dispersed membership. Apple plans to assess all new clients, then refer them for treatment services into its newly recruited provider network. One provider group, confi-

FIGURE 5-5. Capitation

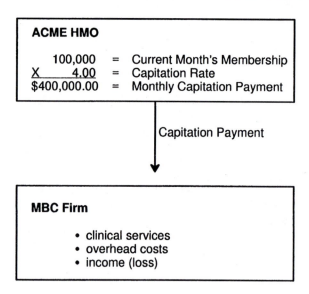

TABLE 5-5. Capitation Funding of MBC Systems

Revenue:	$400,000	(Current month's membership X capitation rate or 100,000 X $4.00)
Cost of Services:	$300,000	(75% of Revenues)
General and Administrative Expenses:	$60,000	(15% of Revenues)
Income:	$40,000	(10% of Revenues)

dent of securing all of Apple's substance abuse clients, expands its practice, leasing new office space and hiring an additional clinician.

For six months all goes well for Apple. Its assessment function guides its members to the appropriate level of care and into its network of cost-effective practitioners. Apple is profitable, its members receive good care, and its providers receive a steady flow of referrals. Then, totally unrelated to Apple MBC's services, the HMO loses two important physician groups from its medical panel. Several large employer accounts choose not to renew their business with the HMO, since its primary medical care panel of physicians is no longer as attractive to their employees as it once was. The HMO looses 40 percent of its membership in a period of a few months. Apple's monthly capitation check shrinks correspondingly. No business can absorb such a dramatic loss of revenue without parallel cutbacks and layoffs. Apple mismanages the necessary transition and is not able to reduce its overhead costs quickly enough. Providers are alienated when referral streams slow down. Apple becomes absorbed with its internal cost of operation issues with resulting poor claims payment and member service problems. The business eventually fails. Client care is disrupted as the HMO must secure a new MBC organization. Providers, especially the ones that expanded their practices to accommodate Apple's referrals, are further alienated as their businesses feel the ripple effect of the failure. The HMO is further damaged in the marketplace by this setback to its MBC firm.

This scenario represents the fact that MBC firms are dependent on a stable HMO population. Changes in the population must be adjusted to quickly and efficiently, with minimal disruption to core MBC functions. In this way the health of a MBC firm is connected to the overall well-being of the HMO customer.

Another example demonstrates how too small a revenue base can affect MBC organizations. In this case, Drs. Smith and Jones decide to pursue a capitated arrangement for Smalltime HMO's mental health needs. Smalltime is actually part of a "big time" insurance carrier, but is in a weak position in Smith and Jones' market. Small-time has only fifteen thousand members, but their parent insurance company is committed to their presence in this market. Drs. Smith and Jones are confident of success as they launch into the new field of managed care!

Contract in hand, they go about restructuring their practice. They decide they will serve as an exclusive provider organization to Smalltime's members. They hope their new service, a partial hospi-talization program, will help them avoid costly inpatient hospital-izations. Also, they hope their managed care contract, with its monthly "cap. check," will finance the partial hospitalization ser-vice which they market in the community, generating more revenue. Smalltime will be their cash cow!

Smith and Jones soon fail. An autopsy reveals their MBC prac-tice underestimated the actual need for inpatient hospitalization and overestimated their partial hospitalization program's ability to cir-cumvent inpatient admissions. Further, the relatively small size of their membership made it difficult for them to negotiate discounted charges from their hospital network. They could not provide the volume of hospital days needed to encourage the hospital adminis-trators to discount their usual rates. Therefore, both the number of hospital days used by their members as well as the cost per day of hospitalization exceeded their estimates. Finally, the doctors were unable to effectively market their partial hospitalization to the com-munity to supplement their contractual revenues.

Had Drs. Smith and Jones anticipated these problems, they would have negotiated a larger cap. rate which would have enabled them to weather the difficult early phase of establishing their man-aged care practice. They may have been able to reduce the rate charged to Smalltime HMO the next year, or reduce the expected increase of the rate over subsequent years, once they became accustomed to "managing" the relatively small membership. As with HMOs, MBC firms often experience higher utilization of hospital beds during the start-up phase of operation. Utilization of bed days on this scenario would probably have trended downward over time as Smith and Jones refined their management of the patient population. Also, over time the doctors may have been able to obtain other managed care contracts so as to achieve a larger revenue base, gain a better negotiating position in the marketplace (due to the additional membership), and achieve the inherent economics of scale associated with a larger MBC population.

Understanding Utilization Data

In the last scenario, mistakes were made in estimating hospital utilization. This is actually a common error throughout the entire managed care field, not just in the mental health area. MBC firms spend much energy in collecting and analyzing utilization data so as to avoid such costly mistakes. Understanding how this data is calculated and used is helpful to all concerned with Managed Behavioral care.

The term "utilization" refers to the quantity of any particular clinical service delivered by a MBC entity. Utilization data is sometimes expressed as a rate per 1,000 members on an annualized basis. Expressing data in this way takes fluctuating membership, or employee populations, into account and gives a meaningful picture of how quickly treatment resources are being used.

Because hospital resources are so costly and because most MBC groups operate with a clinical orientation of treating patients in the least restrictive setting available, utilization data relating to the use of hospital resources is key information, both from financial and clinical perspectives. As we have seen, financial miscalculations in their area can spell ruin for MBC firms. Clinically, the over (or under) utilization of hospital resources may indicate problems in patient access, assessment, treatment, or follow-up. This data may reveal important insights into the quality of services achieved by a MBC firm's network of community practitioners and provider hospitals.

All MBC firms collect and scrutinize three important types of data related to inpatient care. They are hospitalization rates, admission rates, and the average length of stay. The most important statistic is the first, which is the rate at which members are utilizing hospital resources.

As an example, suppose a MBC firm has 100,000 members for which it must provide or purchase all clinical services. In the month of January its members utilize 200 bed days in psychiatric or substance abuse hospitals. Its members are using hospital days, on an annual basis, at twenty-four days per 1,000 members. If this rate continues throughout the rest of the year members will use, and the MBC firm will purchase on their behalf, 2,400 hospital days! The formula used to arrive at this number is:

$$\frac{\text{\# hospital days used per month}}{\text{\# of capitated members}} \times 12,000 = \frac{\text{rate}}{\text{1,000 members (annualized)}}$$

or

$$\frac{200 \text{ days used}}{100,000 \text{ members}} \times 12,000 = \frac{24}{1,000 \text{ members}}$$

By multiplying 24 days by 100 (the number of thousands of members) the figure of 2,400 is reached as a projection of how many hospital days will be utilized in the course of the year (assuming a stable membership).

By April the MBC entity in this example notices a change in its hospitalization patterns. Only 100 hospital days were used by its 100,000 members in that month. Its utilization rate drops to 12 days/1,000 members, or:

$$\frac{100 \text{ days used}}{100,000 \text{ members}} \times 12,000 = \frac{12}{1,000 \text{ members}}$$

It now appears the firm will not need to purchase as many hospital days during the course of the year as it once thought.

Such seasonal variations in hospitalization needs are common and MBC firms budget for them. They give close scrutiny to this key utilization indicator since one day in a hospital may cost the MBC firm $500 to $1,000 or more. If the firm underestimates its hospital utilization rate and budgeting funds accordingly, a shortfall of thousands of dollars may result.

Continuing the example above and estimating each hospital day to cost $500, if the MBC firm underestimates its hospital utilization by 25 percent, it will pay one quarter million dollars extra for its members care that year! Here is how these numbers are reached:

Projection: 20/1,000 = hospitalization rate

20 × 100 = 2,000 hospital days used in one year
20 × $500 = $1,000,000 cost of hospitalization

Actual: 25/1,000 = hospitalization rate

25 × 100 = 2,500 hospital days used in one year
2,500 × $500 = $1,250,000 cost of hospitalization

Actual Cost   = $1,250,000

Projected Cost = $1,000,000

Budget Shortfall = $250,000

MBC firms routinely achieve hospitalization rates in the range of 20 to 50 days per 1,000 members. When these figures are contrasted with unmanaged systems where mental health and substance abuse hospitalization rates are usually in the range of 100 to 200 days per 1,000 members, it is easy to understand the rapid proliferation of MBC! MBC firms use their powerful data to good effect in their sales efforts since it is highly objective information and is in such sharp contrast to unmanaged care data.

The second key inpatient related statistic is the hospital admission rate, which is also expressed as a rate per 1,000 members. This statistic indicates the rate at which members are being admitted to hospitals. The same formula is used to find this rate as in the case of the hospitalization rate.

Suppose the 100,000 member firm had 12 admissions in one month. This equals to 1.44 admissions/1,000 members annually or:

$$\frac{\text{\# of admissions in one month}}{\text{\# of capitated members}} \times 12,000 = \frac{\text{admissions per } 1,0000}{\text{members, annualized}}$$

or

$$\frac{12}{100,000} \times 12,000 = 1.44 \text{ per } 1,000 \text{ members, annualized}$$

The third important inpatient category of data is the Average Length of Stay (ALOS), or how long a typical hospitalization lasts. For example, if 12 admissions in one month used 100 hospital bed days, the ALOS would be 8.33 days (100 ÷ 12 = 8.33). Firms can monitor their data separately for mental health and substance abuse clients, or as a combined statistic. MBC organizations study which physicians and hospitals achieve the shortest ALOS for similar patients. In this way the data can help them select the most effective and efficient providers and hospitals.

MBC firms are interested in similar utilization data about their outpatient services. They wish to understand how quickly members are presenting for care (outpatient admissions per 1,000 members), how long members are in treatment (number of sessions per treatment episode) and the rate at which members are using services (services per 1,000 members, annualized). This information can be found by using the above formulas, but substituting the appropriate outpatient data for the inpatient numbers.

For example, if the 100,000 members of our hypothetical MBC firm used 1,250 units of outpatient services (individual, family, group, medication therapy, etc.) in one month, the rate at which services were used was 150 per 1,000 members annually. This means the firm should have the financial and clinical resources available to accommodate the delivery of 150 outpatient services for each 1,000 of its members over the course of a year. The formula used to calculate this number is:

$$\frac{\text{\# services or visits in one month}}{\text{\# of capitated members}} \times 12{,}000 = \frac{\text{rate of services used per}}{\text{1,000 members (annualized)}}$$

or

$$\frac{1{,}250}{100{,}000} \times 12{,}000 = 150 \text{ per 1,000 members, annualized}$$

MBC operations vary, but outpatient utilization in the range of 150 services or visits per 1,000 members annually is common.

Summary

MBC firms are usually funded through capitated arrangements. Frequently they carry the total financial risk for all contracted clinical services for their members. They carefully estimate utilization for a prospective member population which, along with the type of services called for within the proposed contract, drives the capitation rate charged to the customer. From this monthly revenue, the MBC firm purchases or provides services to its members, pays its overhead costs, and derives an income for itself.

Poor management of the MBC firm or factors beyond its control, such as rapidly fluctuating HMO membership, can result in financial difficulties. The outcome can be disruption in client care and hardships for the MBC firm's providers. Adequate planning, flexibility, and substantial financial resources are needed to avoid such pitfalls.

Understanding how MBC firms measure and analyze key utilization is important in understanding their overall operations. Key among this data is the hospitalization rate. MBC firms usually achieve rates in the 20 to 50 days per 1,000 member range, in contrast to the 100 to 200 day range for unmanaged mental health and substance abuse care.

INDUSTRY CONSOLIDATION

Consistent with the re-structuring of much of America's businesses in the 1990s, managed care companies have experienced a great deal of change. Some have been acquired by large insurance companies, such as CIGNA which owns MCC Behavioral Care, or AETNA which acquired Human Affairs International, both of which were once privately held companies owned by their clinician founders. Others like Preferred Health Care were sold to other managed care companies–in this case, Value Behavioral Care. EAP firms have been acquired by managed care companies to add to their product lines as was the case when Medco acquired Personnel Performance Consultants. Still other managed care companies have embarked upon acquiring group practices, in an attempt to develop treatment delivery capability within their own systems. All of these consolidations have been further evidence of how market forces have come to influence what was traditionally a slow-to-change portion of the health care industry.

Appendix E provides a directory of the nation's largest Managed

Behavioral Care companies. Clinicians or students wishing more information about their operations, customers, product lines, or provider network opportunities should contact respective companies' Provider Relations departments.

TRENDS

Growth

The most apparent trend is the growth of managed care systems, especially among large, self-insured employers. Widespread agreement among many authorities supports this notion. Given employers' and insurers' views that management of benefits is the best way to contain costs and prevent abuse and waste, it is likely that attitudes among practitioners in the mental health field will change. Managed care may well be seen as the only institution that can preserve benefits for consumers. Without this management, many payors may simply be unable to offer mental health and substance abuse benefit plans. In the practice environment of the 1990s, not only will most clinicians be participants in managed care systems, they will also have a large stake in its success—both in the interests of their clients and patients and their own professional futures. Those who practice treatment interventions aimed at the restoration of normal functioning, who are able to contain their operating costs, who are able to document the effectiveness of their services, who are able to demonstrate client satisfaction with their interventions, and who develop innovative marketing approaches toward managed care firms or design and market managed care products themselves, will find the 1990s to be a rewarding practice environment.

New Systems and Applications

Managed behavioral care is still in its infancy. It will continue to evolve in coming years. Clinicians, administrators, consultants, and human resource managers must continue to stay abreast of its evolution, influencing its development when possible.

Whereas much of MBC's focus in the 1980s was on controlling skyrocketing hospitalization rates and costs, focus may shift in the

1990s to managing outpatient and office practices. As in the case of hospitals, outpatient clinicians will increasingly find it necessary to affiliate with a managed care provider network, receiving referrals through these systems. While new managed care products may evolve that offer more choice to the consumer, the choice will have a price tag which will be greater out-of-pocket expenses. This will motivate consumers to utilize such "network providers." MBC will monitor these outpatient providers to ensure cost-conscious and effective care.

Treatment Orientation

Clinicians will increasingly be influenced to utilize interventions aimed at the restoration of normal functioning, not personality change or the restructuring of long-standing personality styles. Clinicians will need increased familiarity with short-term, brief therapy techniques and interventions, which are philosophically compatible with managed care values and benefit constraints. Opportunities will proliferate for clinicians who are able to develop innovative workplace counseling services aimed at maintaining healthy workforces. Other opportunities will exist for new programs and services aimed at treating acute patients outside of hospital walls and preventing rehospitalization. This includes after-hours crisis intervention services and home-based psychiatric treatment programs.

Academia will be challenged to respond to the development of managed care systems by modifying curriculums to include more information about these systems and their impact on clinical practice. Joseph Steiner, PhD, a social work educator at Syracuse University, says graduate students are eager to learn about managed care delivery systems and its implication for their careers. "Many want to understand how it will affect the private practice environment and their futures as clinicians," says Steiner, who teaches seminars on managed care themes. He also believes that academicians should become more involved in outcome research which will better guide managed care decision-makers and practitioners alike in developing cost-effective treatment interventions (personal communication, 1990).

Educators and researchers will also likely investigate many issues related to solution-focused treatments and other techniques that are aimed at rapid change in clients. Understanding the types of problems most amenable to remediation in one or two visits has importance to MBC and EAP practitioners alike. Research concerning these and other managed care-related themes will be an important contribution by academia in the coming years.

The Increased Role of Automated Systems

The role that electronic automated systems play in practice will increase. An example of this is Prudential Insurance Company's project that installed terminals in the offices of many of its primary care physicians in its managed care networks across the United States. These terminals, similar to the familiar grocery store checkout devices verify benefits and produce claims information.

With this system, developed by Health Information Technologies of Princeton, New Jersey, the benefit card is passed through the terminal, or if the member has no card, the identification number is entered. In a few seconds the enrollee's eligibility is verified, benefits are displayed, as well as the status of deductibles, copayments, and needed precertification or authorization information. Other insurance and managed care firms are planning to implement this or similar systems in the near future to help providers better access information.

Automated scheduling systems have also become more common. These systems allow managed care service centers to instantly schedule appointments for clients in any one of a large number of behavioral care offices; an important feature to the care of an after-business hours caller needing an urgent appointment and who does not wish to call back at some other time. Automation will simplify the authorization and claims filing processes, reducing paper flow. In short, technology will continue to revolutionize office practice, customer service, and reimbursement systems while providing impetus to practice consolidation in order to capitalize such innovations.

Nationalized Health Care and Public Policy

Some have questioned whether or not a nationalized health care system, if ever implemented, would supplant managed care technologies and offer an alternative solution to America's health care crisis. Should such a system be developed, it would likely feature more, not fewer managed care procedures. Its managers would continue to be confronted with identical quality of care and access issues, while managing taxpayers' resources to finance the massive endeavor.

Meanwhile, industry leaders say that less, not more government control is needed in the future. According to CIGNA Chairman and Chief Executive Officer Bill Taylor, the delivery of quality, affordable health care can be achieved through enhancing the private-public partnership that exists today. "It can be done without further government intervention, centralization, or additional financing. What is needed first is to make both the private and public sides of the health care equation work more cost-effectively through available managed care techniques," Taylor said in a recent address to the National Association of Manufacturers. He pointed to integrated health care plans as means of achieving affordable, quality health care. He cited the experience of corporate giant Allied-Signal, who reduced the cost of financing health services $750 per employee during an eighteen-month period while utilizing such a plan. Allied-Signal expects to save more than $200 million over three years. Taylor encouraged government to apply managed care systems to Medicare and Medicaid (CIGNA, 1990).

Public policy may be reshaped in the future to accommodate more aspects of managed care technology within existing mental health and substance abuse service delivery systems. Community mental health centers, too frequently characterized by long waiting lists for services, may benefit from the treatment approaches favored by MBC. The introduction of short-term interventions aimed at restoration of normal functioning, not characterological change, may aid in eliminating these waiting lists for outpatient treatment for many clients. At the same time, better management of scarce public hospital resources, through the use of managed care-originated procedures, may well serve the chronically mentally ill populations. Public sector clinicians, administrators, planners, and policy makers will examine managed care systems closely in coming years in an effort to glean their best features and approaches, and to determine how to modify and apply them to public settings.

Quality Assurance and Treatment Outcomes

Managed care organizations have brought new meaning to quality assurance efforts in the behavioral care treatment field. Traditionally the assurance of quality services and the improvement of services was a responsibility of the provider of care and were applied on a case-by-case, not a population-wide basis. Only in the most egregious cases of misconduct or malpractice were civil, criminal, or regulatory sanctions sought. In contrast, today's practice environment is marked by extensive quality assurance efforts conducted by managed care organizations involving large populations and in coordination with medical-surgical care quality assurance processes. The goal of these programs is to monitor service delivery; collect, trend, and analyze key data; and from this information, sustain constant improvement efforts. Summaries of these efforts are routinely reported to the managed care company's customers, or in some cases to regulatory bodies. Often specified-quality indicators are established as performance standards in customer-managed care organization contracts.

A typical quality assurance program may involve studies in three broad areas: quality measurement studies, member services studies, and utilization management studies. For example, a common quality measurement study involves auditing the care of patients who have been re-admitted to a hospital within thirty days of discharge. This audit's objectives would include an evaluation of the appropriateness of care and the opportunity for improvement in future, similar cases. Specifically, the audit might examine the adequacy of the discharge plan, the possibility of poor compliance or case management, or the intervention of additional environmental stressors that contributed to a treatment plan failure and the subsequent deterioration that lead to the readmission.

Another common audit process involves clinical chart reviews. This review's objective might be to evaluate the clinical record kept by the mental health professional as documentation of information that confirms good therapeutic practice. The review might examine the clinical record for documentation of a treatment plan that involved the patient's input and established concrete, specific, and measurable goals. Table 5-6 outlines various other common audits and reviews of quality assurance programs.

Such quality assurance efforts associated with managed care delivery systems are new to the mental health care field. To some clinicians they are controversial and objectionable. Some view them as unneeded intrusions into the clinician-client relationship and as an unwarranted supervision of professional practice. Despite the controversy, these efforts are an increasingly common aspect of practice. Managed care's customers (employers, insurers, unions,

TABLE 5-6. Quality Management Program Overview

Quality Measurement Studies

☐ Inpatient Re-admissions within 30 days

☐ Outpatient Re-admissions within 90 days

☐ Clinical Chart Review

☐ Random Case Reviews

☐ Risk Management Studies

Member Services Studies

☐ Patient Satisfaction Surveys

☐ Complaint Tracking

☐ Provider Credentialing/Recredentialing

Utilization Management Studies

☐ Inpatient Utilization Studies

☐ Outpatient Utilization Studies

☐ Denials of Benefit Coverage Based on Medical Necessity

☐ Under/Over-Utilization of Services

☐ Inter-rator Reliability of Utilization reviewers

public entities) have become accustomed to such efforts in their own field of endeavor. They tend to view quality improvement as an important contribution the managed care industry makes toward their patients' services. Most managed behavioral care companies have integrated these processes into their routine operations, sometimes employing specialists to conduct audits and reviews. Others have collaborated with academia in these efforts. It is likely that quality assurance programs will continue to expand and evolve. They will likely become a cornerstone of managed care's contributions to service delivery.

Because managed care systems involve large numbers of mental health patients, there exists a great potential for treatment outcomes studies. Such processes, if engineered into the managed care system's operations and if they involve large samples, properly case-mix adjusted to assure appropriate comparisons, offer the treatment field much information that may enhance treatment approaches and improve treatment success. During the 1990s managed care organizations began developing these efforts usually in association with academic resources. The following case study describes one type of treatment outcome process developed in 1993 by a large managed care system.

Case Study: Treatment Outcomes Process[5]

This treatment outcomes process is associated with MCC Behavioral Care, a CIGNA company, which operates a system of behavioral care practices across the country and has a national provider network.

The treatment outcomes process is called the Clinical Quality Information System (CQIS). It allows the company to demonstrably measure the impact MCC has on patient outcomes on a case-mix adjusted basis. More important, by combining additional information available within MCC, it is able to evaluate which aspects of care accounts for this improvement. MCC uses this information on an ongoing basis to enhance treatment approaches and delivery systems,while maximizing value to the payor.

---

5. For more information about this process, contact: Clinical Quality Improvement Dept., MCC Behavioral Care, 11095 Viking Drive, Suite 350, Eden Prairie, MN 55344.

MCC's Clinical Quality Information System has four unique characteristics that optimize its usefulness and applicability in the managed care setting. First, in order to assure the highest level of scientific rigor and applicability, MCC entered into a partnership with the University of Minnesota's Institute of Health Services Research, and the University of Arkansas's Comparative Outcomes Research and Evaluation Program. They have assisted MCC in developing data collection instruments that would meet the scientific and methodological rigors imposed by any academic or governmental research facility. Extensive validity and reliability testing has been conducted, verifying that the information provided by the patient is accurate and is not influenced by the individual conducting the assessment. This assures that the subsequent statistical analysis is methodologically sound and statistically conclusive.

Second, MCC has operationally engineered the collection of outcomes evaluation data into the way it does business. That is, they collect, or plan to collect, outcomes information on every substance abuse and mental health patient who receives an assessment within their behavioral care practice offices. Furthermore, the collection of this data is done in a manner that does not add apparent expense, nor interfere with patient-provider rapport. Using this experience as a springboard, MCC plans to initiate the collection of similar data across their entire network of over 10,000 providers.

Third, the outcomes evaluation system collects outcomes data on a comprehensive list of domains of interest. At base line and at six and twelve months post initial assessment, information is collected across several clinical and functional domains of interest including, but not limited to, condition-specific outcomes, social functionality, legal issues, employment status, medical utilization and sense of well-being, psychological health, patient motivation and support, and patient satisfaction. All measures are case-mix adjusted to account for severity and patient characteristic differences. Possible expansion to conduct outcomes data collection at eighteen and twenty-four months post-assessment is being considered.

The MCC computer mainframe architecture is able to incorporate information from other internal data bases including treatment and provider characteristics, benefits, eligibility, appointment scheduling, claims, authorizations, and encounter data. By using this process,

MCC is able to not only measure their effectiveness, but empirically drive quality improvement in practice protocols and delivery systems. In this way it can comprehensively evaluate program appropriateness, effectiveness, and efficiency.

CQIS is actively used within the organization, and is already helping MCC improve the quality of care provided. For example, MCC has noted–along with other managed care organizations–that a considerable proportion of substance abuse patients fail to fully engage in treatment. By using the CQIS data base along with information contained in their encounter and members files, they are able to identify predictors of non-engagement. Analysis is able to predict non-engagement with a confidence level of nearly 75 percent. Their clinicians are now developing proactive interventions that will increase their engagement rates, resulting in improved patient outcomes. This is just one example of how MCC is leveraging CQIS to make sure that they are providing optimal patient care.

Additionally, with necessary safeguards for patient privacy and confidentiality, MCC is able to conduct medical offset studies. By combining CQIS information with employer-based data such as absenteeism/tardiness, accident rates, turnover, and performance measures, the indirect expenses of substance abuse and/or mental health problems can be effectively evaluated. Furthermore, by combining utilization information from other insurance carriers, direct medical, surgical, and pharmacological cost savings associated with appropriate behavioral care intervention may be evaluated. Information gained through this type of study may allow employer groups to comprehensively evaluate the quality and value of behavioral care services provided to its employees, as well as the ability to assess the practical impact of those services on employee health, performance, and other measures of workplace productivity and wellness.

BIBLIOGRAPHY

Berk, M. L., Monheit, A. C., and Hagan, M. M. (1988, Fall). How the U.S. spent its health care dollar, 1929-1980. *Health Affairs,* pp. 46-60.

Bistline, J. L. (November 1990). Personal communication.

Bistline, J. L., Sheridan, S. M., and Winegar, N. (1991). Five critical skills for mental health counselors in managed health care. *Journal of Mental Health Counseling, 13*(1), 147-152.

CIGNA. (1990, December). Quality, affordable health care possible for all Americans. *Cigna News*, p. 1.

Cummings, N. A. (1986). The dismantling of our health care systems: Strategies for the survival of psychological practice. *American Psychologist, 41*, 426-431.

Julius, D. (1990, October). Personal communication.

LaPensee, K. T. (1991). Mental health benefits: What are the real needs and how can we control costs? In *Driving Down Health Care Costs: Strategies and Solutions* (pp. 11-1//nd11.13). New York: Panel Publishers, Inc.

Levin, B. L. and Glasser, J. H. (1989). Mental health service coverage within prepaid health plans. *Administration in Mental Health, 7*, 271-281.

Mullen, P. (1990, December 7). Prudential preps electronic claims verification. *Health Week*, p. 9.

Pigott, H. E. (1990). Psychiatric home health care: One prescription for soaring mental health costs. In *Driving Down Health Care Costs: Strategies and Solutions* (pp. 9-1//nd9.10). New York: Panel Publishers, Inc.

Shadle, M. and Christianson, J. B. (1988). The organization of mental health care delivery in HMOs. *Administration in Mental Health, 15*, 201-225.

Shadle, M. and Christianson, J. B. (1989). The impact of HMO development on mental health and chemical dependency services. *Hospital and Community Psychiatry, 40*, 1145-1151.

Staff. (1990, August-September). Insurance brokers see managed care growing. *AMCRA Newsletter,* p. 6.

Staff. (1990, August-September). Largest Managed Behavioral Care contract awarded. *AMCRA Newsletter,* p. 6.

Steiner, Joseph. (1990). Personal communication.

Wagman, J. B. and Schif, J. (1990). Managed Behavioral Care for employees: Roles for social workers. In *Occupational Social Work Today* (pp. 53-66). New York: The Haworth Press.

William M. Mercer, Inc. (1991). Employer attitudes toward the cost of health care–1990. In *Driving Down Health Care Costs: Strategies and Solutions* (pp. 15-1//nd15-18). New York: Panel Publishers, Inc.

Winegar, N., Bistline, J. L., and Sheridan, S. M. Quality and cost-effectiveness: Establishing a group therapy program in a managed care setting. *Families in Society*, Vol. 73, No. 1, pp. 56-58.

Chapter 6

Contracting with Managed Care

Managed care organizations deliver services to eligible consumers through systems or networks of practitioners, clinics, and facilities which have been screened, credentialed, and contracted to provide services. This section focuses on understanding the contracting process, the salient features of managed care provider contracts, and emerging types of contracting arrangements.

Contracts for professional services are also known as provider agreements. Like other agreements they delineate the various rights and responsibilities held by the two parties. Table 6-1 describes provider rights and responsibilities commonly found in managed care provider agreements.

In addition to discussing rights and responsibilities, provider agreements typically have supplemental attachments documenting fee schedules, product descriptions (the type of service the provider will deliver, such as an Employee Assistance Program assessment visit or a treatment service to a Preferred Provider Organization participant), utilization review protocols and procedures, provider training manuals, and practice guidelines and network directories. Importantly, agreements must delineate for both parties which network(s) is referenced. This is crucial when the managed care firm maintains multiple networks. For example, many organizations credential Employee Assistance Program networks, Preferred Provider Organization networks, and Point-of-Service networks. It is possible for a practitioner to be credentialed for one, but not all networks administered by the managed care company. Delineation of which product the practitioner will deliver on behalf of the managed care firm is another way of designating which network is involved.

TABLE 6-1. Common Provider Rights and Responsibilities Found in Providers Agreements

Responsibilities:

☐   Provide clinical services to referrals.

☐   Maintain necessary licenses or certifications needed for practice.

☐   Participate in utilization review program and protocols.

☐   Participate in the quality assurance program and protocols.

☐   Maintain malpractice insurance.

☐   Maintain clinical and administrative records.

☐   Accept agreed upon fees and not bill consumers (exceptions: copayments, deductibles, etc.).

Rights:

☐   Describe self to consumers and others as a participating provider.

☐   Compensated per an agreed-upon fee schedule, with possible billing/payment time standards.

☐   May bill informed consumers for services which are not a part of their health care benefits.

☐   Terminate the agreement with written notice.

☐   Appeal utilization review decisions per the utilization review program.

CONTRACTING WITH CLOSED NETWORKS

A network is said to be closed to new providers when there exists inadequate business need to justify expansion. That is, the existing network of providers adequately services the managed care company's pool of referrals. A network closed to new contracts may also be an indication that the company does not anticipate new business growth or may actually be losing business to competition. A closed network may also mean that the company is focusing on developing closer referral relationships with providers it has identified as offering the highest quality, most cost-effective, and consumer satisfying services. In this scenario fewer practitioners within the existing network receive a disproportionate number of referrals. Adding additional providers of care to this network would be unnecessary.

The economics of the credentialing and contracting process also create incentives for managed care organizations to maintain minimal networks of contracted practitioners to meet service and marketing objectives. Table 6-2 outlines the steps involved in contracting with a practitioner, clinic, or facility. Each step incurs a cost for the managed care company and the prospective provider of services. This pressure causes managed care companies to carefully consider any new network expansion and provide an incentive for practitioners to not join networks unless there is a likelihood that enough referrals will be forthcoming to offset their costs of the application and contracting process.

Despite these obstacles, practitioners can take measures to increase the probability they may contract with a closed network. First, clinicians should be mindful that most closed networks do not forever remain so. Therefore it may be fruitful to apply to the targeted managed care company. Network managers are likely to archive applications until such time that expansion possibilities exist and a contracting process may be initiated.

Second, understand the business cycle of prospective networks and how that cycle can create network openings. For example, HMOs typically experience a membership growth at the beginning of the calendar year, thus creating a larger referral pool for the managed care company which administers the HMO behavioral care benefits. Network expansion may occur in association with this growth of the managed care company's customer. Likewise, the addition of a new customer, a customer expanding to service a new area of city, or an employer customer opening a new facility or relocating human resources to another site, may all be reasons for network expansion. These temporal windows of opportunity may

TABLE 6-2. The Mechanics of Provider Affiliation with Managed Behavioral Care Networks

Step 1	Application completion
Step 2	Credentialing process — verification of licensure/certification — verification of ethical practice and/or complaint status with regulatory boards — verification of adequate malpractice insurance coverage
Step 3	Applicant interview by network manager(s): 1-2 hours — utilization management procedures — clinical practice guidelines
Step 4	Provider acceptance
Step 5	Provider orientation
Step 6	Ongoing provider training/feedback

come and go unless prospective providers are attuned to their respective markets.

A third strategy that may be employed in joining what is considered a closed network is that of affiliation with an existing contracted provider or group of providers. This opportunity particularly exists with practices that are already high volume providers of services for managed care networks. The addition of another practitioner to these groups gives the clinician exposure to the managed care company and an advantage in pursuing network affiliation.

As referenced in the marketing section, many other opportunities exist for obtaining contracts with managed care firms. These include filling market niches such as geographic needs (especially in rural or underserved areas), clinical specialties, language or cultural needs, hours of office operation or convenience. Professionals in some states have also used political means to enact legislation to facilitate inclusion in provider networks. These statutes are commonly referred to as "Any Willing Provider" laws and mandate that any minimally qualified practitioner who willingly accepts a discounted fee schedule may join Preferred Provider Organization networks. In states with such statutes, PPO networks can never be closed, although wholesale participation in such networks may have the dual effects of diminishing the attractiveness of a "preferred" provider network to some benefit purchasers, while driving down fees for providers as a whole.

RISK-BASED CONTRACTING

Most managed care companies that originated in serving the HMO market, began with risk-based contracts. By the early 1990s employers and managed care firms were also implementing risk-based contracts. Increasingly, providers of services are agreeing to risk-based contracts with managed care companies.

Risk-based or at-risk contracts are those in which a provider group is paid a flat fee per employee or covered life, usually on a monthly basis. The provider group is compensated with the same fee each month regardless of how many services are delivered. Fees, or capitation, fluctuate only as the number of covered lives changes. From this aggregate fee, the provider of services is responsible for the provision of all contracted services for the entire risk pool. Implementing this type of contract must focus not only on providing quality services, and complying with the managed care firm's quality assurance program but also upon managing the amount and type of services delivered to the population as a whole.

Such at-risk or capitated contracting has been a common feature in the HMO industry in its relationship to Primary Care Physicians. In 1993 in fact, capitation was the most common form of reimbursement for physician services with 62 percent of all HMOs using this form of payment. The trend toward capitated arrangements with mental health care providers has accelerated for two reasons. First it eliminates much of the need for oversight of the practitioner through precertification and case management activities, reducing costs to the managed care company. Secondly, it eliminates concerns about benefits-based provision of services (i.e., treatment plans that parallel benefit maximums since there is no economic incentive to provide unnecessary services).

At-risk contracting has many pitfalls, which are outlined in Table 6-3. Most prominent among them is an under estimation of the utilization risk, that is the actual utilization of clinical services the covered population will require. If the population utilizes more care

TABLE 6-3. Types of Risk in Risk-Based Contracts

---

1. Utilization of Services
2. Service Provider Mix (e.g., MD, PhD, LCSW, etc.)
3. Cost of Services
4. Morbidity of the Covered Population
5. Presentation Rates
6. Beta Risk

---

than estimated, costs may escalate making the contract unprofitable. Other risks include estimations of the cost of a unit of service or hospital bed day; the predicted presentation rate of new or returning patients; the morbidity factor (the degree of illness of the population impacts the nature and cost of service provision); and the beta risk or the potentiality of high costs of services to an outlier or catastrophic case within a capitated population that is too small to absorb the financial impact.

Such risk-based contracting may be an attractive alternative arrangement for doing business with managed care for many practition groups but only after a thoughtful analysis of service provision capability, actual practice patterns, anticipated utilization of services, the unit cost of various services required by the population, practice overhead cost, and derived income or profit.

BIBLIOGRAPHY

Marion Merrell Dow, Inc. (1994). *Managed Care Digest–HMO Edition*. Kansas City, MO: (Company publication), p. 12.

Zinser, G.R. (1994). Behavioral Health At-Risk Contracting–A Rate Development and Financial Reporting Guide. *Behavioral Healthcare Tomorrow*, 3(4), 27-35.

Chapter 7

Managing the Utilization Management Process

Utilization management (UM) in MBC systems refers to any of several techniques and procedures used to monitor and evaluate the necessity or appropriateness of care for insurance coverage or provider reimbursement purposes. UM ensures that services delivered are appropriate and necessary and are authorized for reimbursement in advance. UM decisions are based on information concerning clients that includes symptoms, diagnostic impressions, tentative treatment plans, response to treatment, and treatment outcomes.

UM is a term, like several others in the managed care arena, that means different things to different people. It is widely perceived as one of the most controversial areas in Managed Behavioral care. At best, it helps to ensure that care given to consumers is needed and appropriate and that the provider of this care will indeed be reimbursed for services rendered. At worst, UM is perceived as an undue intrusion into the client-therapist relationship, one that is driven by cost reduction at the expense of quality of care. Since UM procedures have demonstrated an ability to reduce hospitalization utilization, its most vocal critics are often hospitals and hospital-affiliated providers who are accustomed to inpatient-based treatment for many patients.

TYPES OF UM PROCEDURES

UM functions may be carried out in one of several ways. Telephonic UM may be conducted by local clinicians or through large centralized operations. Advantages to local UM include a better knowledge by the UM staff of local resources and providers, as well as a better opportunity to develop satisfactory working relationships with provider colleagues. Centralized UM affords cost savings due to the reduced expense of operations since one center eliminates the need for numerous locations. Mental health related utilization management may be provided by MBC firms or by EAPs.

UM may also be provided through on-site interviews, similar to how some HMOs conduct medical/surgical UM. In this example, the UM clinician might visit a hospital, interview the patient or provider(s), and read the clinical record in order to obtain first-hand information.

In MBC systems, UM functions may be the responsibility of one staff member, or they may be diffused throughout several clinicians. In medical/surgical settings, either in HMOs or in utilization management firms, UM is typically provided by nurses and physicians. However in MBC systems, other clinicians such as psychologists, clinical social workers, professional counselors, and other qualified mental health professionals may conduct UM activities. Psychiatrists are utilized directly in oversight and supervisory capacities. UM may be applied to both outpatient and inpatient cases, and UM activities, especially precertification for admission, are provided twenty-four hours per day by MBC entities.

The key task in UM procedures involves the collection of adequate clinical information needed to determine if potential or proposed services for any particular case are necessary and are eligible for reimbursement under the individual's health care or benefit plan. Alternatives may be suggested by the UM clinician if the original proposed treatment was determined to be unnecessary or not a covered service. The core functions of UM are described below.

Eligibility Determination

Eligibility determination is a UM function that ensures that any member is indeed a valid member and is eligible for covered services. This is usually done electronically.

Benefit Interpretation

Benefit interpretation is an important aspect of UM in which the MBC clinician determines whether the presenting condition is one that is eligible for covered services.

Precertification for Admission

Precertification for admission (or "pre-cert") refers to UM personnel making the above determination before an individual is admitted to an inpatient facility or an outpatient episode of treatment. Care is then authorized for reimbursement in advance or alternative (usually less costly) care is recommended. (See Figure 7-1.) An example of how this precertification process works is described below.

Mr. Black is a fifty-year-old, married engineer who receives health insurance coverage through his employer's plan. His drinking problem has gradually accelerated over the years. He has never sought treatment, and never attended Alcoholics Anonymous. On a Sunday morning, after a particularly painful episode of drinking, his wife, who is familiar with Recovery Hospital's substance abuse treatment program, convinces her husband to go there and seek services. The admission nurse at the hospital accesses the UM clinic associated with Mr. Black's health care plan by dialing the twenty-four-hour number on the benefit card Mr. Black presented. The UM clinician obtained clinical data from the admissions nurse and Mr. and Mrs. Black. The UM clinician (after consulting with her physician back-up) determines that the proposed twenty-eight-day hospitalization for alcoholism is not clinically necessary, and that an alternative form of treatment will be appropriate and will be covered by the health care plan. The clinician recommends instead an intensive outpatient treatment program, after a screening by Mr. Black's physician. The new plan is discussed with the patient and his wife. He begins the treatment program authorized the next night, having also returned to work.

Although this vignette is a simplified one, it illustrates several important features of precertification:

Accessibility, twenty-four-hour, 365-day per year accessibility, is required of UM functions. Psychiatric and substance abuse crises occur at all hours, so MBC systems must have easily accessible UM capacity at all times.

Consultation and medical backup, often through a supervising psychiatrist, are important resources to the UM clinician. In the example above, the clinician collected available data about Mr. Black's medical condition both from the hospital's admission

FIGURE 7-1. Precertification for Admissions

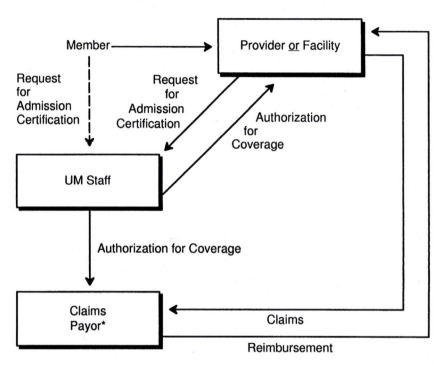

* This entity may be the MBC firm, the HMO, insurance carrier, or another party functioning as a Third Party Administrator (TPA).

worker and the patient. The determination was made that Mr. Black was in no immediate danger from acute alcohol withdrawal symptoms. While treatment at the hospital may have offered the maximum level and intensity of care, the patient was able to participate in an alternative, less costly level of care.

Crisis nature of precertfication situations. Such precertification processes may be conducted in the midst of an emotion-laden series of events. In this instance, both the patient and his spouse as well as the admission worker may have attempted to persuade the UM clinician to authorize care in the hospital setting. At that moment admission to the facility was viewed as a crucial need. This well intended pressure did not prevent the worker from collecting necessary clinical information and making the decision about precertification. In other words the UM clinician had to deny the request for coverage in such a way as to maintain a therapeutic contract with the member and maintain a working relationship with the hospital personnel. Much clinical expertise was needed to frame the hospital presentation by the Blacks as an important milestone and refocus their attention toward outpatient treatment avenues.

Cost savings. In a System without precertification (where essentially the admission worker in this example would have obtained coverage simply by facilitating the admission) the cost of Mr. Black's twenty-eight days of treatment might have been $14,000 or more. Most of the cost would have been borne by the health care plan. Instead, the patient was directed to a treatment program costing only $2,000 over the course of one year. Additionally, the patient continued working. The cost savings amounted to $12,000 directly, and much more in indirect savings to the plan and the member.

Concurrent Review

As implied, this review occurs concurrently with the treatment service provided to MBC members. It assesses the need for continued treatment in a hospital setting or continuation with a course of outpatient treatment. (See Figure 7-2.)

In instances of hospital concurrent review, the UM clinician often will authorize one day or a few days coverage initially. After the inpatient has been assessed, a prospective discharge date is established between the UM clinician and attending physician. Further hospital coverage may be authorized pending the determination of a tentative D/C date. Periodic telephonic updates are used to monitor the patient's progress throughout the hospital stay, and obtain and evaluate any new clinical information that might lengthen or shorten the duration of the necessary hospital care.

UM staff play an active role in discharge planning and clinical case management for inpatients. Discharge planning on the part of the MBC firm is likely to begin at the time of hospital admission.

FIGURE 7-2. Concurrent Review

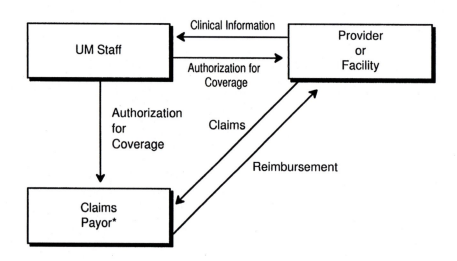

* This entity may be the MBC firm, the HMO, insurance carrier, or another party functioning as a Third Party Administrator (TPA).

The UM clinician may present the case in a clinical staffing or team meeting. Treatment modalities and community resources are reviewed. Often the family is interviewed. The UM clinician becomes the liaison with hospital staff in efforts to coordinate this planning and a smooth transition to outpatient treatment.

In systems that utilize a DRG reimbursement system for hospital stabilization, treatment, or detoxification, the concurrent role is deemphasized. Activity by the UM staff is more focused in the area of discharge planning, since DRGs tend to affix in advance a discharge date for many patients.

Outpatient concurrent review processes begin with an authorization for coverage for "X" number of visits. The initial precertification and authorization may occur after the MBC firm has conducted an initial assessment, after the treatment provider has conducted the assessment and communicated it to the UM clinician, or in some

cases, after another clinician who will not provide treatment services has evaluated the member. Authorizations are typically
mailed to the member as well as the provider. Much outpatient
concurrent review is done through the use of various written updates and summaries. These communicate to the UM staff how the
authorized treatment is progressing and how the patient responded
to the services. Appendix C shows samples of such concurrent
review authorizations, forms, and letters. The following case study
demonstrates the application of several UM techniques.

Ms. Ferguson is twenty-six years old, and employed as an ac-
countant. She presented at the office of her primary care physician,
who contacted the UM staff at the MBC. She was assessed by the
UM staff as exhibiting severe depressive symptomatology. An admission was precertified at a non-network psychiatric hospital and
three days were authorized initially. Initial treatment goals included
further assessment and symptom stabilization.

On the third day telephone concurrent review was conducted
between the UM staff and the treating psychiatrist. The patient had
been diagnosed with major depression, single episode. The psychiatrist indicated that the patient, who had been started on a course of
antidepressant medication on the day of admission, had demonstrated little response to the medication or the hospital milieu. She
judged that the patient could not be treated safely as an outpatient
until further stabilization occurred. The psychiatrist stated that further care could provide close observation of her medication response and provide a safe environment. She also requested coverage for a session with the patient and her spouse to address marital
dysfunction, which seemed to be exacerbating the depression. The
psychiatrist indicated she planned to discuss with the patient and
her husband outpatient treatment services which would follow inpatient care. Three additional days were authorized with a tentative
discharge date being established for the seventh day.

The UM clinician contacted the psychiatrist on the day before the
tentative discharge. The psychiatrist reported the patient had responded favorably, and the outpatient plan for services was con-
firmed. The attending psychiatrist conveyed that Ms. Ferguson's
condition had stabilized enough for her to make the transition to
outpatient care. Her depressive symptoms had diminished and the

lethality risk had declined. The psychiatrist recommended that medication therapy be continued and counseling services initiated with the couple. Ms. Ferguson was seen the day of discharge by the MBC affiliated providers in the outpatient setting.

The case of Ms. Ferguson illustrates several important qualities about inpatient concurrent review. Care is authorized for treatment interventions which are implemented at the onset of the hospital stay. Authorization for coverage of subsequent days is based on specific clinical data regarding the patient's response and progress, and care is expected to be focused toward specific objectives. Another quality illustrated is that discharge planning begins early in the hospital stay. Finally, the working relationship with the attending physician is key. The psychiatrist shared the objectives of the UM staff of stabilizing the patient's condition as quickly as possible and preparing Ms. Ferguson for outpatient treatment as soon as appropriate.

TYPICAL UM QUESTIONS

UM decisions are based on clinical data obtained through the means previously discussed. Below are generalized UM questions which may be used to gather the necessary clinical information. In practice, more specific details are usually elicited.

- What is the member's DSM-III-R diagnosis(es)?
- How, or by what means, was this diagnosis reached?
- What is the member's current mental status and lethality?
- What, if any, treatment history is known? (i.e., number of hospitalizations, length of prior hospital stays, number of outpatient visits)
- What alternative types of treatment have been considered for this member?
- What are the clinical goals for this treatment episode?
- How will more treatment (more hospital days or visits) contribute to achieving these goals?
- How will treatment outcomes (i.e., the achievement of particular goals) be measured?

MEDICAL NECESSITY

The determination of what care or treatment is medically necessary is the central consideration in precertification and concurrent review decisions. Clinical information gathered by UM staff is aimed at this question. The responsibility for making this decision as it pertains to benefit coverage is delegated to the MBC from the firm's customer, an HMO or employer. This issue has been, and will continue to be, the focus of litigation and court rulings. (See Chapter 7 for further discussion of the legal underpinning of UM decisions related to the necessity.)

UM staff are guided by what medically necessary care means in mental health or substance abuse settings through standards or treatment criteria utilized to authorize care for respective diagnoses. These standards do not represent "cookbooks;" they instead are guides requiring clinical interpretation and application on a care-by-care basis (*Clinical Psychiatry News,* 1990).

In the vignette of Mr. Black, the UM criteria in operation helped the clinician arrive at an authorization decision by determining that:

   a. the member was not a medical risk for alcohol withdrawal complications necessitating twenty-four-hour nursing care;
   b. the member was in need of treatment and was motivated for treatment;
   c. the member had never attempted outpatient substance abuse treatment.

Therefore, outpatient substance abuse treatment was recommended to him and was authorized for coverage by his health care plan.

MCC Companies, Inc., which has both centralized and local market UM capabilities, has developed a *Preferred Practice Guide* (1989), which outlines practice standards for the treatment of various disorders. MCC continues to refine and revise it in an effort to assist its UM operations concerning these determinations. Application of such documents helps to ensure MBC customers consistency and uniformity where multiple sites are involved. Although professional groups such as the American Psychiatric Association are now developing standards of treatment documents, the historic lack of such standards and a consensus about them among various professionals has led to the development of MBC. In effect the payors, through MBC firms, have driven the development treatment standards themselves.

DENIALS, APPEALS, AND OTHER UM ASPECTS

All MBC firms have appeal processes to review UM decisions that have resulted in a denial of authorization for coverage. These procedures may require a written appeal; others involve an "expedited appeal process" by which a decision about the appeal may take place while the disputed care is still underway. Quality utilization management firms have clear procedures for these expedited or emergent appeals. UM processes usually involve a physician's approval in cases where a requested authorization (especially hospitalization) is denied.

Often, UM staff will offer to retrospectively review a disputed request. This offer implies that coverage for services may be extended retroactively, pending the review. This review process includes the examination of complete treatment records as well as other supplemental materials. UM staff typically advise providers and members in writing of denials for coverage.

MBC clinicians also apply UM procedures to psychological assessment and evaluations. Not all psychological testing may be covered by a MBC benefit plan, and testing is preauthorized. UM staff frequently authorize testing for the following reasons:

a. To clarify a diagnostic impression. Providers who are unsure of a diagnosis may be authorized to conduct particular assessments to establish or rule out a diagnosis.

b. To focus treatment. Providers who request specific tests that will help establish appropriate treatment goals may have testing authorized by UM staff.

Generally, MBC UM standards do not include routine authorizations for complete psychological evaluations for every client. Again, UM staff view testing as a resource to be authorized for coverage on an as-needed basis, usually centering around the criteria above.

The confidentiality of client information obtained through UM processes is assumed by the provider-MBC agreement. (See the sample agreement in Appendix A.) However, it is wise to obtain a signed authorization for disclosures to the MBC or UM firm and to fully explain to a client that information about his or her treatment is being reported for reimbursement of services rendered.

Provider-UM staff relationships have great potential for difficulty, but it is not necessary that this be the case. Here are some tips on how to create this problematic relationship and how to diffuse it.

Twelve Strategies for Creating Problematic Relationship with UM Staff . . . and Alternatives!

Strategy No. 1: Never use the DSM-III-R diagnostic system and nomenclature.

Alternative: Become familiar with the DSM-III-R diagnostic system and nomenclature. Be prepared to document your diagnosis and communicate it to the UM staff.

Strategy No. 2: Establish vague, or no, treatment goals with the client (and do so slowly).

Alternative: Join with the client in establishing achievable, mutually agreed upon goals quickly. Use a written treatment plan. Clarify goals early in the assessment and treatment process.

Strategy No. 3: Establish vague, or no, outcome measures for any treatment goals (and do so slowly).

Alternative: Develop with the client what outcome measures of the treatment goals will be utilized. Be concise, concrete, and as behaviorally oriented as possible. Be able to explain to UM personnel exactly how you will know when the client has achieved agreed upon goals for the treatment episode.

Strategy No. 4:   Keep vague, or no, clinical notes. Reconstruct important issues about therapy sessions from memory for the UM staff.

Alternative: Keep accurate written notes about all clinical contacts with the client. The S.O.A.P. format, or a variation, is an excellent means of accomplishing this documentation. (See Appendix D.) The ability to access these notes and provide documentation of progress or setbacks is vital to successful working relationships with UM personnel.

Strategy No. 5:   Play "telephone-tag" with the UM staff conducting concurrent review. After a few tries, give up!

Alternative: Schedule a time of day and/or day of the week to discuss cases with the UM staff doing concurrent review. This simplifies your task and theirs.

Strategy No. 6:   Remain as ignorant as possible of the MBC firm's standards for treatment.

Alternative: Ask the UM staff of the MBC firm to share information about their standards of care. Learn what the preferred types and durations of treatment are for particular diagnostic groups, realizing the need for case-by-case variations.

Strategy No. 7:   Assume "precertification" or "preauthorization" does not really mean "pre." Call the MBC firm's UM staff long after the client has been admitted for services.

Alternative: Precertification and preauthorization mean, for reimbursement purposes, that services must be authorized in advance. Not obtaining such advance authorization for benefit coverage can mean the financial responsibility for services may fall upon the provider or the client.

Strategy No. 8:   Interpret the client's benefits yourself. Interpret them as liberally as you wish, including the conditions you feel should be included for coverage in the benefit plan. Express any resentments about benefit limits, exclusions, or UM processes through the client.

Alternative: Do not interpret benefits to the client. This responsibility has been delegated to the MBC firm by the purchaser of benefits, the HMO, or the employer. Refer benefit questions to the UM staff. Do not express resentments or concerns through the client. This is counter-therapeutic. Express concerns about benefit limits or how they are interpreted directly to the MBC firm, employer, or through avenues such as professional associations.

Strategy No. 9:   Do not bother about learning the MBC firm's appeal process for reversing UM decisions.

Alternative: Learn about this appeal process, and how and when to use it. Upon appeal, UM decisions are sometimes reversed. Learn about the UM firm's expedited appeal procedure.

Strategy No. 10:   Do not bother with UM related paperwork. If you do, do so incompletely and slowly.

Alternative: The paperwork related to UM is a necessary fact of practice. It is important for accountability purposes and ignoring it will be problematic. Complete it as expeditiously as possible. Suggest ways to streamline the necessary paperwork or develop alternative ways of processing the paper flow.

Strategy No. 11:   Expect only stable, nonacute referrals from UM staff; expect UM staff to authorize coverage for maximal treatment interventions and durations.

Alternative: Anticipate receiving acute clients with the expectation on the part of the UM staff that the provider will initiate treatment quickly. Expect authorization for care that is not necessarily the maximal intervention, but one that the UM staff has deemed appropriate to the degree of need and that will return the client to normal levels of functioning as soon as possible. Expect the UM staff to be driven by values of efficiency, effectiveness, and cost-consciousness.

Strategy No. 12:   Assume that UM staff are excessively rigid and unlikely to be open to innovation. Approach them by evidencing these qualities yourself.

Alternative: UM staff can be very flexible and innovative. Both they and the MBC firm are interested in exploring innovative programs, services, and arrangements for providing clinically effective and cost-effective assessment and treatment services. Approach UM staff with the intent of forming a mutually satisfactory partnership aimed at providing quality services for both customers: the client and the MBC firm.

BIBLIOGRAPHY

Bartlett, J. (Ed.) (1990). *Preferred Practice Guide.* Minneapolis, MN: MCC Managed Behavioral Care, Inc.

Clinical Psychiatry News (1990, November). Need to develop flexible practice guidelines emphasized.

Gray, B. H. and Field, M. J. (Eds.) (1990). *Controlling Costs and Changing Patient Care: The Role of Utilization Management.* Washington, DC: National Academy Press.

Chapter 8

Legal Issues and Utilization Management

MAJOR CASES

Utilization management (UM) systems can substantially impact the delivery of care. Therefore, UM decisions have the potential for harm to consumers and are subject to legal liabilities. The issues surrounding the exact nature and extent of such liabilities are complex, and are unfolding both through case law and the implementation of new legislation and regulation. It is beyond the scope of this discussion to detail and explore all the intricacies of this topic. Instead, this chapter will focus on major cases in recent years that have been construed as establishing the legal underpinnings of the UM process.[1]

The first case was that of *Sarchett*, which upheld the right of an insurer to participate in the decision making and determination of what care is "medically necessary" and therefore reimbursable. The *Wickline* case dealt with the liability potential of the UM organization resulting from the possibility of harm to the patient as an outcome of a UM decision. Both are medical/surgical cases, but their implications transcend to Managed Behavioral UM as well. The *Wilson* case has not been disposed of by the courts at this writing, but may ultimately have substantial implications for the utilization management field.

---

1. For an excellent and fuller discussion see Helvestine, William A. (1989). Legal Implications of Utilization Review. In Bradford H. Gray and Marilyn J. Field (Eds), *Controlling Costs and Changing Patient Care: The Role of Utilization Management*. Washington, DC: Institute of Medicine National Academy Press, pp. 169-204. Helvestine is the major source for this chapter.

Sarchett v. Blue Shield of California, 1987(43 Cal. 3d. 1,233 Cal. Rptr. 76, 729p. 2d 267)

This case involved a retrospective review by an indemnity insurance company's UM staff. The plaintiff, John Sarchett, had been hospitalized for three days by his primary care physician. Later, Blue Shield UM staff reviewed the hospitalization records. They determined that (1) the hospitalization of Mr. Sarchett had been for diagnostic purposes only, and (2) the hospitalization had not been medically necessary. Their position was that it was not necessary to utilize this level of care–hospitalization–to achieve the diagnostic goals. Coverage for the charges associated with the hospitalization was denied. Blue Shield pointed out that the denial was based on two policy exclusions: (1) hospitalization for diagnostic purposes only, and (2) care that is not medically necessary. Sarchett claimed that he relied upon his physician, and the physician's judgement was that the hospital care was necessary.

The California Supreme Court held that Blue Shield could indeed perform a retrospective review, examining the medical necessity of the hospitalization. The court held that this is an implied right of an insurer. Furthermore, it rejected the premise that only the treating physician could determine medical necessity and that Blue Shield should be bound by the physician's judgement. The court endorsed the practice of preadmission certification as a means of avoiding such disputes.

The importance of Sarchett, then, is twofold. It helped establish the prerogative of insurance carriers, for coverage purposes, to participate in defining what care is medically necessary. Moreover, it denied that only the treating clinician can make this determination and bind an insurance carrier to this decision for coverage purposes.

Wickline v. California (192 Cal. App. 3d 1630, 239 Cal. Rptr. 810, 1986)

Wickline has proven to be a seminal case in the area of UM liability. It relates to the key issue of what is the extent of the UM firm's liability for poor clinical outcomes that may stem from a UM decision. The case pertains to the concurrent review process concerning the care given to a patient in 1977. The concurrent review organization was the state's Medicaid program, Medi-Cal.

The plaintiff, Mrs. Wickline, was being treated for leg and back ailments. Her physicians recommended hospitalization and surgery. Consistent with Medi-Cal's procedures, the admission was precertified. An approved length-of-stay of ten days was authorized; any stay beyond the ten days would require further authorization by Medi-Cal. The patient had complications after the first surgery, however, and two more surgeries were performed. The treating physician requested that eight more hospital days be authorized for coverage by Medi-Cal (for a total LOS of eighteen days). A Medi-Cal nurse, consulting with a Medi-Cal physician, reviewed the case again and responded to the treating physician's request with an authorization for four more days' coverage for the hospital care (for a total LOS of fourteen, not the requested eighteen days). The nurse reviewer did not document the specific reasons for the partial denial of coverage.

The physician discharged Mrs. Wickline after the authorized stay of fourteen days. (All of the physicians involved in the case were aware of the Medi-Cal appeal process, but none appealed the concurrent review decision.) At the time of discharge the patient was stable and was not in danger according to subsequent court testimony. Her physician reported that the last days in the hospital were used for observation of Mrs. Wickline's condition and progress. He stated that he would have continued her hospital treatment, regardless of the Medi-Cal coverage decision, if he had felt she needed more hospital care. One week after the discharge Mrs. Wickline was seen in her physician's office for follow-up. Nothing remarkable was found. Then, nine days after discharge, Mrs. Wickline grew worse and was readmitted to a hospital. Eventually her right leg had to be amputated at the hip. Mrs. Wickline later sued Medi-Cal for negligence, alleging that Medi-Cal's decision to not authorize the additional eight hospital days requested by her physician resulted in her injury (the injury being the subsequent amputation of her right leg).

A jury trial was held in the Wickline case. The jury awarded the patient $500,000 in damages for her injury, but the California Court of Appeals reversed the jury verdict.

The *Wickline* case and decision involved several key issues. First, the UM firm (Medi-Cal itself in this case) was sued for negligence, the most likely cause for legal actions brought against UM firms. In order to prove negligence, the plaintiff must demonstrate that the defendant owed the plaintiff a duty of reasonable care, that the duty was not fulfilled, and that, as a result, an injury occurred. Courts have agreed that UM firms have a duty of care to patients (since nonauthorization of care may mean that the patient will not seek care), and that there must be reasonable standards of care as well as reasonable processes to apply the standards. Plaintiffs have the greatest difficulty in proving negligence when attempting to demonstrate that UM decisions are causative (i.e., result in injury that would not have otherwise occurred).

The appellate court's ruling related to these aspects of proving negligence on the part of a UM firm. First, the Court of Appeals ruled the UM organization played a role in the discharge decision, but that *ultimate responsibility for Mrs. Wickline's discharge lay with her physicians.* In other words, Medi-Cal was not proximately responsible for the decision to discharge her after fourteen days.

Second, the court did not find that the decision to discharge was causative of the later amputation. Mrs. Wickline's own physicians said, in effect, that she was stable when she left the hospital. Moreover, she was doing well seven days after the hospital discharge, three days beyond the hospital time originally requested for authorization.

Finally, the court held that UM groups are participants in important treatment decisions and therefore can be liable for defects of design in their systems, or for poor implementation of such systems. The decision served to put such firms on notice that their processes must be adequately designed and administered in order to reduce their liability in cases with unfortunate outcomes.

The *Wickline* decision points out to clinicians some interesting features of our judicial system. First is the difficulty of proving that any UM decision results in an injury. The plaintiff in this case was not able to show that her deterioration and subsequent amputation could have been prevented if she had been authorized for the extra four hospital days. In the realm of psychiatric and behavioral medicine, a demonstration of causation might be even more difficult to prove.

Second, the *Wickline* case clearly demonstrates the sympathetic nature of the jury system. A jury of her peers assessed that Mrs. Wickline, who presented before them as an infirmed amputee, had been wronged by the bureaucratic blunders of an uncaring, quasi-governmental insurance carrier. It easily awarded her $500,000 (only to have the decision reversed later by the appellate court). A lesson insurance companies have learned from this is to settle out of court with plaintiffs who are particularly "attractive" to sympathetic jurors, thus avoiding costly legal proceedings in jury trials and appeals courts.

Wilson v. Blue Cross of Southern California et al. (No. B04597, Cal. Ct App filed July 27, 1990)

The same division of the state court of appeals that handed down the landmark *Wickline* decision recently made another important ruling concerning a case that is unfolding. Its implications may be far reaching. In this case a patient was admitted to an inpatient facility for the treatment of depression. The physician estimated the needed length of stay as three to four weeks of hospital-based care. Blue Cross' utilization review firm informed the hospital that it would not cover the extended stay, and the patient was discharged. A few weeks later he committed suicide. His heirs then sued the insurer, the UM firm, and its physician consultant for wrongful death.

The trial court decided to grant the defendant's (Blue Cross et al.) motion for a summary judgement. The appeal court reversed this decision and remanded the case for a trial on its merits. The court held that the facts presented by the plaintiffs constituted sufficient evidence for a triable issue concerning a causal link between the denial of insurance coverage and the death of the patient a few weeks later. The court also said that the UM program's emphasis on cost containment inappropriately affected medical judgement, with a result of a premature discharge. This was in contrast to the *Wickline* case, in which the court held that the provider was responsible for the decision to discharge the patient.

IMPLICATIONS FOR EMPLOYERS

UM firms, their employees and consultants, and/or their insurance carrier or self-insured employer who hires them, may be brought to court concerning a range of other charges. Plaintiff's attorneys usually pursue the "deepest pocket," that is, the insurance company, the state (as in the *Wickline* case), or an employer, instead of a UM or managed care firm. Charges may involve infliction of emotional distress through a UM decision, breach of contract, product liability, or other concerns.

UM firms may also be sued by treatment providers. In *Slaughter v. Friedman* (32 Cal. 3d. 148, 185 Cal Rptr. 244, 649 p. 2d a66, 1982), the plaintiff, an oral surgeon, successfully claimed a dental insurance company's medical director defamed his professional reputation when denying claims for his services. The director had said that he was overcharging his patients. Statements such as these, when made by a UM firm to a patient, may indicate malice toward a particular provider. UM firms should be careful, for this reason, to not use unnecessarily inflammatory language to patients about providers.

Employers who attempt to contain costs for their employee benefit programs by designing their own benefit plan or by contracting with MBC or UM firms may take several steps to limit their exposure to liability claims. Here are some strategies and examples of how they may be applied.

Although unlikely, it is possible that an employer who purchases services for employees through an HMO or PPO can have potential liability for the malpractice of the HMO or PPO sanctioned provider. (In this instance the employer's liability would be premised on negligent selection of the HMO or PPO, a difficult point to establish.) Employers can avoid this situation by selecting accredited HMOs or PPOs who have adequate credentialing policies and procedures.

Despite the protections afforded by the Employee Retirement and Income Security Act (ERISA), employers who self-insure still have the responsibility to act in the employee's best interests concerning the administration of benefits, a high standard of operation requiring close scrutiny of MBC or UM vendors acting on the employer's behalf. Here are some steps these employers may consider to assume quality service delivery.

- Use a written selection process as a guide to selecting a MBC/ UM vendor. Follow the process.
- Use a corporate panel of appropriate staff to review and monitor the services of MBC/UM firms. These panels may include the medical director, attorney, benefits manager, human resources manager, and Employee Assistance Program director or consultant.
- Inspect the MBC/UM firm's credentialing process for its providers. Does the firm have adequate policies and procedures to screen out unethical or poor quality practitioners? Does it ensure that its providers have adequate malpractice insurance and that it is always current? Are its providers licensed or certified for delivering the services they intend to perform?
- Ensure that the MBC/UM firm employs licensed and/or certified staff who practice within the scope of their licensure. Are the MBC/UM firm's programs licensed where applicable?
- Ensure that the MBC/UM firm bases its operations upon written clinical standards and level of care guidelines. Are these standards consistently employed? Ensure that there are adequate safeguards to prevent abuse of the standards for the financial gain of the firm.
- Educate employees about benefit plans and about their interface with the company's Employee Assistance Programs. Ensure that employees understand that benefits may be limited to medically necessary care, if this is the case.

STATE REGULATIONS AND ERISA

Several states have enacted or are proposing legislation to regulate UM processes and entities. This will likely be a trend for several years to come. State legislation in this arena pertains to confidentiality of patient records, minimum personnel qualifications, and processes for the appeal of decisions made by UM firms. It is important that clinicians and providers have input into legislation in this realm. Professional associations usually should monitor any relevant legislative initiatives.

In a 1987 case (reaffirmed in 1990) the U.S. Supreme Court ruled that when insurance is provided through a self-insured or ERISA qualified plan, state law is preempted by ERISA. (See Chapter 1 for a fuller description of ERISA.) Most private employers' plans are thus preempted from many of the liability concerns discussed above. If the employer's UM firm is judged, under ERISA, to have "fiduciary" responsibility (discretionary authority or control) on the plan's behalf, the firm is also exempted. The exact scope of ERISA preemption is still being clarified by the courts. Uncertainty remains.

ERISA also limits the extent of damages awarded against ERISA qualified plans. The monetary award is usually equivalent to the recovery of the plan's benefits, *not* awards for pain and suffering. Also, jury trials are not a right under ERISA regulations, while awards for the plaintiff's attorney fees are allowed. These aspects of ERISA provide a substantial disincentive to bring litigation against employer plans.

SUMMARY

The Supreme Court's interpretation of ERISA limits much litigation against MBC entities that have UM functions. Under the HMO rubric, much more litigation is precluded by the arbitration clause in provider contracts. These clauses often bind the parties to settle any disputes through a predetermined arbitration process. Despite these protections, UM firms, employers, insurance carriers, and their personnel are at risk for litigation by dissatisfied consumers and providers. This is especially the case when UM processes are not clearly defined, followed, and documented. The courts, state legislatures (in absence of national health care policies and universal health care systems), and governmental regulatory agencies are likely to make, interpret, and implement statutes and regulations concerning utilization review. Clinicians and employers should keep abreast of these developments and offer their input. Utilization management and MBC firms surely will.

BIBLIOGRAPHY

Helvestine, W. A. (1989). Legal implications of utilization review. In B. H. Gray and M. J. Field (Eds.), *Controlling Costs and Changing Patient Care: The Role of Utilization Management* (pp. 169-204). Washington, DC: Institute of Medicine National Academy Press.

Pollard, M. R. and Rinn, C. C. (1990). Employee benefit plans: New liabilities for employers. *HMO/PPO Trends, 3* (5), 12-15.

Staff. (1990, October). Wickline court backtracks in Wilson, says UR firms bear liability for bad decision making. *Managed Care Law Outlook,* pp. 2-4.

Chapter 9

Marketing to Managed Care

IMPLICATIONS FOR CLINICIANS

As the market share of managed care directed referrals grows, practitioners must re-examine traditional service offerings, practice structures, and sales strategies. Since managed care organizations value services that are effective, consumer-friendly, and efficiently delivered, these qualities must be interwoven in demonstratable ways into practice strategies. This challenge creates exciting marketing opportunities for practitioners and managers. This chapter discusses some of the most salient implications for change in clinical practice brought about by MBC entities. It also suggests strategies that will assist the mental health professional in retaining as much control as possible of his or her professional future. Refer to the Appendix section which provides comprehensive information about HMOs operating in respective markets, as well as a directory of managed behavioral care companies. Since most HMOs provide behavioral care services, practitioners may discern which managed behavioral care organization they utilize, or what referral arrangements have been made for mental health and substance abuse patients. Likewise, the mental health care company directory affords the reader a means of assessing opportunites to market services, contract with, and receive referrals from the organizations that manage mental health care services for HMOs, employers, unions, and public entities.

OUTPATIENT PRACTICE

Employment Opportunities

MBC represents the corporatization of mental health services and a diminution of the "cottage industry" nature of the field. One important aspect of this corporatization is that more and more clinicians are employed directly by these MBC firms. The exact number of therapists employed by MBC and EAP firms is not known. The largest of these firms employ hundreds of clinicians directly. Thousands more are employed indirectly as network providers or affiliates. These numbers will grow dramatically in the coming years as MBC continues to expand in both size and acceptance.

As this growth occurs, competition for competent staff will escalate salary and benefit packages, making MBC and EAP settings increasingly attractive to clinicians as career opportunities. Individuals whose treatment backgrounds feature experience with interventions that are successful at promoting rapid change in patients will be especially in demand. Also in demand will be clinicians who have practice experience in both inpatient and outpatient settings, who have keen assessment and diagnostic skills, and who enjoy a treatment team milieu as a work environment. A knowledge of the workings of MBC systems will be essential to all clinicians interested in careers in these challenging settings.[1]

While excellent skills are essential, of even more importance to these clinicians may be a sharing of values associated with managed care entities. "Clinicians most suited to managed care are those who receive their reward from seeing patients recover rapidly and in seeing mental health and substance abuse (benefits) extended to cover all employees," according to Nicholas A. Cummings, PhD, Chief Executive Officer of American Biodyne, Inc., a national MBC firm based in San Francisco. A former president of the American Psychological Association, Cummings points out that therapists who are successful in managed care settings share a belief that unless managed care is successful in its mission, many employers will choose to reduce or eliminate benefit coverage altogether due to increasing costs (Personal communication, 1990).

For clinicians interested in careers in the MBC industry, there are several types of positions in most such systems. Clinical managers in MBC hold positions such as Executive Director or Network

---

1. See Bistline, J. L. et al. (January 1991). "Five Critical Skills for Mental Health Counselors in Managed Health Care." *Journal of Mental Health Counseling 13*(1), 147-152.

Manager. These are challenging positions involving much clinical and managerial skills. These individuals must have the knowledge of clinical, financial, and administrative systems necessary to manage the complexities of MBC operations, while interfacing with employer, HMO, or insurance carrier customers. The recruitment and development of provider networks is a key task of this position.

A variety of clinical positions are found in these systems, including challenging supervisory roles. Important aspects of supervisors' roles include facilitating training and staff development, leading clinical case staffings, monitoring the delivery of clinical services, providing customer service functions, and interacting with network providers. Supervisors in MBC systems must have a thorough knowledge of managed care operations as well as diverse clinical skills and knowledge of community resources.

The clinical case manager is a key position in MBC systems. In some operations this individual provides direct assessment and treatment services. In systems that heavily utilize a provider network for treatment services, the clinical case manager may serve a utilization management role, interacting with the treatment provider in developing treatment plans, providing peer consultation, and maintaining an ongoing dialogue with the provider to ensure the timely and appropriate delivery of care. At the same time, this case manager explores and evaluates the totality of applicable community resources available to the client, recommending such resources as would supplement direct treatment services. Examples include self-help and support groups, educational programs, or social services. Substantial skills for interacting with various individuals, as well as clinical acumen are essential in this role.

Another key clinical role is that of utilization management worker. The tasks and skills associated with this position parallel that of the clinical case manager. The role involves the interpretation of clinical criteria for admission to inpatient or outpatient treatment, as well as the determination of length of stay at all levels of care. Psychiatric nurses often fulfill these roles in MBC, but other professionals such as clinical social workers, psychologists, and professional counselors as well as physicians are also involved in utilization management functions.

Besides these positions, many other evolving professional roles are found in MBC systems. Psychiatrists and addictionologists serve in clinical and clinical managerial positions, often playing major roles in utilization and peer review, and quality assurance efforts. As MBC and EAP systems merge, more and more specialists with experience and skills in both areas of practice will be employed in the emerging generation of products that have features of both MBC and EAPs. Other specialty positions center upon network development, customer services, and technical sales.

Private Practice Survival Skills

While MBC offers various employment opportunities for practitioners, it presents important implications for clinicians who choose to pursue private practice careers. Many private practitioners are understandably concerned about the changes brought about by MBC. Some wonder if managed care may mean the demise of private therapy and counseling practices. Undoubtedly, for some this will be this case, as they are unable to accommodate the necessary changes in practice patterns or are too inefficient or ineffective to withstand the test of increased accountability and structure demanded by managed care.

Table 9-1 summarizes the changes in traditional office-based therapy that managed care has brought about, and will bring about increasingly. Some of these involve attitudinal change by practitioners, others involve changes in clinical techniques, while still others involve new marketing and strategic approaches to the business of private practice.

Attitudinal Changes

Most clinicians have been schooled to view the client as the "customer." Much clinical focus by private practitioners has been upon client service and the fostering of the client-therapist relationship to the exclusion of other influences. Managed care forces a reevaluation and modification of this attitude to include the MBC (or EAP firm) as the customer as well, taking into consideration the overall goals and objectives of the referral source. These goals may include the return of the client to an optimal, if not maximal, state of

TABLE 9-1. The Effects of Managed Care on Practice

Traditional Approaches	Emerging Approaches
Client as Customer	Client and MBC/EAP Firms as Customer
Uni-dimensional Client Advocacy	Multi-dimensional Client Advocacy
Minimal Accountability	Increased Accountability
Minimal Focus on Time-Sensitive Treatments	Increased Focus on Time-Sensitive Treatments
Minimal Focus on Resource Management	Increased Focus on Resource Management
Retrospective Authorization for Reimbursement of Services	Pre-Authorization for Reimbursement of Services
Self-Directed Client Referrals	Other-Directed Client Referrals
Solo Practice	Group Practice
Marketing Aimed at the Public (Retail)	Marketing Aimed at MBC and EAP Firms (Wholesale)
Less Entrepreneurial Approach	Increased Entrepreneurial Focus

functioning as soon as possible; the compliance with utilization review procedures; and the adequate documentation of services delivered and outcome achieved.

EAP professionals, accustomed to serving both the employer's goals and the individual client's goals, are familiar with the duality. Similarly, school social workers, psychologists, and guidance counselors are also familiar with this mindset, as are professionals employed in various agency settings.

Traditionally, client advocacy has centered upon a more narrow, individual perspective than that favored by managed care. Advocacy must be redefined to include an enlarged perspective, with a view toward benefit protection and client education. Clinicians working within managed care systems "advocate" for clients by educating them about the limitations to therapy, as well as its benefits; by educating clients as to their financial responsibilities and options within the benefit plan they and their employer have purchased; and by thoroughly documenting and communicating treatment needs, goals, and progress toward such ends. Misguided efforts at client advocacy include expressing resentments toward managed care indirectly through the client. This is a nonproductive and nontherapeutic approach.

Accountability in private mental health practice has long meant accountability to client service, while meeting the minimal requirements for maintenance of licensure and professional affiliation. Accountability for efficiency and effectiveness have long been absent, unlike many other fields of endeavor.

Managed care demands much more accountability, both for efficacy and efficiency. In an era in which the insurance carrier served mostly as a passive claims payor, reimbursement for clinical services was not necessarily related to the client improvement. Since reimbursement was not outcome-related, an incentive existed to continue to see the client as long as the client felt therapy was beneficial, regardless of significant change or in the absence of it. Managed care has reversed this dynamic. MBC seeks to select effective therapists for inclusion in its networks. It asks practitioners to set realistic treatment goals, to document progress, recommend new therapy approaches to replace ones that are not successful, and terminate therapy when goals have been achieved.

Clinical Changes

With its goal of returning clients to normal levels of functioning as quickly as possible, managed care has provided impetus to the development of new clinical innovations. Clinicians are examining how to modify a variety of approaches that are more compatible to managed care philosophies.

Prominent among these approaches are the so-called "time-sensitive," "solution-focused," or "brief" therapy strategies. A central theme of these approaches is that therapy is delivered intermittently, as needed, over the course of human development and that the least invasive treatment needed to achieve change is the most desirable one. (Table 9-2 compares and contrasts the values of practitioners utilizing these interventions with traditional therapists, as viewed by two well-known practitioners in this area.) Practitioners of these interventions believe that much therapy work can be done in short periods of therapy, sometimes even one or two visits. (See Table 9-3.)

Research on treatment outcomes and client preferences supports the use of these strategies, even though such interventions have commonly been perceived by many clinicians as inferior to "long-term" treatment. MBC will likely provide support for the development and acceptance of these and other innovative approaches to outpatient treatment. Much more research is needed in this area and should be aimed at guiding clinicians as to when such brief interventions are most effective.

The management of treatment resources on an aggregate level is a key task of the MBC industry. In practice this means clinicians must develop and provide services whenever possible that are effective alternatives to more costly interventions, such as hospitalization. For example, a benefit plan may provide for a maximum of twenty outpatient visits per calendar year, yet the member may need more than one course of treatment in that period. The clinician must be sensitive to these resource limitations and design interventions accordingly. Outpatient practitioners working with managed care systems must also be sensitive to treatment resource management.

Traditionally, practitioners have become accustomed to providing services, submitting claims, having these claims retrospectively reviewed and—hopefully—paid. Managed care changes this process as well, with its focus on the preauthorization of services that it reimburses. This assures the clinician that payment will be made for services rendered. The implication of this system is that the practitioner must comply with the MBC's authorization and utilization review procedures, providing only services authorized in advance. This system eliminates the guesswork of whether or not payors will reimburse providers for services rendered, helping clinicians have a more successful practice.

TABLE 9-2. Comparative Dominant Values of the Long-Term and Short-Term Therapist (From Budman and Gurman [1983]. The Practice of Brief Therapy. *Professional Psychology: Research and Practice, 14,* pp. 277-292).

Long-Term Therapist	Short-Term Therapist
1. Seeks change in basic character.	Prefers pragmatism, parsimony, and least radical intervention, and does not believe in notion of "cure."
2. Believes that significant psychological change is unlikely in everyday life.	Maintains an adult developmental perspective from which significant psychological change is viewed as inevitable.
3. Sees presenting problems as reflecting more basic pathology.	Emphasizes patient's strengths and resources; presenting problems are taken seriously (although not necessarily at face value).
4. Wants to "be there" as patient makes significant changes.	Accepts that many changes will occur "after therapy" and will not be observable to the therapist.
5. Sees therapy as having a "timeless" quality and is patient and willing to wait for change.	Does not accept the timelessness of some models of therapy.
6. Unconsciously recognizes the fiscal convenience of maintaining long-term patients.	Fiscal issues often muted, either by the nature of the therapist's practice or by the organizational structure for reimbursement.
7. Views psychotherapy as almost always benign and useful.	Views psychotherapy as being sometimes useful and sometimes harmful.
8. Sees patient's being in therapy as the most important part of patient's life.	Sees being in the world as more important than being in therapy.

TABLE 9-3. Treatment Goals Suitable for a One- to Two-Visit Treatment Course

1. Disabuse clients of false notion that their or their children's behavior is abnormal.

2. Confirm that a strategy (for dealing with a problem) devised by a client is a reasonable one (i.e., reassure clients that they are "on the right course").

3. Refer clients to self-help groups, bibliotherapy, or other such resources when available.

4. Acknowledge that a problem is not amenable to psychotherapy.

5. Describe a simple technique that is effective for treating a circumscribed problem.

6. Inform clients that another agency or institution is available and/or obligated to assist the client, especially when there is no cost (e.g., the school system's obligation to assess suspected learning disabilities).

Adapted from: Pekarik, Gene. *Rationale, Training, and Implementation of Time Sensitive Treatments.* Unpublished Manuscript, 1990.

Clinical Innovation:
Prescription for Escalating Mental Health Care Costs

America's health care bill will soon exceed $750 billion, or over 12 percent of the gross national product. Western Europe and Japan, by contrast, spend only about 6 percent to 9 percent of their GNP on health care with little difference in outcomes.

Between 1980 and 1984 adolescent admissions to psychiatric hospitals increased 350 percent. At any time, as much as 25 percent of all hospital beds are occupied by psychiatric or substance abuse patients. During the last decade the cost of psychiatric care, fueled in large part by hospital costs, rose at twice the rate of the overall medical consumer price index. Today as much as 70 percent of employers' mental health benefit dollars go toward mental health related hospitalization. Rather than eliminate these benefits, employers may turn to Managed Behavioral Care specialists for solutions.

One clinical innovation is Psychiatric Home Health Care (PHHC). This service provides intensive, outpatient treatment to clients whose conditions would traditionally warrant hospitalization. Unlike partial hospitalization programs, which are often associated with psychiatric hospitals and may sometimes produce ever longer treatment episodes, these services are offered in the client's home. Clients and families are seen when needed, twenty-four hours a day, seven days a week. PHHC services teach clients how to cope and resolve problems in living and support independence. They may even provide more direct treatment hours per day, at less cost than hospital-based care. Clients who are acutely suicidal, homicidal, or are severely psychotic or manic are inappropriate for such care but may utilize such services after stabilization in a hospital setting. However, many acute clients can be treated by these intensive in-home services, averting hospitalizations. These and other clinical innovations aimed at reducing unnecessary psychiatric hospitalizations are increasingly of interest to EAP and MBC professionals.[2]

The Practitioner as Entrepreneur

The managed care environment creates an atmosphere more conducive to the success of creative, entrepreneurally oriented therapists. Such therapists will be quick to see how MBC is influencing the business of their practices and adjust accordingly. Here are some examples of these changes.

Managed care represents the introduction of a wholesaling influence in the market for therapy and counseling services. The prevailing hypothesis among employers and other purchasers of needed treatment services is that complete freedom of choice to access treatment on the part of consumers results in unnecessary costs and that management of this process by qualified professionals is needed. The translation of this hypothesis into action means that through a single agreement between an employer and a MBC or EAP firm, tens of thousands of consumers will be directed toward a selected group of treatment providers. Self-referrals by individuals to therapists will represent diminishing volumes of clients in com-

---

2. For a discussion of these services and the literature concerning their effectiveness see: Pigott, H. E. (1991). "Psychiatric Home Health Care: One Prescription for Soaring Mental Health Costs." In *Driving Down Health Care Costs, Strategies & Solutions,* 1991 (pp. 9.1-9.10). New York: Panel Publishers.

ing years. More the norm will be referrals directed to the practitioner by others (MBC case managers or EAP professionals), or by the design of the client's benefit plan which provides a financial incentive to the consumer to utilize certain clinicians endorsed by the plan's managers. This endorsement (inclusion in provider networks) will, of course, be based on the practitioners' practice patterns, efficiency, and acceptance of fee discounts.

Because MBC uses alternative fee arrangements such as fee discounting and fixed fee maximums, outpatient, office-based practitioners affiliated with MBC system have a need to keep their operational cost as low as is feasible. An increase in managed care in the future will give momentum toward the establishment of more group practices, where overhead costs may be shared and reduced in relation to each practitioner. These arrangements may also facilitate the development of group therapies as an efficient and effective treatment modality. Group therapy is often not compatible with the reduced client volume associated with a solo practice.

Managed care holds the potential to revolutionize how practitioners have approached the marketing of their services. In the past, many practitioners have become successful by analyzing their communities' needs, developing a specialization or niche to fit a particular need or needs, and publicizing the service provided through mass media advertising, promotional literature, workshops, and the cultivation of collegial referral sources. Today, practitioners, especially newcomers, must aim marketing efforts at the managed care markets in their respective communities, while recognizing that competition for the decreasing number of potential clients who have total freedom of choice concerning reimbursable treatment providers will increase.

Below are several strategies to employ in marketing to the managed care industry:

1. Assess the managed care referral sources.[3] They include MBC

---

3. Appendix B of this book contains a current list of the nation's HMOs as compiled by InterStudy, a Minnesota-based managed care research organization. Appendix E contains a list of the nation's leading MBC and EAP firms. PPOs are referral sources, i.e., how well are they managed, how well do they reimburse for services rendered to their members? Listings of PPOs, which may or may not include a MH/SA component, can be obtained from the American Association of Preferred Provider Organizations, whose address is in the Resource Directory.

firms (local and national), EAPs, PPOs, and self-insured employers. Determine their size and attractiveness potential.

2. Assess the special needs of this market. Potential specialty needs include services for:

- assessment services
- twenty-four-hour crisis intervention services
- substance abuse programs
- eating disorders
- marital counseling
- parenting skills
- sex therapy
- partial hospitalization services
- crisis intervention services
- in-home psychiatric interventions
- ambulatory detoxification
- specialized testing or diagnostic services, such as evaluation for attention-deficit/hyperactivity disorder

3. Consider developing MBC services as a part of your practice. While the capital and expertise to fund and operate an at-risk MBC system is beyond the scope of most practitioners, other avenues are available to enter the market as a vendor. Employee assistance programs can be offered with little capital investment, can be designed to incur marginal or no financial risk for clinical services on the vendor's behalf, and require no license in most settings. Specialized training in the EAP field is required, but is readily available through seminars and university sponsored programs. A nationally recognized credential (Certified Employee Assistance Professional) is available through the Employee Assistance Professionals' Association. This credential indicates to prospective customers that you have specialized skills in this area of practice.

Also be aware that self-insured employers, which include most of the larger employers in any community, constitute a market for the vendor of a preferred provider organization, or network. PPOs are largely unregulated and small PPOs require minimal capital to develop.

4. Recognize that MBC firms represent an important secondary market for practitioner's services. Such secondary markets can pro-

vide a steady stream of referrals to boutique practices. For example, Acme HMO does not have a benefit for marital counseling, therefore its MBC firm does not provide these counseling services when the assessment reveals only a V code diagnosis of marital problem (DSM-III-R Code V61.10). Yet the MBC firm has numerous potential referrals of these clients to a clinician who specializes in this area of practice and is willing to adjust his or her fees in such a way that clients can purchase services themselves, outside their health care benefits plan. This may also be the case for clients presenting other excluded diagnoses or who have requests for therapy services that are not covered within their benefit plan. Table 9-4 lists these and other suitable practice strategies.

Finally, the managed care environment will reward the creative, entrepreneurial practitioners who can efficiently manage their practices while developing innovative ways to serve clients and customers. In many instances this will mean reevaluation of what skills the practitioner community has to offer to MBC clients and a rethinking of how to develop and package them in a manner that is compatible to managed care systems.

MANAGED CARE-HOSPITAL PARTNERSHIPS: IMPLICATIONS FOR SUBSTANCE ABUSE TREATMENT

Psychiatric hospitals and substance abuse inpatient facilities were a growth industry in the late 1970s and throughout the 1980s. These institutions face an inevitable contraction in the near term, due to the fact that MBC focuses strongly on the containment of unnecessary hospital-based care. Fewer inpatients and shorter lengths of stay are likely to be a continuing trend and source of concern to hospital-based programs and providers.

Managed care entities have produced fewer inpatient referrals with shorter lengths of stay through several strategies. First, clinical systems for outpatient care have been developed and implemented to treat very acute patients who, without such specialized care, might need hospitalization. Features to these systems include: easy access for emergent cases, intensive visits and aggressive monitoring of acute clients, special case management programs for clients

TABLE 9-4. Successful Strategies for Private Practice Growth in a Managed Care Environment

- Use current *Diagnostic and Statistical Manual* codes and terminology.
- Make clinical notes for each visit or interaction with the client. Use a standard format such as S.O.A.P.
- Reduce overhead costs and increase economies of scale by joining with colleagues in group practices.
- Provide patient advocacy by informing patients of their rights and responsibilities within their benefit plan.
- Become familiar with MBC utilization review procedures, forms, and appeals processes.
- View managed care as an increasingly important market for counseling and treatment services.
- View MBC firms as important secondary markets for referrals.
- Assess the managed care market carefully, choosing the most attractive organization(s) for network affiliation. Evaluate on the basis of financial stability, competent management, reimbursement levels, claims payment history, and volume of referrals. Be aware that some firms may use your professional credibility to help market their networks. Inquire carefully about their business reputation, programmatic licensure, and individual license where applicable.
- Become familiar with the benefit plan and the staff that manage its clients' care.
- Stress convenience and accessibility.
- Document clinical effectiveness and client satisfaction.
- Adopt an entrepreneurial approach.

at high risk for hospitalization, after-hours crisis intervention services, and alternative programming such as partial hospital services.

Once hospitalized, MBC firms have monitored care through utilization management processes (see Chapter 6) to determine that hospital care is necessary; that no less restrictive, lower cost alternative treatment setting is available; that the patient is improving as a result of care at that level of intensity; and that appropriate discharge plans are in place well before discharge.

When ready for discharge, MBC systems have attempted to begin clients in treatment as soon as possible, ideally the day of the hospital discharge. These and other strategies have resulted in the lower admission rates and in the shorter lengths-of-stay lamented by many hospital staff and affiliates.

The inpatient substance abuse treatment field has possibly been impacted the most by managed care. This industry, which developed the twenty-eight-day inpatient treatment program to parallel insurance reimbursement patterns, is now faced with a proliferation of alternatives favored by managed care. Intensive outpatient treatment programs and partial hospitalization (or day hospitals) in their various permutations are largely replacing the traditional, fixed length of stay, hospital-based substance abuse rehabilitation programs.

A comment in a recent issue of the *U.S. Journal of Drug and Alcohol Dependence* by alcoholism treatment consultant Terence Gorski typifies the anger toward managed care by many in the inpatient substance abuse rehabilitation community. "The system as it is discriminates against alcoholics and denies them benefits they've paid for," Gorski said about denials for inpatient rehabilitation coverage. He and many others in this industry charge that managed care clinicians are concerned only with cost reductions, not client care (Meacham, 1990). The same article went on to correctly predict that MBC would be a factor in even more admission decisions as the decade progressed.

Private psychiatric hospitals are confronted with similar implications as managed care becomes more and more the norm. Writing in the Fall 1990 edition of *Psychiatric Hospital,* Peter Boland, a health care consultant, says that these institutions themselves are partly to blame for their dilemma. "Those in the mental health care industry—and particularly in psychiatric hospitals–have largely failed to provide employers and insurers with an adequate range of treatment service options . . . " (p. 155). Boland also noted that fewer and fewer of the purchasers of services accept the argument that quality of care should be the main reason to preserve traditional treatment patterns.

Psychiatrists with inpatient-based practices have seen managed care affect them in similar ways–fewer patients and an increased emphasis on shorter lengths of stay. Since they have the responsibility for making decisions that greatly affect the cost of services, this group has felt the impact of managed care more than other professions. Like the hospital groups, they too have actively resisted managed care, undoubtedly because of its financial impact but also on grounds of quality of care issues and managed care's perceived intrusion into the special doctor-patient relationship.

One of the reasons for the development of managed care has been the lack of widely accepted standards of treatment–ones that would guide all treating clinicians toward similar patterns of care, while still allowing the adequate exercise of professional judgement. Both the American Psychiatric Association and the American Society of Addiction Medicine are developing such standards. In part, they hope to encourage employers and insurers to use them in administration of benefits in relation to hospitalization and other treatment issues. Meanwhile, MBC has already tackled this controversial and difficult challenge, producing its own standards for their members. This issue of treatment standards and how they may impact inpatient care will likely be an evolving topic of controversy and debate for years to come.

Strategies

How can hospitals and hospital-based practitioners respond successfully to managed care? Although the need for substance abuse and psychiatric beds decrease as managed care becomes more widespread, the need for treatment will not. Jobs formerly based in hospital settings will follow clients to less restrictive treatment settings, such as intensive outpatient treatment programs, partial hospitalization programs, and others. Clinicians must anticipate these shifts in service delivery patterns and plan accordingly.

Just as clinical employment will follow clients from private hospitals into less restrictive treatment settings, so too may psychiatric and substance abuse beds move to other settings that can provide care at reduced costs. The use of scatter beds is one such example. Scatter beds are found in general hospitals without formal psychiatric or substance abuse treatment units. Beds, dispersed throughout the facility (or grouped together in the case of "cluster beds"), are designated for mental health or substance abuse use. When supervised by a psychiatrist or addictionologist, and cared for by a properly trained nursing staff, many clients whose lethality risk does not require a secure unit can be successfully treated in these beds (Olfson, 1990).

The absence of treatment staffs and facilities helps to reduce the cost of these beds. Lengths of stay in such beds are shorter than in traditional, freestanding psychiatric or substance abuse hospital settings (Hendryx and Bootzin, 1986). This is due to the nature of the service provided through these settings. The physician and nursing staff provide observation, assessment, and short-term stabilization with a goal in mind of discharge to outpatient treatment. These objectives often mirror those of MBC concerning the use of hospital resources. One strategy hospitals may employ is to deemphasize formal treatment units, instead transitioning to the use of scatter or cluster beds.

The coming decade will likely witness the demise of the traditional, twenty-eight-day inpatient substance abuse treatment program, long the bellwether of the rehab field. Research has not shown that such very expensive programs are any more effective than treatment in less restrictive settings (Miller and Hester, 1986). Yet their cost is many times more than treatment in other settings. Unless proponents of these "dinosaurs" of substance abuse rehabilitation can document their superior client outcomes vis-à-vis less restrictive interventions (thus moving away from the "quality of care" arguments) such programs face a precarious future.

The need for quality hospital-based care will not go away regardless of the extent to which managed care grows. In assessing the needs of managed care entities to develop new programs and alternative services with different clinical goals, hospital-based clinicians and administrators will use the same methods discussed earlier concerning outpatient practice. For example, clinicians are implementing crisis assessment and stabilization units in some facilities. These units have as their goal the rapid diagnosis and stabilization of acute clients in a secure environment. Treatment dispositions (i.e., transfer to a hospital-based treatment unit or discharge to a less restrictive level of care) are made after one or two days of careful evaluation and observation.

Another emerging inpatient program is the variable-length-of-stay substance abuse unit. These programs provide medically necessary inpatient detoxification, with discharge decisions based on the individual client's medical status and psychosocial features. Like the staff of assessment units, the staff of these variable-length-of-stay units share a goal of discharging the client to an outpatient based treatment program whenever possible. Hospitals with such detoxification services coupled with intensive outpatient treatment programs or partial hospital programs will be attractive to managed care groups.

In short, a challenge for hospitals in the 1990s will be to develop partnerships with Managed Behavioral care firms and to offer services compatible to managed care philosophies. This will present opportunities for innovative programming on the part of clinical managers in hospital settings. Hospitals may dialogue with managed care firms as in the case of other referral sources. Marketing efforts must be redefined and targeted toward these organizations. Marketing activities aimed at the shrinking pool of clients who may self-refer with complete freedom of choice in selecting a treatment setting will receive less attention, and more attention will be directed to this new and growing market. Some writers have encouraged hospital-based administrators and clinicians to go even further and develop managed care services themselves (Fry, 1990)! Fry encourages hospitals to consider marketing PPOs, HMOs, EAPs, and other managed care products. A more viable option is that hospitals will develop and market their own provider networks of clinicians, with the hospital as the focus point of inpatient treatment. In this scenario, the hospital can offer employers an array of services: inpatient assessment and stabilization, variable length-of-stay detoxification, partial hospitalization, intensive outpatient substance abuse treatment, and crisis intervention and outpatient therapy through a provider network of community based practitioners.

Hospital staffs and physicians can employ several strategies to facilitate a smoother working relationship with MBC in providing covered services to clients. These strategies are as follows:

- Learn about the values, operations, benefit plans, and goals of respective MBC firms.
- Study the MBC firm's level of care guidelines carefully. Train staff and physicians to ensure familiarity with how and when the firm authorizes admission or ends coverage for specific conditions.

- Offer to increase the level of interaction with MBC staff so as to facilitate a collegial relationship (i.e., joint case staffings, training programs, inservices, quality assurance programs).
- Adopt clinical objectives and services compatible with MBC benefit plans and coverages. These objectives include: assessment, diagnosis, short-term stabilization of acute clients, and discharge planning focused on a rapid transition to outpatient treatment.
- Utilize hospital/MBC liaison personnel to work with physicians to modify their treatment patterns to focus on stabilization of acute symptoms, not long-term therapy goals. (MBC firms frequently are disinclined to rely on these liaison workers at psychiatric and substance abuse hospitals for primary communication about client's clinical status. Some firms report that these workers are not adequately trained or do not possess the necessary clinical information. Others prefer to obtain clinical information solely from the attending physician. Utilizing these workers in this manner may be more productive for hospitals interested in receiving MBC referrals.)
- Document clinical data thoroughly, accurately, and in a timely manner. Include information such as:

    a. specific, behavioral indicators for hospital admission or continued hospital-based treatment.
    b. specific, behavioral, short-term treatment goals that have measurements for outcome.
    c. specific indicators of progress toward treatment goals, or the lack thereof.
    d. specific estimates of length-of-stay needed to achieve the treatment goals.
    e. specific interventions and responses.

- Begin the discharge planning process upon admission. Quality MBC firms begin planning for post-hospitalization treatment services at the time the client is admitted. Hospital staff can facilitate a better working relationship that will ensure better care by recognizing and joining this process.
- Document client outcomes. Develop a data base of information concerning the clinical outcome of services provided.

- Conduct client satisfaction research. Be able to demonstrate that clients received quality care as measured by their own reports about the facility, physician staff, nursing care, and mental health professionals.
- Do not express resentments toward MBC through the client care or improvement. Address concerns through direct contact with MBC staff, through professional associations, or through direct communication with the employer and insurer community.
- Learn about respective MBC firms' appeal processes for disputed coverage decisions. Train staff about these processes. Most firms have three levels of appeal:

    a. Appeal to the review staff.
    b. Appeal to the supervising clinician or medical director.
    c. Appeal to a committee or group, less directly involved with the particular case. This appeal may involve the review of all clinical records. Another reason to be sure that hospital records are well documented.

- A fourth level of appeal is via a specified arbitration process described in facility-MBC agreements. (See Appendix A for an example of such contracts.)

    It is important to learn about the MBC firm's process for appeals concerning clients whose care may be interrupted, to the client's detriment, by a UM decision. These are known as expedited or emergent appeals and are conducted while care is still being provided rather than after discharge. It is reasonable to expect such appeals to be available within twenty-four- to forty-eight-hours. They should be conducted by a physician on a peer review basis. The physician should be empowered by the MBC firm to make an immediate disposition.

    Hospitals should initiate an appeal after receiving written notice that coverage has been denied. Quality MBC operations promptly issue such notices to the facility, physician provider, and the client whenever such a decision is made. If the firm does not follow this procedure, the facility should request such a notice. Facilities benefit from written policies to assist staff in when and how to initiate such appeals. Staff should be well trained in these procedures.

• Explore alternative contracting arrangements, including per diems, bed leasing, or discounted daily rates based on referral volume.

SUMMARY

As the revolution of managed care unfolds, it brings change: new employment opportunities, dramatic impacts on treatment services, implications for new marketing strategies. It is a revolution that presents challenges, pitfalls, and opportunities for all concerned, with the question of how. adequate mental health care services can be preserved for the insured population of Americans at costs that they and employers can afford.

BIBLIOGRAPHY

American Psychiatric Association. (1994). *Diagnostic and Statistical Manual Of Mental Disorders* (4th ed.). Washington, DC: Author.

APA initiates series of actions in managed care. (1990). *Hospital and Community Psychiatry, 37,* 1106-1111.

Bartlett, J., Prest, S., and Soper, M. (1991). *Cigna Level Of Care Guidelines.* Hartford, CT: Cigna Corporation.

Beigel, J. K. and Earle, R. H. (1990). *Successful Private Practice in the 1990's.* New York: Brunner/Masel Publishers.

Bistline, J. L., Sheridan, S. M., and Winegar, N. (1991). Five critical skills for mental health counselors in managed health care. *Journal of Mental Health Counseling, 13,* 147-152.

Borenstein, D. B. (1990). Managing care: A means of rationing psychiatric treatment. *Hospital and Community Psychiatry, 41,* 1095-1098.

Budman, S. H. and Gurman, A. S. (1983). The practice of brief psychotherapy. *Professional Psychology: Research and Practice, 14,* 277-292.

Budman, S. H. and Gurman, A. S. (1988). *Theory and Practice of Brief Therapy.* New York: Guilford Press.

Dennison, R. (1990). The impact of cost containment on psychiatric practice: Implications and options. *Psychiatric Hospital, 21,* 159-164.

De Shazer, S. (1988). *Clues: Investigating Solutions in Brief Therapy.* New York: Norton.

Developing practice parameters: An interview with John McIntyre. (1990). *Hospital and Community Psychiatry, 41,* 1103-1105.

Dorwart, R. A. (1990). Managed Behavioral care: Myths and realities in the 1990's. *Hospital and Community Psychiatry, 41,* 1087-1091.

Forecast 1991: Managed care. (1990, December 17). *Health Week.*

Fry, J. D. (1990). Rationale for a hospital-based Managed Behavioral care system. *Psychiatric Hospital, 21*(4), 171-173.

Health Insurance Association of America. *HIAA on State Health Insurance Issues.* Washington, DC (pp. 1-3).

Hendryx, M. and Bootzin, R. R. (1986). Psychiatric episodes in general hospitals without psychiatric units. *Hospital and Community Psychiatry, 37,* 1025-1029.

Hill, L. K. (1990). The future of mental health counseling in the new era of health care. In G. Seiles (Ed.), *The Mental Health Counselors Sourcebook* (pp. 105-138). New York: Plenum Press.

Hiraisuka, J. (1990). Brief mental health care can reduce medical bills, four-year study confirms. *NASW NEWS, 31,* 1.

Kimball, Merit C. (1990, December 17). New year, same old song: Can health costs be controlled? *Health Week,* p. 23.

Meacham, A. (1990, December). Treatment and managed care: An uneasy mix. *U.S. Journal of Drug and Alcohol Dependence,* pp. 1, 17.

Miller, W. R. and Hester, R. K. (1986). Inpatient alcoholism treatment: Who benefits? *American Psychologist, 41,* 794-805.

National Institute of Mental Health. (1978-1979). Provisional data on federally funded community mental health centers. Report prepared by the Survey and Reports Branch, Division of Biometry & Epidemiology. Washington, DC: U.S. Government Printing Office.

Need to develop flexible practice guidelines emphasized. (1990, November). *Clinical Psychiatry News,* p. 9.

O'Hanlon, W. H. and Weiner-Davis, M. (1989). *In Search of Solutions: A New Direction in Psychotherapy.* New York: Norton.

Olfson, M. (1990). Treatment of depressed patients in general hospitals with scatter beds, cluster beds, and psychiatric units. *Hospital and Community Psychiatry, 41,* 1106-1111.

Patterson, D. Y. (1990). Managed care: An approach to national psychiatric treatment. *Hospital and Community Psychiatry, 41,* 1092-1095.

Pekarik, G. (1983). Follow-up adjustment of outpatient dropouts. *American Journal of Orthopsychiatry, 53*(3)501-511.

Pekarik, G. (1990, January 22-24). *Rationale, Training, and Implementation of Time Sensitive Treatments.* Unpublished paper presented at the MCC Companies, Inc. Executive Director's Meeting in Scottsdale, AZ.

Reding, G. R. and Maguire, B. (1973). Nonsegregated acute psychiatric admissions to general hospitals: Continuity of care within the community hospital. *New England Journal of Medicine, 289,* 185-188.

Rodriguez, A. R. (1990, Fall). Directions in contracting for psychiatric services managed care firms. *Psychiatric Hospital,* pp. 165-170.

Straussner, S. L. A. (Ed.). (1989). *Occupational Social Work Today.* Binghamton, NY: The Haworth Press.

Taube, C. A., Burns, B. J., and Keesler, L. (1984). Patients of psychiatrists and psychologists in office-based practice: 1980. *American Psychologist, 39,* 1435-1447.

Using In-Patient Psychiatric Benefits Wisely. (1988). National Association of Private Psychiatric Hospitals, Washington: DC (pp. 1-12).

Wagman, J. B. and Schiff J. (1990). Managed Behavioral care for employees: Roles for social workers. In S. L. A. Straussner (Ed.), *Occupational Social Work Today.* Binghamton, NY: The Haworth Press (pp. 53-66).

Winegar, N., Bistline, J. L., and Sheridan, S. M. Combining quality and cost effectiveness: Establishing a group therapy program in a managed care setting. *Families in Society, 73*(1), 56-58.

Winegar, N. and Bistline, J.L. (1994). *Marketing Services to Managed Care.* Binghamton, NY: The Haworth Press.

Chapter 10

Critical Issues

Obviously consumers are affected by changes in the mental health care delivery system. Employers, insurers, and providers should assist consumers in understanding the nature and extent of services available to them and the role of managed care systems in them. Consumers should become aware of the nature of their mental health and substance abuse benefits at the time they select a benefit option or plan. Most employers cooperate with vendors in offering orientation programs about benefits to employees. Various intracompany communications may also be used for this purpose.

The most prominent way managed care varies from traditional benefits according to many consumers is the matter of choice. Consumers in managed care systems have less choice in selecting the type, intensity, duration, and setting for care. Choice in selecting a provider is diminished as well. In managed care systems consumers are usually not able to choose a provider from the telephone book and make an appointment. Instead their health care benefit information or card directs them to a preapproved assessor or other clinician who can provide services under the plan's coverage. In other plan designs consumers must have their first visit to a treatment provider approved by a primary care physician or a company-sponsored EAP counselor. Many MBC plans increase access to different types of providers. While traditional plans sometimes cover only the service of psychiatrists or psychologists, MBC networks often include these professionals as well as clinical social workers, professional counselors, marriage and family therapists, and clinical nurse specialists.

When changing to a MBC system from a traditional one, consumers may be faced with changing a long-standing professional relationship, in favor of starting a new one with a MBC provider. This is a relatively common scenario, given that many employer groups are redesigning their benefit plans and that MBC firms do not include all providers in a community in this network. Instead, they screen providers and facilities. MBC firms select only the number of providers needed to fulfill their business needs for a particular community. Importantly, they also screen for quality of services delivered, cost-effective practice patterns, provider interest, and willingness to participate in utilization management procedures. Many providers and facilities are not members of a particular network for these reasons.

Yet another change often experienced by consumers who are new to MBC practice is a new treatment orientation on the part of the provider. Providers in MBC systems or networks focus on the rapid restoration of normal functioning on the part of their clients. They employ techniques that are aimed at helping clients resolve their problems as quickly as possible. They take the approach toward their clients that they may return at any time in the future for more therapy should the need arise. This approach is sometimes referred to as "intermittent" therapy; that is, recognizing that there is no "cure" to many emotional and interpersonal problems, but that they can be successfully resolved and addressed again in the future if they arise. Clients learn that "more" is not necessarily better, and that results can be achieved quickly in many instances.

Consumers also find that MBC's approach to the use of hospital care varies from tradition. MBC uses hospital-based care primarily to stabilize symptoms and prepare clients or families for outpatient treatment. Generally, traditional benefit plans allowed for treatment to occur in hospitals, producing lengths of stay sometimes measured in weeks. MBC systems tend to operate in much the same manner in which physicians use medical/surgical hospitals. Only clients who require hospital care to stabilize acute symptoms, or to receive treatments that are unavailable on an outpatient basis, are hospitalized. MBC staff begin planning for outpatient treatment services when the client is admitted to a hospital.

This approach to hospital care may seem troublesome to some consumers who associate treatment for alcoholism or drug abuse with an extended hospital-based treatment program. These costly programs are often fixed at twenty-eight or thirty days in length. This length of stay was derived from the maximum amount of hospital-based care covered by traditional benefit plans. For many years the only available form of treatment for addictions, these programs have helped many people. Consumers understandably are often not aware of the literature that indicates that today's outpatient treatment programs, sometimes after brief medical detoxification in a hospital or detoxification facility, are as effective in treating addiction (Miller and Hester, 1986). Families who view such hospitalization programs as a means of gaining control over a troubled family member by removing a disruptive influence from the home environment, or who do not wish to participate in outpatient treatment, may have difficulty accepting this approach. MBC clinicians and network providers should anticipate these concerns and be prepared to address them with their clients.

Consumers find that the client payment system in MBC is often greatly simplified in comparison to traditional benefits. The need for filing a health care claim is reduced or eliminated. Frequently the only out-of-pocket expense is a small copayment, one that is only a fraction of the actual cost of the service.

Consumers are sometimes able to receive services at no out-of-pocket expense. Often, assessment visits in MBC networks are at no charge to the client. An increasingly popular benefit is the employee assistance program, which provides prepaid counseling services to employees and family members at no out-of-pocket expense.

Consumers in MBC systems are protected from unscrupulous practices by providers which would put them at financial risk. For example, MBC agreements with providers prohibit them from charging their clients more than the allowable copayment, or from continuing to provide services not authorized by the MBC system and then charging the client. (This may be permissible, but only with the client's knowledge and permission. See the sample Individual Provider Agreement, Section 5, in Appendix A.)

Quality of services provided are often enhanced for consumers in MBC systems, particularly through their emphasis on clinical case management. This emphasis provides better coordination of care and increased linkage to available community resources. A case from the author's practice illustrates this fact.

Diane was a forty-two-year-old homemaker whose husband had recently joined a MBC benefit plan through his employer. Diane had become known to us through an emergency admission to a network hospital due to psychotic symptoms and out-of-control behaviors. She was quickly stabilized and began treatment at our clinic, where she was assigned a case manager. Our assessment revealed that Diane had never been in a managed care system before. She had seen seven different psychiatrists since her first psychotic episode–at the age of nineteen. She had also taken various psychotropic medications from at least five nonpsychiatrist physicians, and had been treated in hospitals seven different times. On one occasion, she had been transferred to a state hospital after exhausting her insurance benefits. Diane had never had a nonpsychiatrist case manager. Neither she nor her husband had ever been involved in available community-based services. Her treatment was poorly coordinated with her primary care physician.

Obviously Diane needed case management services. Our clinic provided her with these services, in addition to medication maintenance by our staff psychiatrist, and a regular support group. Diane was referred to a club house program at a local mental health center. This service gave her day needed structure and provided support for achieving therapeutic gains. Care was coordinated with her primary care physician and her husband was involved in treatment. Such case management services, providing linkage and coordination of care across various systems, are inherent to well-run MBC systems and are often absent in traditional benefit plans.

Consumers who are entering an MBC benefit program should be aware that transition visits are typically a feature available to new members. This means that the MBC firm may authorize visits with the client's current provider until the client may enter the new benefit plan. If treatment is nearing completion, the MBC firm may authorize enough care so that the client can complete treatment with the present provider, avoiding a disruptive change in therapists. If therapy is not approaching completion, visits necessary to ensure a smooth transition to a MBC network provider may be authorized and covered by the MBC firm. Many consumers do not always understand they may have out-of-network benefits available, though at a reduced level and with greater out-of-pocket expenses.

Such benefits, when available in the employer's health care plan, allow consumers greater choice in selecting providers.

Americans seem to value the freedom of choice and resist being locked into a particular system. Consumers should be given choice in their benefit plan whenever possible. They should encourage their human resource managers and benefit managers to develop such programs. They should also be aware that with increased choice comes an inherent increase in costs. After all, maximal consumer choice in traditional benefit plans is perceived as one part of the problem of escalating mental health care costs. In practice this means that overall benefit levels, premium payments, and copayments must be adjusted and be substantially different between managed and unmanaged benefits.

Consumers should view access to quality mental health related benefits as vital and understand that most employers see these benefits as worthwhile and important. Managed care strategies used by employers are ultimately aimed at preserving these benefits by ensuring quality care at reasonable costs.

IMPORTANT MBC FEATURES FOR CONSUMERS

- Services must be preauthorized, or there is a risk of nonpayment by the benefit plan, or payment at reduced levels with greater out-of-pocket expenses.
- Treatment services eligible for benefit coverage are aimed at a quick resolution of problems.
- Hospital-based treatment programs, especially for substance abuse, are deemphasized, since most problems may be treated on an outpatient basis with less disruption to work and academic routines and increased family participation.
- MBC networks often provide access to different types of counseling professionals, not just psychiatrists or psychologists. However not all providers in any given community are members of a particular MBC network.
- Transition visits with current, non-network providers may be authorized for new members who are in therapy at the time they join a managed benefit plan.

• MBC clients are responsible for copayments to providers. They usually do not file claim forms and cannot be charged for nonauthorized services without the client's permission.

EAPs AND MANAGED CARE

The last decade has seen a proliferation both of employee assistance and managed care programs. Many internal EAPs have taken on aspects of managed care systems or plan to, while large EAP companies such as PPC and HAI have been acquired by insurance companies or other managed care companies and have added managed care functions or products to their offerings. Meanwhile, firms more closely associated with managed care, such as MCC, have expanded their lines of EAP products. Can EAPs perform MBC functions and can MBC deliver services traditionally associated with EAPs?

Some point to differences in the two fields that argue against any merging of functions. The first disparity, they say, is in the scope and mission of the two services. EAPs have historically had a mission of early case finding and client advocacy, whereas MBC has minimal focus in these areas, instead concentrating on cost savings to their customers.

They also point out differences in staffing patterns. Some MBC professionals view EAP staff as untrained and poorly qualified for the sophisticated clinical tasks found in managed care. They say that EAP professionals are too often naive about important clinical issues that dramatically influence costs. They view EAP staff as a frequent "obstacle" to managed care, saying they attempt to confound referral decisions, dispute treatment planning, and generally favor traditional treatment approaches. Meanwhile, some EAP professionals view managed care systems and staff as "barriers" to good clinical services. They see MBC processes as impersonal and decisions as being driven more by costs than by quality of care or concern for clients.

Others point to the commonalities between EAPs and MBC that may help in a merging of these systems in the future. Both share a mission of ensuring cost-effective care for their clients. Both entities are organizationally comfortable with serving two clients: the individual and the corporate customer. Both entities have long been involved with clinical case management activities, both are accustomed to screening for appropriate referral resources, and both have had as their function the identification of cost-effective providers.

It seems likely that as both systems evolve, an increased merging of functions will occur. Already most EAPs are provided by outside vendors and the largest of these firms are already providing both EAP and managed care functions and services. In some instances employers may go to one vendor to purchase insurance products, HMO services, MBC services, and EAPs.

To accommodate these changes and compete in the marketplace of the 1990s, EAPs must be able to add three key elements to their existing services: *utilization management components, formalized cost-effective treatment provider networks,* and *an added treatment capacity.* The first will require the addition of new skills and technologies; the second requires only a refinement of existing functions; while the third may require changes in staffing patterns, as some old style EAPs used unlicensed individuals in counseling capacities. These changes will also provide an increased need for EAP administrators with managed care experience and knowledge.

In contrast, MBC will be challenged to develop an orientation and approach more heavily focused on prevention, case finding, and customer service in order to provide EAP services or to blend them into existing products. MBC staff will also need to develop more EAP-specific skills and knowledge. Meeting these challenges while continuing to manage costs will be critical to MBC entities.

The uncertainty as to if and how one of these entities will supersede and supplant the other presents a range of opportunities to many organizations and entrepreneurially oriented individuals who can provide new service models. While no perfect, hybrid model exists, two possible EAP/MBC products are found in Tables 10-1 and 10-2. The first can be adapted to smaller practice settings, while the second requires the administrative and financial resources associated with large insurance and employee benefit companies.

Discussion

This model can be sold as an "at-risk" product for MH/SA services or without risk. It utilizes local EAP/MBC staff to provide the

TABLE 10-1. A Model EAP/MBC Product Suitable for Delivery to Employer Accounts by Small Clinical Practices

Features

- Prevention and case finding activities

    - Wellness seminars
    - Educational materials
    - Employee orientation

- Training and consultation

    - Executive orientation
    - Supervisory training
    - Human resource policy consultation

- Assessment, clinical case management, and extended treatment*

    - Clinical assessment and referral to community resources as appropriate (broad brush approach).
    - Brief treatment component, with a session limit paralleling the average number of treatment sessions required per presentation of most clinical problems.

- Provider network, contracted and credentialed

    - Outpatient services
    - Inpatient facilities

- Quality assurance programs

    - Monitor outcomes, client satisfaction, complaints, and assure clinical standards. Performance features in the contract can be tied to these indicators, penalizing the vendor for excess complaints, poor outcomes, and excess claims costs.

* Mandatory/nonmandatory options regarding accessing MH/SA benefits.

ongoing account service, training, consultation, assessment, UM, MH/SA treatment services, provider network management, and QA functions. MIS functions involve an interface between local and central operations. This product can be sold by sales forces to employers wanting a "friendly" MBC product or a nontraditional looking EAP.

TABLE 10–2. A Model EAP/MBC Product Suitable for Delivery to Employer Accounts by Employee Benefit Companies

Features

- Prevention and case finding activities

  - Wellness seminars
  - Educational materials
  - Employee orientation

- Training and consultation

  - Executive orientation
  - Supervisory training
  - Human resource policy consultation

- Assessment, clinical case management, and extended treatment*

  - Clinical assessment and referral to community resources as appropriate (broad brush approach).
  - Brief treatment component, with a session limit paralleling the average number of treatment sessions required per presentation of most clinical problems.

- Provider network, contracted and credentialed

  - Outpatient providers
  - Inpatient facilities

- Quality assurance programs

  - Monitor outcomes, client satisfaction, complaints, and assure clinical standards. Performance features in the contract can be tied to these indicators, penalizing the vendor for excess complaints, poor outcomes, and excess claims costs.

- Utilization management

  - Preadmission certification
  - Concurrent review

- MIS reporting

  - Utilization and trending data

*Mandatory/nonmandatory options regarding accessing MH/SA benefits.

QUALITY OF SERVICES

MBC systems have been frequently criticized as evidencing multiple deficits concerning the delivery of quality services, both to clients and providers. Some criticisms focus on administrative services, while others are related to clinical services and philosophies. Many are testimony to the impact of managed care on traditional service delivery systems. Common criticisms include poor management, poor claims payment services, poor provider network relations, inadequate reimbursement (or excessive discounting requested) for services rendered, confusing UM procedures, excessive paperwork, and a concern that needed care is denied or not authorized for reimbursement, and that such decisions are made by unqualified staff.

While some of these concerns have been generated by the inherent structure and accountability requirements associated with managed care, others are legitimate criticisms. Managed mental health is an emerging, growth industry. There are no "standardized" models of MBC. Just as the lack of a national health care policy has allowed the marketplace to largely shape the health care industry, in conjunction with various regulatory bodies, so too has it shaped the MBC field. Some MBC firms, interested mostly in short-term gains, have promised enormous savings to employers and insurers. After garnering these immediate profits, such firms have lost accounts due to practices that do not provide adequate care or provide poor customer services.

MBC firms that will be successful in the long term are those that make a commitment to quality service delivery to three constituent groups: (1) individual clients or patients; (2) customers; and (3) providers. This commitment to quality will be found within a larger social mission of providing needed services, preserving benefits, and managing the resources society provides for mental health and substance abuse treatment services in the private sector.

What are some indicators of quality in the MBC field? In addition to adequate administrative expertise and the financial resources to operate these delivery systems, here are some essential features indicating a quality focus in MBC.

Clinical Care Standards or Guides. These documents must allow flexibility for individualized care, but provide a consistent and reasonable framework for recommending treatment options and services. Toward this end, the MBC system must be able to ensure the consistent application of such standards across operating sites. Without such standards as safeguards, important treatment choices can be overly or inappropriately influenced by financial incentives or constraints, or by the idiosyncratic views of particular clinicians or clinical managers. Clinical care standards should be viewed as ongoing processes and require regular modification as new treatments or technologies become accepted.

Client Complaint Systems. The MBC firm should have written policies describing these processes and these must be made known to consumers. Mechanisms should be in place for both local and nonlocal resolution of complaints as quickly as possible. (Some firms have a corporate-wide customer service department in addition to local customer service staff.)

Client Satisfaction Surveys. MBC firms should regularly monitor the level of satisfaction the consumer experiences toward the MBC firm, as well as its individual providers and facilities.

Written Treatment Plans. MBC firms should require adequate, written treatment plans for each client, by which treatment outcomes may be evaluated.

Level of Care Guidelines. Firms should have written guides, decision trees, and policies to be utilized in guiding clinicians in referring clients to the most appropriate level of care. Again, such guidelines can reduce the possibility that level of care decisions will be influenced by financial or other such motives. These guides should be clearly enunciated to the firm's network of providers and facilities.

Qualified, Licensed Staff. MBC firms should employ fully credentialed staff functioning in capacities within the parameters of their respective professions.

Licensed Programs. Many MBC firms offer treatment services directly through their own staff. These programs should be licensed, where applicable, by respective regulatory bodies.

Credentialed and Adequate Provider Networks. Individual providers or facility providers should be licensed, where applicable. The MBC firm should have policies and procedures for credentialing all providers. Networks should be adequate to conveniently service the MBC firm's members.

Staff Training and Development. MBC firms should adequately provide for ongoing training of their staff and network providers.

Adequate Physician Involvement. Psychiatrists should be utilized in oversight capacities, and especially in utilization management activities and in expedited appeals processes.

Quick Claims Payment. Prompt payment of claims should be made to providers who submit timely and "clean" claims documents.

Table 10-3 summarizes these indicators of quality in these systems.

TABLE 10-3. Twelve Essential Quality Indicators in MBC Systems

- Clinical Care Standards or Guides

- Quality Assurance Programs

- Client Complaint Systems

- Client Satisfaction Surveys

- Written Treatment Plans

- Level of Care Guidelines

- Qualified, Licensed Staff

- Licensed Programs

- Credentialed and Adequate Provider Networks

- Staff Training and Development

- Adequate Physician Involvement

- Quick Claims Payment

ETHICAL ISSUES FOR PRACTITIONERS

Practice in the era of managed care presents dilemmas for many clinicians. As managed care proliferates, these issues will affect more and more practitioners.

MBC often places clinicians, long accustomed to relating to colleagues in an atmosphere of mutual respect and cooperation, in the sometimes uncomfortable position of having to say no to a peer's professional judgement or recommendation. Saying no appropriately and respectfully while maintaining successful working relationships presents a challenge, especially to the staff of MBC firms.

Equally trained in and accustomed to saying yes to clients, clinicians involved in the MBC field also find themselves in the difficult position of saying no to client requests. They must often interpret benefits in a manner that will not please the client. At these times the clinician may seem to the client as an impediment to the service desired. This type of reaction by clients is frequently described by those in the field as one of the most difficult aspects of practice.

Some view MBC's insertion into traditional client-therapist relationships as an undue intrusion. They believe that the clinician's ethical responsibility toward colleagues cannot be maintained in these systems. Some critics feel that MBC exposes clinicians to an inevitable conflict concerning the best interests of clients, given these and other reasons. They are concerned that serving in part a cost management, and in part a clinical service delivery or authorization function for the client's care, is a conflictual relationship–one to be avoided. They also point out that MBC may provide incentive for clinicians to precipitously withdraw services from clients, or that in other ways financial incentives may overly influence clinician's decisions about care.

At the same time these clinicians must also be aware of ethical standards annunciated by several groups, that point out practitioners' responsibility to society as a whole. Is it not the professional's responsibility, while providing adequate care, to also help keep mental health care costs as low as possible and thus help preserve these benefits for private sector employees? This implies that counseling professionals be aware of and efficient in utilizing the most effective therapies as well as evidencing a sensitivity to managing mental health care resources.

Others point out that there is a widespread perception on the part of the payors of the private health care system in this country that financial incentives on various levels have created the need for managed care. They believe that clinicians involved in MBC must accept the challenge of interpreting and applying ethical standards appropriately in new settings and evolving relationships. They believe this to be a valuable form of client advocacy, without which the trend toward the extension of health care benefits for the treatment of psychological or substance abuse problems may be reversed.

As the managed behavioral care revolution spreads, as its processes and technologies are refined, and as it gains wider acceptance in the treatment community, these ethical questions and issues surely will confront more and more clinicians, and will bear much more discussion.

BIBLIOGRAPHY

Miller, W. R. and Hester, R. K. (1986). Inpatient alcoholism treatment: Who benefits? *American Psychologist, 41,* 794–805.

Appendix A

Mental Health Provider Agreement

This Agreement (the "Agreement") is by and between _____ ("MCC") and _____ ("PROVIDER").

WITNESSETH

1. Purpose

WHEREAS, MCC is a corporation engaged in providing, managing, and/or arranging for mental health and substance abuse services ("MH/SA Services") to Participants of various health maintenance organizations, health service plans, preferred provider organizations, insurance, labor trusts, self-insurance, and ERISA plans under agreements between MCC and the entities which fund or administer such Plans ("Health Services Agreements"); and

WHEREAS, PROVIDER is duly licensed and/or certified as required by law to practice the profession of _____ in the State or Commonwealth of _____ and wishes to provide certain MH/SA Services ("Covered Services") under the terms and conditions set forth herein to Participants; and

WHEREAS, MCC desires to contract with PROVIDER to provide Covered Services for the benefit of Participants;

NOW, THEREFORE, in consideration of the premises and mutual promises herein, the parties agree as follows:

2. Definitions

a. *Accounts*–Means an employer or other entity which has established a welfare benefit plan, and which has contracted with MCC or Payor to make available the Provider Network.

Note: This is a sample document.

b. *Coinsurance*–Means that portion of the MCC considered charge for Covered Services, calculated as a percentage of the charge of such services, which is to be paid by Participants.

c. *Copayment or Deductible*–Means a fixed dollar portion of the charge of Covered Services which is to be paid by Participants.

d. *Covered Services*–Means those PROVIDER services which are listed on Exhibit A attached hereto.

e. *Medical Management Programs*–Means the quality management, credentialling, case management, and other programs ad or established by MCC.

f. *Medically Necessary*–Means services or supplies which, under the provisions of this Agreement, are: (1) necessary for the symptoms, diagnosis, or treatment of the mental health or substance abuse condition; (2) provided for diagnosis or direct care and treatment of the mental health or substance abuse condition; (3) not primarily for the convenience of the Participant, the Participant's physician or another PROVIDER; and (4) the most appropriate supply or level of service which can safely be provided. For inpatient stays, this means that acute care as an inpatient is necessary due to the kind of services the Participant is receiving or the severity of the Participant's condition, and that safe and adequate care cannot be received as an outpatient or in a less intensified setting.

g. *Participant*–Means any individual, or eligible dependent of such individual, whether referred to as "Insured," "Subscriber," "Member," "Participant," "Covered Life or Individual," "Enrollee," "Dependent," or otherwise, who is eligible for Covered Services pursuant to Health Services Agreements.

h. *Participating Providers*–Means those MH/SA Service providers and other health care providers or institutions who have entered into agreements with MCC to provide Covered Services to Participants.

i. *Payor*–Means MCC, or an insurer, or health maintenance organization, or employer, or other entity which funds or administers a Plan.

j. *Plan*–Means the welfare benefit plan funded, arranged, or administered by Payor for Payor's or Account's Participants.

k. *Provider Network*–Means the network of Participating Providers established and maintained by MCC to provide Covered Services to Participants.

l. *Provider Services*–Means those mental health and substance abuse services provided by a Participating Provider and covered by a Plan.

3. Provider's Obligations

a. PROVIDER shall personally provide the Medically Necessary Covered Services listed on Exhibit A to Participants in accordance with the program(s) set forth in Exhibit(s) B of this Agreement.

b. PROVIDER will maintain sufficient facilities and personnel to provide Participants with timely access to Covered Services in accordance with the standards set forth in the Medical Management Programs.

c. PROVIDER agrees to keep valid all licenses and/or certifications which are required under federal, state, or local laws for the provision of Covered Services to Participants.

d. PROVIDER agrees to fully cooperate with MCC and the Plans to resolve complaints from Participants and shall use his/her best efforts to comply with the complaint procedures established by MCC and/or each of the Plans.

e. PROVIDER represents and warrants that the information contained on his/her Provider Application, which is incorporated herein by reference, is true and accurate, and he/she will notify MCC promptly of any material change in the information on such Application.

f. PROVIDER will procure and maintain adequate policies of comprehensive general liability, professional liability, and other insurance, in amounts deemed appropriate by MCC based on the PROVIDER's mode of practice/specialty, necessary to insure the PROVIDER against any claim or claims for damages arising out of personal injuries or death occasioned directly or indirectly in connection with the provision of services pursuant to this Agreement. PROVIDER will submit evidence of such coverage to MCC upon request, and will notify MCC at least thirty (30) days prior to the expiration, termination, or material change in the coverages listed on the Provider's Application.

g. PROVIDER will not discriminate against any Participant on the basis of source of payment, race, color, gender, sexual orientation, age, religion, national origin, handicap, or health status in providing services under this Agreement.

h. PROVIDER will render Covered Services to all Participants in an appropriate, timely, and cost effective manner. Further, PROVIDER agrees to furnish the services according to generally accepted medical, mental health, and substance abuse practice, community standards and applicable laws and regulations. In the event PROVIDER discovers that a claim, suit, or criminal or administrative proceeding has been brought or may be brought against PROVIDER relating to the quality of services provided to Participants by PROVIDER or relating to PROVIDER's compliance with community standards and applicable laws and regulations, then PROVIDER shall notify MCC of such claims, suit, or proceeding, within five (5) working days and MCC shall determine whether to terminate this Agreement pursuant to section 9.

i. PROVIDER will maintain the confidentiality of information contained in Participants' medical records and will only release such records: (1) in accordance with this Agreement, (2) subject to applicable laws, regulations, or orders of any court of law, or (3) with the written consent of the Participant.

j. PROVIDER will cooperate with Medical Management Programs. PROVIDER shall use best efforts to obtain an appropriate release and keep MCC and the primary care physician or referring physician, if different, informed of the diagnosis or prognosis of treatment provided to Participant.

k. PROVIDER agrees to participate in a Provider Network for additional Accounts of MCC or Payor or with additional Payors on the terms set forth herein. No further consent of PROVIDER shall be required for FCC to add or delete an Account or Payor.

4. Compensation

PROVIDER agrees to accept reimbursement from Payor in the amount set forth in the appropriate Exhibit(s) C and in accordance with this Agreement, its Exhibit(s), and the terms of the Participant's Plan as full payment for Covered Services rendered to such Participant. Payor shall notify PROVIDER of the Copayment, Deductible, or Coinsurance, if any, which shall be charged to the Participant pursuant to the Participant's coverage under Participant's Plan.

PROVIDER shall submit an itemized bill for Covered Services personally rendered by PROVIDER on forms acceptable to Payor within sixty (60) days from the date of Covered Services being rendered. PROVIDER shall supply any additional information reasonably requested by MCC to verify that PROVIDER rendered Covered Services and the usual charges for such services. Payor may deny payment not submitted within the sixty (60) days from the date of Covered Services being rendered, unless PROVIDER can demonstrate to Payor's satisfaction that there was good cause for such delay. Payor may deny payment for services that are not Covered Services or not Medically Necessary.

5. Charges to Participants

PROVIDER agrees that it will hold harmless and will not seek reimbursement from Participants for Covered Services for which Payor is financially responsible, or for non-Covered Services for which authorization was denied by MCC, unless Participant agreed in writing prior to the delivery of the services to be billed. PROVIDER further agrees that PROVIDER shall only bill Participants for Copayments, Coinsurance, and Deductible amounts required by the Plan, and for those non-Covered Services for which Participant's agreement has been obtained as described herein.

PROVIDER further agrees (1) this provision shall survive the termination of the Agreement for Covered Services rendered prior to its termination regardless of the cause giving rise to termination and that (2) this provision supersedes any oral or written contrary agreement heretofore entered into between PROVIDER and Participants or anyone acting on their behalf.

6. Access to Books and Records

PROVIDER will maintain medical, financial, and administrative records, concerning services provided to Participants pursuant to this Agreement, in accordance with applicable Federal and state laws. MCC, its authorized representatives and duly authorized third parties, such as but not limited to governmental and regulatory agencies, will have the right to inspect, review, and make copies of such records directly related to services rendered to Participants. Such review and duplication shall be allowed upon reasonable notice during regular business hours and shall be subject to all applicable laws and regulations concerning confidentiality of such data or records. This provision shall survive the termination of this Agreement.

7. Relationship of Parties

The parties to this Agreement are independent contractors. This Agreement shall not create an employer-employee partnership or a joint venture relationship between or among Payor, PROVIDER, or any of their respective directors, officers, employees, or other representatives. This Agreement shall not be deemed to create any rights or remedies in persons who are not parties to this Agreement except as otherwise set forth herein.

PROVIDER agrees not to allow determinations pursuant to Medical Management Programs or any other terms and conditions of this Agreement to alter or affect his/her standards of care, medical judgement, or the PROVIDER-patient relationship.

Each party agrees to refrain from making disparaging statements that interfere with the contractual relationships between the other party and its existing or prospective Participants, Accounts, Participating Providers, or patients during the term of or following the termination of this Agreement.

8. Dispute Resolution Procedure

In the event any dispute shall arise with respect to the performance or interpretation of this Agreement, all matters in controversy shall be submitted to MCC for review and resolution pursuant to MCC's Medical Management Programs. If PROVIDER is not satisfied with the resolution, PROVIDER may submit the matter to MCC's President or his designee who will review the matter and may seek written statements as appropriate. The decision of MCC will be binding on MCC and PROVIDER if the resolution is accepted by PROVIDER. Neither party shall cease or diminish its performance under the Agreement pending dispute resolution.

If PROVIDER is not satisfied with such resolution and to the extent permitted by law, the matter in controversy shall be submitted either to a dispute resolution entity, or to a single arbitrator selected by the American Arbitration Association, as the parties shall agree within sixty (60) days of MCC's final decision. If the matter is submitted to arbitration, it shall be conducted in accordance with the commercial arbitration rules of the American Arbitration Association. The arbitrator shall be a person who has knowledge of and is experienced in the health care delivery field. Arbitration shall take place in _____. Both parties expressly covenant and agree to be bound by the decision of the dispute resolution entity or arbitrator as final determination of the matter in dispute. Each party shall assume its own costs, but shall share the cost of the resolution entity equally. Judgement upon the award rendered by the resolution entity may be entered in any court having jurisdiction.

9. Term and Termination

a. *Term*–The initial term of this Agreement shall begin on the Effective Date and shall continue unless terminated as set forth below.

b. This Agreement may be terminated by either party, without cause, upon ninety (90) days prior written notice to the other party.

c. Either party may terminate this Agreement for cause upon thirty (30) days written notice to the other party specifying the manner in which that party has materially breached its obligations pursuant to the Agreement. The Agreement shall terminate automatically at the expiration of such thirty (30) day period if that party has not cured its breach within such period and delivered evidence of such cure to nonbreaching party.

d. MCC may terminate this Agreement immediately upon the occurrence of any of the following: (1) PROVIDER fails to maintain any license or certification required to provide Covered Services; (2) any of PROVIDER's insurance required by this Agreement is canceled; (3) PROVIDER willfully breaches, habitually neglects, or continually fails to perform professional duties; (4) PROVIDER commits or fails to commit an act which is determined by MCC to be detrimental to the reputation, operation, or activities of MCC or Payor; (5) an administrative finding or judgement of professional misconduct on the part of PROVIDER or PROVIDER's Professional Staff.

e. This Agreement may be terminated without the consent of or notice to any Account, Payor, Participant, other Participating Providers, or other third parties.

10. Effect of Termination

The Agreement will be of no further force or effect as of the date of termination except that:

a. PROVIDER shall continue to accept reimbursement from Payor in accordance with the terms of this Agreement and its Exhibits as payment in full for care provided to a Participant for the balance of any MH/SA Services in progress at the time of termination. For purposes of this section, the rates set forth in the appropriate Exhibit(s) C in effect at the time of termination of this Agreement shall apply. This requirement applies only to those MH/SA Services that would have been Covered Services had the Agreement not terminated. Termination of this Agreement shall in no way be construed as affecting the provider/patient relationship.

b. The parties shall cooperate to promptly resolve any outstanding financial, administrative, or patient care issues upon the termination of this Agreement.

11. References to PROVIDER

PROVIDER consents to lawful references to his/her participation in Programs, Provider Network, and any informational efforts initiated by MCC or any third party on behalf of MCC. Neither party will otherwise use the other party's name, symbol, trademarks, or service marks without the prior written consent of that party and will cease any such use as soon as is reasonably possible upon termination of this Agreement.

12. Coordination of Benefits

a. PROVIDER will cooperate with MCC to coordinate Plan's coverage with that of other Payors or entities that have primary responsibility to pay for Covered Services in accordance with the Participant's Plan.

b. PROVIDER shall not withhold or refuse to render Covered Services to Participants nor require Participants to pay for Covered Services pending a decision about which Payor is primarily responsible for paying for such services.

c. If Plan's coverage is considered primary coverage, in accordance with Plan's Order of Benefits Determination rules, MCC or Payor shall reimburse PROVIDER in accordance with Section II.A of the appropriate Exhibit(s) B to this Agreement.

d. If Plan's coverage is not primary, PROVIDER shall supply MCC or Payor with copies of statements from third parties related to the payment or denial of payment for Covered Services rendered to the Participant.

e. If MCC or Payor is required to coordinate Plan's benefits with the primary Payor, MCC or Payor will reimburse PROVIDER the agreed upon amount, in accordance with Section II.A of the appropriate Exhibit(s) B to this Agreement, less the amount for which the primary Payor is responsible, and less any applicable Copayments, Deductibles, or Coinsurance charges. Neither MCC nor Payor shall participate in coordination of benefits or be required to provide any reimbursement if the total received from the Primary Payor exceeds the reimbursement rates agreed to in this Agreement.

13. *Miscellaneous*

a. *Amendment*–This Agreement or its Exhibits may be amended by MCC upon thirty (30) days prior written notice to PROVIDER at any time during the term of the Agreement. If an amendment is not acceptable to PROVIDER, he/she may terminate this Agreement, as of the date the amendment becomes effective, by giving written notice to MCC within thirty (30) days of receipt of the amendment. Otherwise, PROVIDER will be deemed to have accepted such amendment as of its effective date.

b. *Assignment and Subcontracting*–Neither party shall assign to or contract with another party for the performance of any of its obligations under this Agreement without the prior written consent of the other party, which shall not be unreasonably withheld. However, an assignment by MCC to a parent, affiliate, or subsidiary shall not constitute an assignment for purposes of this Agreement.

c. *Entire Agreement*–This Agreement, its Exhibits, and any documents incorporated by reference constitute the entire Agreement between the parties. It supersedes any prior Agreements, promises, negotiation, or representations, either oral or written, relating to the subject matter of this Agreement.

d. *Governing Law*–This Agreement shall be governed by and construed under the laws of the State or Commonwealth of _____ and in accordance with applicable Federal laws and regulations.

e. *Impossibility of Performance*–Neither party shall be deemed to be in violation of this Agreement if it is prevented from performing its obligations for reasons beyond its control, including without limitations, acts of God or of the public enemy, flood or storm, strikes, or statute, rule or action of any Federal, State, or local government or agency. The parties shall make a good faith effort, however, to ensure that Participants have access to Covered Services.

f. *Non-Exclusivity*–This Agreement shall not be construed to be an exclusive Agreement between MCC and PROVIDER, nor shall it be deemed to be an Agreement requiring MCC, Participating Providers, or other PROVIDERS to refer any minimum number of Participants to PROVIDER.

g. *Notice*–Any and all notices required to be given pursuant to the terms of this Agreement must be given by United States mail, postage prepaid, return receipt requested, and forwarded to the addresses on the signature page. The parties may agree to substitute the service of the U. S. Postal Service with those of nationally recognized courier services that provide signed receipt of correspondence.

h. *Regulatory Approval*–This Agreement shall be deemed to be a binding letter of intent if MCC has not received any required license or certification, or MCC or Payor has not received applicable regulatory approval as of the date of the execution of this Agreement. The Agreement shall become effective on and after the date MCC receives such regulatory approval. If MCC notifies PROVIDER of its inability to obtain such licensure, certification, or regulatory approval, after due diligence, both parties shall be released from any liability pursuant to this Agreement.

i. *Severability*–In the event that a provision of the Agreement is rendered invalid or unenforceable by Federal or State Statute or Regulations, or declared null and void by any court of competent jurisdiction, the remaining provisions of this Agreement will remain in full force and effect.

j. *Waiver of Breach*–Waiver of a breach of any provision of this Agreement will not be deemed a waiver of any other breach of the Agreement.

IN WITNESS WHEREOF, the parties have executed this Agreement intending to be bound on and after _____, 19____. (Effective Date)

PROVIDER

NAME: _____
(Please Print)

SIGNATURE: ——————————————————————————

DATE: ——————————————————————————————

MCC: ————————————————————————————————

BY: —————————————————————————————————
                          (Please Print)

ITS: ————————————————————————————————
                          (Title)

SIGNATURE: ——————————————————————————

DATE: ——————————————————————————————

Attachments:

Exhibits: A. Covered Services
             B-1. HMO Programs
             B-2. PPO Programs

EXHIBIT A
COVERED SERVICES

These services checked below shall be Covered Services. PROVIDER shall be reimbursed according to the appropriate Exhibit(s) C under the Agreement only for those Covered Services provided to a Participant in accordance with the Participant's Plan.

*Check
If
Applicable*   *Service*

————————   1. Inpatient Consultation

————————   2. Inpatient Attending Services

————————   3. Outpatient Mental Health Services (Group)

———————— 4. Outpatient Mental Health Services (Individual)

———————— 5. Medication Management

———————— 6. Electroconvulsive Treatment

———————— 7. Intensive Outpatient Substance Abuse Treatment

———————— 8. Intensive Outpatient Eating Disorder Treatment

———————— 9. Biofeedback

———————— 10. Miscellaneous (Specify)

_____

_____

EXHIBIT B-1
HMO PROGRAMS

I. PROVIDER's Responsibilities

A. *Covered Services*–Payor shall reimburse PROVIDER as described in this Exhibit for providing Covered Services to Participants in accordance with Health Services Agreements.

B. *Referrals to Other PROVIDERS*–PROVIDER will only make referrals pursuant to MCC's Medical Management Programs.

II. Reimbursement for Covered Services

A. PROVIDER will bill Payor his/her usual charges for Covered Services rendered to Participants. Payor will only reimburse PROVIDER as a Participating Provider for Covered Services which were appropriately authorized, pursuant to MCC's Medical Management Programs. Reimbursement for Covered Services provided in an emergency shall be pursuant to MCC's Medical Management Programs. PROVIDER shall receive the lesser of: (1) PROVIDER's usual and customary charges; or (2) the maximum allowable reimbursement for such services as set forth in the appropriate Exhibit(s) C ("Maximum Reimbursement Rate"); less applicable Copayment, Deductible, and Coinsurance payments received from Participants, and payments from third parties through coordination of benefits as described in section 12 of the Agreement. If a Covered Service has not been assigned a Maximum Reimbursement Rate in the appropriate Exhibit(s) C, PROVIDER will be paid at an hourly rate equivalent to the hourly psychotherapy rate in the appropriate Exhibit(s) C.

B. Payor may deny all or a portion of PROVIDER's claim specifically attributable to PROVIDER's failure to comply with the requirements of MCC's Medical Management Programs.

III. Billing

A. PROVIDER will submit all statements for Covered Services directly to MCC or Payor, as designated by MCC. The statements shall include, at a minimum, the following information: (1) Participant's name, sex, date of birth, and identification number; (2) the date or dates services were rendered; (3) CPT-4 codes describing those services; (4) primary and secondary DSM–III–R diagnosis number(s); (5) PROVIDER's usual and customary fee for services rendered; and (6) the authorization number and the name of the provider actually providing care.

B. PROVIDER shall bill MCC or its designee for Covered Services within sixty (60) days from the date he/she renders such services.

C. MCC will make reasonable efforts to require Payor to make payment to PROVIDER within thirty (30) days of the receipt by MCC or its designee of a properly completed bill for Covered Services. Such payment period may be extended, however, if MCC or Payor, in good faith, requires additional time to investigate whether it is responsible for such billed services.

D. PROVIDER agrees to refrain from duplicate billing within thirty (30) days after submitting a bill for Covered Services to MCC or its designee.

EXHIBIT B-2
PPO PROGRAMS

I. PROVIDER's Responsibilities

A. *Covered Services*–MCC shall arrange for PROVIDER to be reimbursed by Payor as described in this Exhibit for providing Covered

Services to Participants in accordance with Health Services Agreements.

B. *Referrals to Other PROVIDERS*–PROVIDER will only make referrals pursuant to MCC's Medical Management Programs.

II. Reimbursement for Covered Services

A. PROVIDER will charge his/her usual charges for Covered Services rendered to Participants. Payor will only reimburse PROVIDER as a Participating Provider for Covered Services which were appropriately authorized, pursuant to MCC's Medical Management Programs. Reimbursement for Covered Services provided in an emergency shall be pursuant to MCC's Medical Management Programs. PROVIDER shall receive the lesser of: (1) PROVIDER's usual and customary charges; or (2) the maximum allowable reimbursement for such services as set forth in the appropriate Exhibit(s) C ("Maximum Reimbursement Rate"); less applicable Copayment, Deductible, and Coinsurance payments received from Participants, and payments from third parties through coordination of benefits as described in Section XIII of the Agreement. If a Covered Service has not been assigned a Maximum Reimbursement Rate in the appropriate Exhibit(s) C, PROVIDER will be paid at an hourly rate equivalent to the hourly psychotherapy rate in the appropriate Exhibit(s) C.

B. Payor may deny all or a portion of PROVIDER's claim specifically attributable to PROVIDER's failure to comply with the requirements of MCC's Medical Management Programs.

III. Billing

A. PROVIDER agrees to accept an assignment of benefits which has been submitted by a Participant.

B. PROVIDER will submit all statements for Covered Services pursuant to assignments of benefits directly to MCC or Payor, as designated by MCC. The statements shall include, at a minimum, the following information: (1) Participant's name, sex, date of birth, and identification number; (2) the date or dates services were rendered; (3) CPT-4 codes describing those services; (4) primary and secondary DSM–III–R diagnosis number(s); (5) PROVIDER's usual and customary fee for services rendered; and (6) the authorization number and the name of the provider actually providing care.

C. Pursuant to assignments of benefits, PROVIDER shall submit all statements to MCC or its designee for Covered Services within sixty (60) days from the date he/she renders such services.

D. MCC will make reasonable efforts to require Payor to make payment to PROVIDER within thirty (30) days of the receipt by MCC or its designee of a properly completed bill for Covered Services. Such payment period may be extended, however, if MCC or Payor, in good faith, requires additional time to investigate whether it is responsible for such billed services.

E. PROVIDER agrees to refrain from duplicate billing within thirty (30) days after submitting a bill for Covered Services to MCC or its designee.

F. MCC will make best efforts to verify a Participant's eligibility. If it is later determined that a patient was not a Participant, PROVIDER may bill patient directly.

MENTAL HEALTH PROVIDER AGREEMENT
(Clinic)

This Agreement (the "Agreement") is by and between

_____ ("MCC") and _____ ("PROVIDER").

WITNESSETH

1. Purpose

WHEREAS, MCC is a corporation engaged in providing, managing, and/or arranging for mental health and substance abuse services ("MH/SA Services") to Participants of various health maintenance organizations, health service plans, preferred provider organizations, insurance, labor trusts, self-insurance, and ERISA plans under agreements between MCC and the entities which fund or administer such Plans ("Health Services Agreements"); and

WHEREAS, PROVIDER employs professional mental health and/or substance abuse staff, and other qualified health personnel and staff ("Professional Staff"); is licensed to provide mental health and/or substance abuse services under the laws of the State of _____; and is equipped with the appropriate, licensed, and duly accredited facilities ("Facilities") necessary to provide mental health and substance abuse services to Participants; and

WHEREAS, MCC desires to contract with PROVIDER to provide Covered services for the benefit of Participants;

NOW, THEREFORE, in consideration of the premises and mutual promises herein, the parties agree as follows:

2. Definitions

a. *Accounts*–Means an employer or other entity which has established a welfare benefit plan, and which has contracted with MCC or Payor to make available the Provider Network.

b. *Clinical Staff*–Those licensed or certified members of PROVIDER's Professional Staff who directly provide Covered Services to Participants.

c. *Coinsurance*–Means that portion of the MCC considered charge for Covered Services, calculated as a percentage of the charge of such services, which is to be paid by Participants.

d. *Copayment or Deductible*–Means a fixed dollar portion of the charge of Covered Services which is to be paid by Participants.

e. *Covered Services*–Means those PROVIDER services which are listed on Exhibit A attached hereto.

f. *Medical Management Programs*–Means the quality management, credentialling, case management, and other programs adopted or established by MCC.

g. *Medically Necessary*–Means services or supplies which, under the provisions of this Agreement, are: (1) necessary for the symptoms, diagnosis, or treatment of the mental health or substance abuse condition; (2) provided for diagnosis or direct care and treatment of the mental health or substance abuse condition; (3) not primarily for the convenience of the Participant, the Participant's physician, or another PROVIDER; and (4) the most appropriate supply or level of service which can safely be provided. For inpatient stays, this means that acute care as an inpatient is necessary due to the kind of services the Participant is receiving or the severity of the Participant's condition, and that safe and adequate care cannot be received as an outpatient or in a less intensified setting.

h. *Participant*–Means any individual, or eligible dependent of such individual, whether referred to as "Insured," "Subscriber," "Member," "Participant," "Covered Life or Individual," "Enrollee," "Dependent," or otherwise, who is eligible for Covered Services pursuant to Health Services Agreements.

i. *Participating Providers*–Means those MH/SA Service providers and other health care providers or institutions who have entered into agreements with MCC to provide Covered Services to Participants.

j. *Payor*–Means MCC, or an insurer, or health maintenance organization, or employer, or other entity which funds or administers a Plan.

k. *Plan*–Means the welfare benefit plan funded, arranged, or administered by Payor for Payor's or Account's Participants.

l. *Provider Network*–Means the network of Participating Providers established and maintained by MCC to provide Covered Services to Participants.

m. *Provider Services*–Means those mental health and substance abuse services provided by a Participating Provider and covered by a Plan.

3. Provider's Obligations

a. PROVIDER shall have all of its Clinical Staff complete MCC's Provider Application and submit such additional information as MCC requests for credentialling purposes. Further, PROVIDER shall submit evidence to MCC of initial and recurring licensing or certification for each member of its Clinical Staff approved by MCC for participation. MCC will notify PROVIDER regarding which Clinical Staff have been approved for participation. PROVIDER shall be reimbursed for Covered Services rendered only by Clinical Staff whose credentials have been reviewed and approved by MCC.

b. PROVIDER, through its Clinical Staff, shall provide the Medically Necessary Covered Services listed on Exhibit A to Participants in accordance with the program(s) set forth in the appropriate Exhibit(s) B of this Agreement.

c. PROVIDER will maintain sufficient facilities and personnel to provide Participants with timely access to Covered Services in accordance with the standards set forth in the Medical Management Programs.

d. PROVIDER agrees and shall require its Clinical Staff to agree to keep valid all licenses and/or certifications which are required under federal, state, or local laws for the provision of Covered Services to Participants.

e. PROVIDER agrees and shall require its Clinical Staff to agree to fully cooperate with MCC and the Plans to resolve complaints from Participants and use best efforts to comply with the complaint procedures established by MCC and/or each of the Plans.

f. PROVIDER shall require its Clinical Staff to represent and warrant that the information contained on his/her Provider Application, which is incorporated herein by reference, is true and accurate. PROVIDER will notify MCC promptly of any material change in the information on such Application.

g. PROVIDER will procure and maintain adequate policies of comprehensive general liability, professional liability, and other insurance, in amounts, deemed appropriate by MCC based on the PROVIDER's mode of practice/specialty, necessary to insure the PROVIDER against any claim or claims for damages arising out of personal injuries or death occasioned directly or indirectly in connection with the provision of services pursuant to this Agreement. PROVIDER will submit evidence of such coverage to MCC upon request, and will notify MCC at least thirty (30) days prior to the expiration, termination, or material change in the coverages.

h. PROVIDER agrees and shall require its Clinical Staff to agree not to discriminate against any Participant on the basis of source of payment, race, color, gender, sexual orientation, age, religion, national origin, handicap, or health status in providing services under this Agreement.

i. PROVIDER, through its Clinical Staff, will render Covered Services to all Participants in an appropriate, timely, and cost effective manner. Further, PROVIDER, through its Clinical Staff, agrees and shall require its Clinical Staff to agree to furnish the services according to generally accepted medical, mental health, and substance abuse practice, community standards, and applicable laws and regulations. In the event PROVIDER discovers that a claim, suit, or criminal or administrative proceeding has been brought or may be brought against PROVIDER or a member of its Clinical Staff relating to the quality of services provided to Participants by PROVIDER, or a member of its Clinical Staff or relating to the compliance of PROVIDER, or a member of its Clinical Staff with community standards and applicable laws and regulations, then PROVIDER shall notify MCC of such claim, suit, or proceeding, within five (5) working days and MCC shall determine whether to terminate this Agreement pursuant to section 9.

j. PROVIDER agrees and shall require its Clinical Staff to agree to maintain the confidentiality of information contained in Participants' medical records and will only release such records: (1) in accordance with this Agreement, (2) subject to applicable laws, regulations, or orders of any court of law, or (3) with the written consent of the Participant.

k. PROVIDER agrees and shall require its Clinical Staff to agree to cooperate with Medical Management Programs. PROVIDER agrees and shall require its Clinical Staff to use best efforts to obtain an appropriate release and keep MCC and the primary care physician or referring physician, if different, informed of the diagnosis or prognosis of treatment provided to Participant.

l. PROVIDER agrees to participate in a Provider Network for additional Accounts of MCC or Payor or with additional Payors on the terms set forth herein. No further consent of PROVIDER shall be required for MCC to add or delete an Account or Payor.

4. Compensation

PROVIDER agrees to accept reimbursement from Payor in the amount set forth in the appropriate Exhibit(s) C and in accordance with this Agreement, its Exhibit(s) and the terms of the Participant's Plan as full payment for Covered Services rendered to such Participant. Payor shall notify PROVIDER of the Copayment, Deductible, or Coinsurance, if any, which shall be charged to the Participant pursuant to the Participant's coverage under Participant's Plan.

PROVIDER shall submit an itemized bill for Covered Services rendered by PROVIDER on forms acceptable to Payor within sixty (60) days from the date of Covered Services being rendered. PROVIDER shall supply any additional information reasonably requested by MCC to verify that PROVIDER rendered Covered Services and the usual charges for such services. Payor may deny payment not submitted within the sixty (60) days from the date of Covered Services being rendered, unless PROVIDER can demonstrate to Payor's satisfaction that there was good cause for such delay. Payor may deny payment for services that are not Covered Services or are not Medically Necessary.

5. Charges to Participant

PROVIDER agrees that it will hold harmless and will not seek reimbursement from Participants for Covered Services for which Payor is financially responsible, or for non-Covered Services for which authorization was denied by MCC, unless Participant agreed in writing prior to the delivery of the services to be billed. PROVIDER further agrees that PROVIDER shall only bill Participants for Copayments, Coinsurance, and Deductible amounts required by the Plan, and for those non-Covered Services for which Participant's agreement has been obtained as described herein.

PROVIDER further agrees (1) this provision shall survive the termination of the Agreement for Covered Services rendered prior to its termination regardless of the cause giving rise to termination; and that (2) this provision supersedes any oral or written contrary agreement heretofore entered into between PROVIDER and Participants or anyone acting on their behalf.

6. Access to Books and Records

PROVIDER will maintain medical, financial, and administrative records, concerning services provided to Participants pursuant to this Agreement, in accordance with applicable Federal and state laws. MCC, its authorized representatives and duly authorized third parties, such as but not limited to governmental and regulatory agencies, will have the right to inspect, review, and make copies of such records directly related to services rendered to Participants. Such review and duplication shall be allowed upon reasonable notice during regular business hours and shall be subject to all applicable laws and regulations concerning confidentiality of such data or records. This provision shall survive the termination of this Agreement.

7. Relationship of Parties

The parties to this Agreement are independent contractors. This Agreement shall not create an employer-employee partnership or a joint venture relationship between or among Payor, PROVIDER, or any of their respective directors, officers, employees, or other representatives. This Agreement shall not be deemed to create any rights or remedies in persons who are not parties to this Agreement except as otherwise set forth herein.

PROVIDER agrees and shall require its Clinical Staff to agree not to allow determinations pursuant to Medical Management Programs or any other terms and conditions of this Agreement to alter or affect standards of care, medical judgement, or the PROVIDER-patient relationship.

PROVIDER agrees and shall require its Clinical Staff to agree, and MCC agrees to refrain from making disparaging statements that interfere with the contractual relationships between the parties and existing or prospective Participants, Accounts, Participating Providers, or patients during the term of or following the termination of this Agreement.

8. Dispute Resolution Procedure

In the event any dispute shall arise with respect to the Performance or interpretation of this Agreement, all matters in controversy shall be submitted to MCC for review and resolution pursuant to MCC's Medical Management Programs. If PROVIDER is not satisfied with the resolution, PROVIDER may submit the matter to MCC's President or his designee who will review the matter and may seek written statements as appropriate decision of MCC wilt be binding on MCC and PROVIDER if the resolution is accepted by PROVIDER. Neither party shall cease or diminish its performance under the Agreement pending dispute resolution.

If PROVIDER is not satisfied with such resolution and to the extent permitted by law, the matter in controversy shall be submitted either to a dispute resolution entity, or to a single arbitrator selected by the American Arbitration Association, as the parties shall agree within sixty (60) days of MCC's final decision. If the matter is submitted to arbitration, it shall be conducted in accordance with the commercial arbitration rules of the American Arbitration Association. The arbitrator shall be a person who has knowledge of and is experienced in the health care delivery field. Arbitration shall take place in _____. Both parties expressly covenant and agree to be bound by the decision of the dispute resolution entity or arbitrator as final determination of the matter in dispute. Each party shall assume its own costs, but shall share the cost of the resolution entity equally. Judgement upon the award rendered by the resolution entity may be entered in any court having jurisdiction.

9. Term and Termination

a. *Term*–The initial term of this Agreement shall begin on the Effective Date and shall continue unless terminated as set forth below.

b. This Agreement may be terminated by either party, without cause, upon ninety (90) days prior written notice to the other party.

c. Either party may terminate this Agreement for cause upon thirty (30) days written notice to the other party specifying the manner in which that party has materially breached its obligations pursuant to the Agreement. The Agreement shall terminate automatically at the expiration of such thirty (30) day period if that party has not cured its breach within such period and delivered evidence of such cure to nonbreaching party.

d. MCC may terminate this Agreement immediately upon the occurrence of any of the following: (1) PROVIDER or any member of its Clinical Staff fails to maintain any license or certification required to provide Covered Services; (2) any of PROVIDER's insurance required by this Agreement is canceled; (3) PROVIDER or any member of its Clinical

Staff willfully breaches, habitually neglects, or continually fails to perform professional duties; (4) PROVIDER or any member of its Clinical Staff commits or fails to commit an act which is determined by MCC to be detrimental to the reputation, operation, or activities of MCC or Payor; (5) an administrative finding or judgement of Professional misconduct on the part of PROVIDER or PROVIDER'S Professional Staff.

e. This Agreement may be terminated without the consent of or notice to any Account, Payor, Participant, other Participating Providers, or other third parties.

10. Effect of Termination

The Agreement will be of no further force or effect as of the date of termination except that:

a. PROVIDER shall continue to accept reimbursement from Payor in accordance with the terms of this Agreement and its Exhibits as payment in full for care Provided to a Participant for the balance of any MH/SA Services in progress at the time of termination. For Purposes of this section, the rates set forth in the appropriate Exhibit(s) C in effect at the time of termination of this Agreement shall apply. This requirement applies only to those MH/SA Services that would have been Covered Services had the Agreement not terminated. Termination of this Agreement shall in no way be construed as affecting the PROVIDER-Patient relationship.

b. The parties shall cooperate to Promptly resolve any outstanding financial, administrative, or Patient care issues upon the termination of this Agreement.

11. References to PROVIDER

PROVIDER consents and shall require its Clinical Staff to consent to lawful references to participation in Programs, Provider Network, and any informational efforts initiated by MCC or any third party on behalf of MCC. Neither party will otherwise use the other party's name, symbol, trademarks, or service marks without the prior written consent of that party and will cease any such use as soon as is reasonably possible upon termination of this Agreement.

12. Coordination of Benefits

a. PROVIDER will cooperate with MCC to coordinate Plan's coverage with that of other Payors or entities that have primary responsibility to pay for Covered Services in accordance with the Participant's Plan.

b. PROVIDER shall not withhold or refuse to render Covered Services to Participants nor require Participants to pay for Covered Services pending a decision about which Payor is primarily responsible for paying for such services.

c. If Plan's coverage is considered primary coverage, in accordance with Plan's Order of Benefits Determination rules, MCC or Payor shall reimburse PROVIDER in accordance with Section II.A of the appropriate Exhibit(s) B to this Agreement.

d. If Plan's coverage is not primary, PROVIDER shall supply MCC or Payor with copies of statements from third parties related to the payment or denial of payment for Covered Services rendered to the Participant.

e. If MCC or Payor is required to coordinate Plan's benefits with the primary Payor, MCC or Payor will reimburse PROVIDER the agreed upon amount, in accordance with Section II.A of the appropriate Exhibit(s) B to this Agreement, less the amount for which the primary Payor is responsible, and less any applicable Copayments, Deductibles, or Coinsurance charges. Neither MCC nor Payor shall participate in coordination of benefits or be required to provide any reimbursement if the total received from the Primary Payor exceeds the reimbursement rates agreed to in this Agreement.

13. Miscellaneous

a. *Amendment*–This Agreement or its Exhibits may be amended by MCC upon thirty (30) days prior written notice to PROVIDER at any time during the term of the Agreement. If an amendment is not acceptable to PROVIDER, PROVIDER may terminate this Agreement, as of the date the amendment becomes effective, by giving written notice to MCC within thirty (30) days of receipt of the amendment. Otherwise, PROVIDER will be deemed to have accepted such amendment as of its effective date.

b. *Assignment and Subcontracting*–Neither party shall assign to or contract with another party for the performance of any of its obligations under this Agreement without the prior written consent of the other party, which shall not be unreasonably withheld. However, an assignment by MCC to a parent, affiliate, or subsidiary shall not constitute an assignment for purposes of this Agreement.

c. *Entire Agreement*–This Agreement, its Exhibits, and any documents incorporated by reference constitute the entire Agreement between the parties. It Supersedes any prior Agreements, promises, negotiation, or representations, either oral or written, relating to the subject matter of this Agreement.

d. *Governing Law*–This Agreement shall be governed by and construed under the laws of the State or Commonwealth of _____ and in accordance with applicable Federal laws and regulations.

e. *Impossibility of Performance*–Neither party shall be deemed to be in violation of this Agreement if it is Prevented from performing its obligations for reasons beyond its control, including without limitations, acts of God or of the public enemy, flood or storm, strikes, or statute, rule or action of any Federal, State, or local government or agency. The parties shall make a good faith effort, however, to ensure that Participants have access to Covered Services.

f. *Non–Exclusivity*–This Agreement shall not be construed to be an exclusive Agreement between MCC and PROVIDER, nor shall it be deemed to be an Agreement requiring MCC, Participating Providers, or other PROVIDERS to refer any minimum number of Participants to PROVIDER.

g. *Notice*–Any and all notices required to be given pursuant to the terms of this Agreement must be given by United States mail, postage prepaid, return receipt requested, and forwarded to the addresses on the signature page. The parties may agree to substitute the service of the U.S. Postal Service with those of nationally recognized courier services that provide signed receipt of correspondence.

h. *Regulatory Approval*–This Agreement shall be deemed to be a binding letter of intent if MCC has not received any required license or certification or MCC or Payor has not received applicable regulatory approval as of the date of the execution of this Agreement. The Agreement shall become effective on and after the date MCC receives such regulatory approval. If MCC notifies PROVIDER of its inability to obtain such licensure, certification, or regulatory approval, after due diligence, both parties shall be released from any liability pursuant to this Agreement.

i. *Severability*–In the event that a provision of the Agreement is rendered invalid or unenforceable by Federal or State Statute or Regulations, or declared null and void by any court of competent jurisdiction, the remaining provisions of this Agreement will remain in full force and effect.

j. *Waiver of Breach*–Waiver of a breach of any provision of this Agreement will not be deemed a waiver of any other breach of the Agreement.

IN WITNESS WHEREOF, the parties have executed this Agreement intending to be bound on and after _____, 19____. (Effective Date)

PROVIDER

NAME: ——————————————————————————
                    (Please Print)

SIGNATURE: —————————————————————————

DATE: ————————————————————————————

MCC: ————————————————————————————

BY: ——————————————————————————————
                    (Please Print)

ITS: ——————————————————————————————
                    (Title)

SIGNATURE: —————————————————————————

DATE: ————————————————————————————

Attachments:

Exhibits: A. Covered Services
             B-1. HMO Programs
             B-2. PPO Programs

EXHIBIT A
COVERED SERVICES

These services checked below shall be Covered Services. PROVIDER shall be reimbursed according to the appropriate Exhibit(s) C under the Agreement only for those Covered Services provided to a Participant in accordance with the Participant's Plan.

Check
If
Applicable   *Service*

——————— 1. Inpatient Consultation

——————— 2. Inpatient Attending Services

——————— 3. Outpatient Mental Health Services (Group)

——————— 4. Outpatient Mental Health Services (Individual)

——————— 5. Medication Management

——————— 6. Electroconvulsive Treatment

——————— 7. Intensive Outpatient Substance Abuse Treatment

——————— 8. Intensive Outpatient Eating Disorder Treatment

——————— 9. Biofeedback

——————— 10. Miscellaneous (Specify)

_____

_____

EXHIBIT B-1
HMO PROGRAMS

I. PROVIDER's Responsibilities

A. *Covered Services*–Payor shall reimburse PROVIDER as described in this Exhibit for providing Covered Services to Participants in accordance with Health Services Agreements.

B. *Referrals to Other PROVIDERS*–PROVIDER agrees and will require its Clinical staff to agree to only make referrals pursuant to MCC's Medical Management Programs.

II. Reimbursement for Covered Services

A. PROVIDER will bill Payor its usual charges for Covered Services rendered to Participants. Payor will only reimburse PROVIDER as a Participating Provider for Covered Services which were appropriately authorized, pursuant to MCC's Medical Management Programs. Reimbursement for Covered Services provided in an emergency shall be pursuant to MCC's Medical Management Programs. PROVIDER shall receive the lesser of: (1) PROVIDER's usual and customary charges; or (2) the maximum allowable reimbursement for such services as set forth in the appropriate Exhibit(s) C ("Maximum Reimbursement Rate"); less applicable Copayment, Deductible, and Coinsurance payments received from Participants, and payments from third parties through coordination of benefits as described in section 12 of the Agreement. If a Covered Service has not been assigned a Maximum Reimbursement Rate in the appropriate Exhibit(s) C, PROVIDER will be paid at an hourly rate equivalent to the hourly psychotherapy rate in the appropriate Exhibit(s) C.

B. Payor may deny all or a portion of PROVIDER's claim specifically attributable to PROVIDER's failure to comply with the requirements of MCC's Medical Management Programs.

III. Billing

A. PROVIDER will submit all statements for Covered Services directly to MCC or Payor, as designated by MCC. The statements shall include, at a minimum, the following information: (1) Participant's name, sex, date of birth, and identification number; (2) the date or dates services were rendered; (3) CPT-4 codes describing those services; (4) primary and secondary DSM–III–R diagnosis number(s); (5) PROVIDER's usual and customary fee for services rendered; and (6) the authorization number and the name of the provider actually providing care.

B. PROVIDER shall bill MCC or its designee for Covered Services within sixty (60) days from the date services are rendered.

C. MCC will make reasonable efforts to require Payor to make payment to PROVIDER within thirty (30) days of the receipt by MCC or its designee of a properly completed bill for Covered Services. Such payment period may be extended, however, if MCC or Payor, in good faith, requires additional time to investigate whether it is responsible for such billed services.

D. PROVIDER agrees to refrain from duplicate billing within thirty (30) days after submitting a bill for Covered Services to MCC or its designee.

EXHIBIT B-2
PRO PROGRAMS

I. PROVIDER's Responsibilities

A. *Covered Services*–MCC shall arrange for PROVIDER to be reimbursed by Payor as described in this Exhibit for providing Covered Services to Participants in accordance with Health Services Agreements.

B. *Referrals to Other PROVIDERS*–PROVIDER agrees and will require its Clinical Staff to agree to only make referrals pursuant to MCC's Medical Management Programs.

II. Reimbursement for Covered Services

A. PROVIDER will charge its usual charges for Covered Services rendered to Participants. Payor will only reimburse PROVIDER as a Participating Provider for Covered Services which were appropriately authorized, pursuant to MCC's Medical Management Programs. Reimbursement for Covered Services provided in an emergency shall be pursuant to MCC's Medical Management Programs. PROVIDER shall receive the lesser of: (1) PROVIDER's usual and customary charges; or (2) the maximum allowable reimbursement for such services as set forth in the appropriate Exhibit(s) C ("Maximum Reimbursement Rate"); less applicable Copayment, Deductible, and Coinsurance payments received from Participants, and payments from third parties through coordination of benefits as described in Section XIII of the Agreement. If a Covered Service has not been assigned a Maximum Reimbursement Rate in the appropriate Exhibit(s) C, PROVIDER will be paid at an hourly rate equivalent to the hourly psychotherapy rate in the appropriate Exhibit(s) C.

B. Payor may deny all or a portion of PROVIDER's claim specifically attributable to PROVIDER's failure to comply with the requirements of MCC's Medical Management Programs.

III. Billing

A. PROVIDER agrees to accept an assignment of benefits which has been submitted by a Participant.

B. PROVIDER will submit all statements for Covered Services pursuant to assignments of benefits directly to MCC or Payor, as designated by MCC. The statements shall include, at a minimum, the following information: (1) Participant's name, sex, date of birth, and identification number; (2) the date or dates services were rendered; (3) CPT-4 codes describing those services; (4) primary and secondary DSM–III–R diagnosis number(s); (5) PROVIDER's usual and customary fee for services rendered; and (6) the authorization number and the name of the provider actually providing care.

C. Pursuant to assignments of benefits, PROVIDER shall submit all statements to MCC or its designee for Covered Services within sixty (60) days from the date services are rendered.

D. MCC will make reasonable efforts to require Payor to make payment to PROVIDER within thirty (30) days of the receipt by MCC or its designee of a properly completed bill for Covered Services. Such payment period may be extended, however, if MCC or Payor, in good faith, requires additional time to investigate whether it is responsible for such billed services.

E. PROVIDER agrees to refrain from duplicate billing within thirty (30) days after submitting a bill for Covered Services to MCC or its designee.

F. MCC will make best efforts to verify a Participant's eligibility. If it is later determined that a patient was not a Participant, PROVIDER may bill patient directly.

INSTITUTIONAL SERVICES AGREEMENT

This Agreement (the "Agreement") is by and between

_____ ("MCC") and _____ ("PROVIDER").

WITNESSETH

1. Purpose

WHEREAS, MCC is a corporation engaged in providing, managing, and/or arranging for mental health and substance abuse services ("MH/SA Services") to Participants of various health maintenance organizations, health service plans, preferred provider organizations, insurance, labor trusts, self-insurance, and ERISA plans under agreements between MCC and the entities which fund or administer such Plans ("Health Services Agreements"); and

WHEREAS, PROVIDER employs professional mental health and substance abuse staff, and other qualified health personnel and staff ("Professional Staff"); is licensed to provide MH/SA Services under applicable state law; and is equipped with the appropriately licensed and duly accredited facilities ("Facilities") necessary to provide MH/SA Services to Participants; and

WHEREAS, PROVIDER wishes to provide certain MH/SA Services ("Covered Services") under the terms and conditions set forth herein to Participants; and WHEREAS, MCC desires to contract with PROVIDER to provide Covered Services for the benefit of Participants;

NOW, THEREFORE, in consideration of the premises and mutual promises herein, the parties agree as follows:

2. Definitions

a. *Accounts*–Means an employer or other entity which has established a welfare benefit plan, and which has contracted with MCC or Payor to make available the Provider Network.

b. *Coinsurance*–Means that portion of the MCC considered charge for Covered Services, calculated as a Percentage of the charge of such services, which is to be paid by Participants.

c. *Copayment or Deductible*–Means a fixed dollar portion of the charge of Covered Services which is to be paid by Participants.

d. *Covered Services*–Means those PROVIDER services which are listed on Exhibit A attached hereto.

e. *Medical Management Programs*–Means the quality management, credentialling, case management, and other programs adopted or established by MCC.

f. *Medically Necessary*–Means services or supplies which, under the provisions of this Agreement, are: (1) necessary for the symptoms, diagnosis or treatment of the mental health or substance abuse condition; (2) provided for diagnosis, or direct care and treatment of the mental health or substance abuse condition; (3) not primarily for the convenience of the Participant, the Participant's physician, or another PROVIDER; and (4) the most appropriate supply or level of service which can safely be provided. For inpatient stays, this means that acute care as an inpatient is necessary due to the kind of services the Participant is receiving or the severity of the Participant's condition, and that safe and adequate care cannot be received as an outpatient or in a less intensified setting.

g. *Participant*–Means any individual, or eligible dependent of such individual, whether referred to as "Insured," "Subscriber," "Member," "Participant," "Covered Life or Individual," "Enrollee," "Dependent," or otherwise, who is eligible for Covered Services pursuant to Health Services Agreements.

h. *Participating Providers*–Means those MH/SA Service providers and other health care providers or institutions who have entered into agreements with MCC to provide Covered Services to Participants.

i. *Payor*–Means MCC, or an insurer, or health maintenance organization, or employer, or other entity which funds or administers a Plan.

j. *Plan*–Means the welfare benefit plan funded, arranged, or administered by Payor for Payor's or Account's Participants.

k. *Provider Network*–Means the network of Participating Providers established and maintained by MCC to provide Covered Services to Participants.

l. *Provider Services*–Means those mental health and substance abuse services provided by a Participating Provider and covered by a Plan.

3. Provider's Obligations

a. PROVIDER shall personally provide the Medically Necessary Covered Services listed on Exhibit A to Participants in accordance with the program(s) set forth in Exhibit(s) B of this Agreement.

b. PROVIDER will maintain sufficient facilities and personnel to provide Participants with timely access to Covered Services in accordance with the standards set forth in the Medical Management Programs. PROVIDER agrees to notify MCC of any additions or reductions in services as soon as possible.

c. PROVIDER agrees to keep valid all licenses and/or certifications which are required under federal, state, or local laws for the maintenance of its Facilities and Professional Staff and for the provision of Covered Services to Participants. If a hospital, PROVIDER also agrees to maintain its accreditation by the Joint Commission on Accreditation of Health Organizations relative to its Facilities and Professional Staff.

d. PROVIDER agrees to fully cooperate with MCC and the Plans to resolve complaints from Participants and shall use its best efforts to comply with the complaint procedures established by MCC and/or each of the Plans.

e. PROVIDER represents and warrants that the information contained on its Provider Application, which is incorporated herein by reference, is hue and accurate and PROVIDER will notify MCC promptly of any material change in the information on such Application.

f. PROVIDER will procure and maintain general and professional liability insurance as set forth in Section 13 of this Agreement.

g. PROVIDER will not discriminate against any Participant on the basis of source of payment, race, color, gender, sexual orientation, age, religion, national origin, handicap, or health status in providing services under this Agreement.

h. PROVIDER agrees that Covered Services shall be provided by qualified Professional Staff and shall be delivered to all Participants in an appropriate, timely, and cost effective manner. PROVIDER agrees to furnish the services according to generally accepted medical, mental health, and substance abuse practice, community standards, and applicable laws and regulations.

PROVIDER agrees to provide Professional Staff with ongoing training and supervision according to generally accepted medical, mental health, and substance abuse practice. PROVIDER shall furnish a summary of such training and supervision efforts upon request by MCC.

In the event PROVIDER discovers that a claim, suit, or criminal or administrative proceeding has been brought or may be brought against PROVIDER relating to the quality of services provided to Participants by PROVIDER or relating to PROVIDER's compliance with community standards and applicable laws and regulations, then PROVIDER shall notify MCC of such claim, suit, or proceeding within five (5) working days, and MCC shall determine whether to terminate this Agreement pursuant to section 9.

i. PROVIDER will cooperate with Medical Management Programs. PROVIDER shall use best efforts to obtain an appropriate release and keep MCC and the primary care physician or referring physician, if different, informed of the diagnosis or prognosis of treatment provided to Participant.

j. PROVIDER will permit representatives designated by MCC to visit hospitalized Participants and will provide information reasonably necessary to conduct Medical Management Programs in accordance with PROVIDER policies and procedures governing such activity. PROVIDER further agrees that MCC's utilization review coordinators may call designated representatives of PROVIDER for reports concerning the status of Participants receiving inpatient services from PROVIDER subject to Section 6 of this Agreement.

k. PROVIDER agrees to participate in a Provider Network for additional Accounts of MCC or Payor or with additional Payors on the terms set forth herein. No further consent of PROVIDER shall be required for MCC to add or delete an Account or Payor.

4. Compensation

PROVIDER agrees to accept reimbursement from Payor in the amount set forth in the appropriate Exhibit(s) C and in accordance with this Agreement, its Exhibit(s), and the terms of the Participant's Plan as full payment for Covered Services rendered to such Participant. Payor shall notify PROVIDER of the Copayment, Deductible, or Coinsurance, if any, which shall be charged to the Participant pursuant to the Participant's coverage under Participant's Plan.

PROVIDER shall submit an itemized bill for Covered Services rendered by PROVIDER on forms acceptable to Payor within sixty (60) days from the date of Covered Services being rendered. PROVIDER shall supply any additional information reasonably requested by MCC to verify that PROVIDER rendered Covered Services and the usual charges for such services. Payor may deny payment not submitted within the sixty (60) days from the date of Covered Services being rendered, unless PROVIDER can demonstrate to Payor's satisfaction that there was good cause for such delay. Payor may deny payment for services that are not Covered Services or not Medically Necessary.

5. Charges to Participants

PROVIDER agrees that it will hold harmless and will not seek reimbursement from Participants for Covered Services for which Payor is financially responsible, or for non-Covered Services for which authorization was denied by MCC, unless Participant agreed in writing prior to the delivery of the services to be billed. PROVIDER further agrees that PROVIDER shall only bill Participants for Copayments, Coinsurance, and Deductible amounts required by the Plan, and for those non-Covered Services for which Participant's agreement has been obtained as described herein.

PROVIDER further agrees (1) this provision shall survive the termination of the Agreement for Covered Services rendered prior to its termination regardless of the cause giving rise to termination; and that (2) this provision supersedes any oral or written contrary agreement heretofore entered into between PROVIDER and Participants or anyone acting on their behalf.

6. Access to and Confidentiality of Books and Records

PROVIDER will maintain medical, financial, and administrative records concerning services provided to Participants pursuant to this Agreement in accordance with applicable Federal and state laws, JCAHO guidelines, and generally accepted business practice. MCC, its authorized representatives, and duly authorized third parties, such as but not limited to governmental and regulatory agencies, will have the right to inspect, review, and make copies of such records directly related to services rendered to Participants. Such review and duplication shall be allowed upon reasonable notice during regular business hours and shall be subject to all applicable laws and regulations concerning confidentiality of such data or records. This provision shall survive the termination of this Agreement.

PROVIDER will maintain the confidentiality of information contained in Participants' medical records and will only release such records: (1) in accordance with this Agreement; (2) subject to applicable laws, regulations, or orders of any court of law; or (3) with the written consent of the Participant. This section will not be construed to prevent the PROVIDER from releasing information which it has taken from or based on such records to organizations or individuals taking part in research, experimental, educational or similar programs, if no identification of the Participant is made in the released information.

7. Relationship of Parties

The parties to this Agreement are independent contractors. This Agreement shall not create an employer-employee, partnership or a joint venture relationship between or among Payor, PROVIDER, or any of their respective directors, officers, employees, or other representatives. This Agreement shall not be deemed to create any rights or remedies in persons who are not parties to this Agreement except as otherwise set forth herein.

PROVIDER agrees not to allow determinations pursuant to Medical Management Programs or any other terms and conditions of this Agreement to alter or affect its standards of care, medical judgement, or the PROVIDER-patient relationship.

Each party agrees to refrain from making disparaging statements that interfere with the contractual relationships between the other party and its existing or prospective Participants, Accounts, Participating Providers, or patients during the term of or following the termination of this Agreement.

8. Dispute Resolution Procedure

In the event any dispute shall arise with respect to the performance or interpretation of this Agreement, all matters in controversy shall be submitted to MCC for review and resolution pursuant to MCC's Medical Management Programs. If PROVIDER is not satisfied with the resolution, PROVIDER may submit the matter to MCC's President or his designee who will review the matter and may seek written statements as appropriate. The decision of MCC will be binding on MCC and PROVIDER if the resolution is accepted by PROVIDER. Neither party shall cease or diminish its performance under the Agreement pending dispute resolution.

If PROVIDER is not satisfied with such resolution and to the extent permitted by law, the matter in controversy shall be submitted either to a dispute resolution entity, or to a single arbitrator selected by the American Arbitration Association, as the parties shall agree within sixty (60) days of MCC's final decision. If the matter is submitted to arbitration, it shall be conducted in accordance with the commercial arbitration rules of the American Arbitration Association. The arbitrator shall be a person who has knowledge of and is experienced in the health care delivery field. Arbitration shall take place in _____. Both parties expressly covenant and agree to be bound by the decision of the dispute resolution entity or arbitrator as final determination of the matter in dispute. Each party shall assume its own costs, but shall share the cost of the resolution entity equally. Judgement upon the award rendered by the resolution entity may be entered in any court having jurisdiction.

9. Term and Termination

a. *Term*–The initial term of this Agreement shall begin on the Effective Date and shall continue unless terminated as set forth below.

b. This Agreement may be terminated by either party, without cause, upon ninety (90) days prior written notice to the other party.

c. Either party may terminate this Agreement for cause upon thirty (30) days written notice to the other party specifying the manner in which that party has materially breached its obligations pursuant to the Agreement. The Agreement shall terminate automatically at the expiration of such thirty (30) day period if that party has not cured its breach within such period and delivered evidence of such cure to nonbreaching party.

d. MCC may terminate this Agreement immediately upon the occurrence of any of the following: (1) PROVIDER fails to maintain any license or certification required to provide Covered Services; (2) any of PROVIDER's insurance required by this Agreement is canceled; (3) PROVIDER willfully breaches, habitually neglects, or continually fails to perform professional duties; (4) PROVIDER commits or fails to commit an act which is determined by MCC to be detrimental to the reputation, operation, or activities of MCC or Payor; (5) an administrative finding or judgement of professional misconduct on the part of PROVIDER or PROVIDER's Professional Staff.

e. This Agreement may be terminated without the consent of or notice to any Account, Payor, Participant, other Participating Providers, or other third parties.

10. Effect of Termination

The Agreement will be of no further force or effect as of the date of termination except that:

a. PROVIDER shall continue to accept reimbursement from Payor in accordance with the terms of this Agreement and its Exhibits as payment in full for care provided to a Participant for the balance of any MH/SA Services in progress at the time of termination. For purposes of this section, the rates set forth in the appropriate Exhibit(s) C in effect at the time of termination of this Agreement shall apply. This requirement applies only to those MH/SA Services that would have been Covered Services had the Agreement not terminated. Termination of this Agreement shall in no way be construed as affecting the provider/ patient relationship.

b. The parties shall cooperate to promptly resolve any outstanding financial, administrative, or patient care issues upon the termination of this Agreement.

11. References to PROVIDER

PROVIDER consents to lawful references to his/her participation in Programs, Provider Network, and any informational efforts initiated by MCC or any third party on behalf of MCC. Neither party will otherwise use the other party's name, symbol, trademarks, or service marks without the prior written consent of that party and will cease any such use as soon as is reasonably possible upon termination of this Agreement.

12. Coordination of Benefits

a. PROVIDER will cooperate with MCC to coordinate Plan's coverage with that of other Payors or entities that have primary responsibility to pay for Covered Services in accordance with the Participant's Plan.

b. PROVIDER shall not withhold or refuse to render Covered Services to Participants nor require Participants to pay for Covered Services pending a decision about which Payor is primarily responsible for paying for such services.

c. If Plan's coverage is considered primary coverage, in accordance with Plan's Order of Benefits Determination rules, MCC or Payor shall reimburse PROVIDER in accordance with Section II.A of the appropriate Exhibit(s) B to this Agreement.

d. If Plan's coverage is not primary, PROVIDER shall supply MCC or Payor with copies of statements from third parties related to the payment or denial of payment for Covered Services rendered to the Participant.

e. If MCC or Payor is required to coordinate Plan's benefits with the primary Payor, MCC or Payor will reimburse PROVIDER the agreed upon amount, in accordance with Section II.A of the appropriate Exhibit(s) B to this Agreement, less the amount for which the primary Payor is responsible, and less any applicable Copayments, Deductibles, or Coinsurance charges. Neither MCC nor Payor shall participate in coordination of benefits or be required to provide any reimbursement if the total received from the Primary Payor exceeds the reimbursement rates agreed to in this Agreement.

13. Insurance and Indemnification

During the term of this Agreement PROVIDER will procure and maintain adequate policies of comprehensive general liability, professional liability, or self-insurance, in amounts deemed appropriate by MCC based on the PROVIDER's mode of practice/specialty, necessary to insure PROVIDER against any claim or claims for damages arising out of personal injuries or death occasioned directly or indirectly in connection with the provision of services pursuant to this Agreement. PROVIDER will submit evidence of such coverage to MCC upon request, and will notify MCC with at least thirty (30) days written notice to MCC of any material change in or termination of such coverage. Neither party shall be liable for any loss, expense, injury, claim, demand, judgement, or attorney's fees arising out of any action or failure to act by the other party, its directors, officers, employees, agents, or representatives, while acting within the scope of their employment. The responsible party shall indemnify and hold the other party harmless against any and all liability and expenses arising from such claims, actions, or judgements.

14. Miscellaneous

a. *Amendment*–This Agreement or its Exhibits may be amended by MCC upon thirty (30) days prior written notice to PROVIDER at any time during the term of the Agreement. If an amendment is not acceptable to PROVIDER, he/she may terminate this Agreement, as of the date the amendment becomes effective, by giving written notice to MCC within thirty (30) days of receipt of the amendment. Otherwise, PROVIDER will be deemed to have accepted such amendment as of its effective date.

b. *Assignment and Subcontracting*–Neither party shall assign to or contract with another party for the performance of any of its obligations under this Agreement without the prior written consent of the other party, which shall not be unreasonably withheld. However, an assignment by MCC to a parent, affiliate, or subsidiary shall not constitute an assignment for purposes of this Agreement.

c. *Entire Agreement*–This Agreement, its Exhibits, and any documents incorporated by reference constitute the entire Agreement between the parties. It supersedes any prior Agreements, promises, negotiation, or representations, either oral or written, relating to the subject matter of this Agreement.

d. *Governing Law*–This Agreement shall be governed by and construed under the laws of the State or Commonwealth of _____ and in accordance with applicable Federal laws and regulations.

e. *Impossibility of Performance*–Neither party shall be deemed to be in violation of this Agreement if it is prevented from performing its obligations for reasons beyond its control, including without limitations, acts of God or of the public enemy, flood or storm, strikes, or statute, rule or action of any Federal, State, or local government or agency. The parties shall make a good faith effort, however, to ensure that Participants have access to Covered Services.

f. *Non-Exclusivity*–This Agreement shall not be construed to be an exclusive Agreement between MCC and PROVIDER, nor shall it be deemed to be an Agreement requiring MCC, Participating Providers, or other PROVIDERS to refer any minimum number of Participants to PROVIDER.

g. *Notice*–Any and all notices required to be given pursuant to the terms of this Agreement must be given by United States mail, postage prepaid, return receipt requested, and forwarded to the addresses on the signature page. The parties may agree to substitute the service of the U.S. Postal Service with those of nationally recognized courier services that provide signed receipt of correspondence.

h. *Regulatory Approval*–This Agreement shall be deemed to be a binding letter of intent if MCC has not received any required license or certification or MCC or Payor has not received applicable regulatory approval as of the date of the execution of this Agreement. The Agreement shall become effective on and after the date MCC receives such regulatory approval. If MCC notifies PROVIDER of its inability to obtain such licensure, certification, or regulatory approval, after due diligence, both parties shall be released from any liability pursuant to this Agreement.

i. *Severability*–In the event that a provision of the Agreement is rendered invalid or unenforceable by Federal or State Statute or Regulations, or is declared null and void by any court of competent jurisdiction, the remaining provisions of this Agreement will remain in full force and effect.

j. *Waiver of Breach*–Waiver of a breach of any provision of this Agreement will not be deemed a waiver of any other breach of the Agreement.

IN WITNESS WHEREOF, the parties have executed this Agreement intending to be bound on and after _____, 19____. (Effective Date)

PROVIDER

NAME: ———————————————————————————————
(Please Print)

SIGNATURE: —————————————————————————————

DATE: ————————————————————————————————

MCC: —————————————————————————————————

BY: ————————————————————————————————
(Please Print)

ITS: ————————————————————————————————
(Title)

SIGNATURE: ————————————————————————————

DATE: ———————————————————————————————

Attachments:

Exhibits: A. Covered Services
            B-1. HMO Programs
            B-2. PPO Programs

EXHIBIT A
COVERED SERVICES

These services checked below shall be Covered Services. PROVIDER shall be reimbursed according to the appropriate Exhibit C under the Agreement only for those Covered Services provided to a Participant in accordance with the Participant's Plan.

*Check
If
Applicable   Service*

————————   1. Inpatient Mental Health Services
              (Adult) (Open Unit)

————————   2. Inpatient Mental Health Services
              (Adult) (Closed Unit)

————————   3. Inpatient Mental Health Services
              (Adolescent) (Open Unit)

————————   4. Inpatient Mental Health Services
              (Adolescent) (Closed Unit)

———————— 5. Inpatient Mental Health Services (Child)

———————— 6. Partial Hospital Mental Health Services (Adult)

———————— 7. Partial Hospital Mental Health Services (Adolescent)

———————— 8. Outpatient Mental Health Services (Group)

———————— 9. Outpatient Mental Health Services (Individual)

———————— 10. Inpatient Attending Services

———————— 11. Ancillary Services Not Otherwise Included

———————— 12. Emergency Room and/or Urgent Care Unit Services

———————— 13. Inpatient Detoxification Services (Adult)

———————— 14. Inpatient Detoxification Services (Adolescent)

———————— 15. Inpatient Substance Abuse Rehabilitation (Adult)

———————— 16. Inpatient Substance Abuse Rehabilitation (Adolescent)

———————— 17. Intensive Outpatient Substance Abuse Services (Adult)

———————— 18. Intensive Outpatient Substance Abuse Services (Adolescent)

———————— 19. Inpatient Eating Disorder Rehabilitation Services (Variable Length of Stay)

———————— 20. Intensive Outpatient Eating Disorder Treatment Services

———————— 21. Treatment of nuclear family members and/or
significant other of substance abusing patients

———————— 22. Miscellaneous (Specify)

_____

_____

EXHIBIT B-1
HMO PROGRAMS

I. PROVIDER's Responsibilities

A. *Covered Services*–Payor shall reimburse PROVIDER as described in
this Exhibit for Providing Covered Services to Participants in accordance with Health Services Agreements.

B. *Referrals to Other PROVIDERS*–PROVIDER will only make referrals
pursuant to MCC's Medical Management Programs.

II. Reimbursement for Covered Services

A. PROVIDER will bill Payor its usual charges for Covered Services
rendered to Participants. Payor will only reimburse PROVIDER as a
Participating Provider for Covered Services which were appropriately
authorized, pursuant to MCC's Medical Management Programs. Reimbursement for Covered Services Provided in an emergency shall be
pursuant to MCC's Medical Management Programs. PROVIDER shall
receive the lesser of: (1) PROVIDER'S usual and customary charges;
or (2) the maximum allowable reimbursement for such services as set
forth in the appropriate Exhibit(s) C ("Maximum Reimbursement
Rate"); less applicable Copayment, Deductible, and Coinsurance payments received from Participants, and payments from third parties
through coordination of benefits as described in Section 12 of the
Agreement. If a Covered Service has not been assigned a Maximum
Reimbursement Rate in the appropriate Exhibit(s) C, PROVIDER will
receive _____ percent of its billed charges subject to a standard reasonable and customary screening.

B. Payor may deny all or a portion of PROVIDER's claim specifically attributable to PROVIDER's failure to comply with the requirements of MCC's Medical Management Programs.

III. Billing

A. PROVIDER will submit all statements for Covered Services directly to MCC or Payor, as designated by MCC. Payor shall have the right to require that all statements be on form UB82 or HFCA 1500 or other similar form. The statements shall include, at a minimum, the following information: (1) Participant's name, sex, date of birth, and identification number; (2) the date or dates services were rendered; (3) CPT-4 codes describing those services; (4) primary and secondary DSM-III-R diagnosis number(s); (5) PROVIDER's usual and customary fee for services rendered; and (6) the authorization number and the name of the Provider actually providing care.

B. PROVIDER shall bill MCC or its designee for Covered Services within sixty (60) days from the date PROVIDER renders such services.

C. MCC will make reasonable efforts to require Payor to make payment to PROVIDER within thirty (30) days of the receipt by MCC or its designee of a properly completed bill for Covered Services. Such payment period may be extended, however, if MCC or Payor, in good faith, requires additional time to investigate whether it is responsible for such billed services.

D. PROVIDER agrees to refrain from duplicate billing within thirty (30) days after submitting a bill for Covered Services to MCC or its designee.

EXHIBIT B-2
PPO PROGRAMS

I. PROVIDER's Responsibilities

A. *Covered Services*–MCC shall arrange for PROVIDER to be reimbursed by Payor as described in this Exhibit for providing Covered Services to Participants in accordance with Health Services Agreements.

B. *Referrals to Other PROVIDERS*–PROVIDER will only make referrals pursuant to MCC's Medical Management Programs.

II. Reimbursement for Covered Services

A. PROVIDER will charge its usual charges for Covered Services rendered to Participants. Payor will only reimburse PROVIDER as a Participating Provider for Covered Services which were appropriately authorized, pursuant to MCC's Medical Management Programs. Reimbursement for Covered Services provided in an emergency shall be pursuant to MCC's Medical Management Programs. PROVIDER shall receive the lesser of: (1) PROVIDER's usual and customary charges; or (2) the maximum allowable reimbursement for such services as set forth in the appropriate Exhibit(s) C ("Maximum Reimbursement Rate"); less applicable Copayment, Deductible, and Coinsurance payments received from Participants, and payments from third parties through coordination of benefits as described in Section 12 of the Agreement. If a Covered Service has not been assigned a Maximum Reimbursement Rate in the appropriate Exhibit(s) C, PROVIDER will receive _____ percent of its charges subject to a standard reasonable and customary screening.

B. Payor may deny all or a portion of PROVIDER's claim specifically attributable to PROVIDER's failure to comply with the requirements of MCC's Medical Management Programs.

III. Billing

A. PROVIDER agrees to accept an assignment of benefits which has been submitted by a Participant.

B. PROVIDER will submit all statements for Covered Services pursuant to assignments of benefits directly to MCC or Payor, as designated by MCC. Payor shall have the right to require that all statements be on form UB82 or HFCA 1500 or other similar form. The statements shall include, at a minimum, the following information: (1) Participant's name, sex, date of birth, and identification number; (2) the date or dates services were rendered; (3) CPT-4 codes describing those services; (4) primary and secondary DSM–III–R diagnosis number(s); (5) PROVIDER's usual and customary fee for services rendered; and (6) the authorization number and the name of the provider actually providing care.

C. Pursuant to assignments of benefits, PROVIDER shall submit all statements to MCC or its designee for Covered Services within sixty (60) days from the date PROVIDER renders such services.

D. MCC will make reasonable efforts to require Payor to make payment to PROVIDER within thirty (30) days of the receipt by MCC or its designee of a properly completed bill for Covered Services. Such payment period may be extended, however, if MCC or Payor, in good faith, requires additional time to investigate whether it is responsible for such billed services.

E. PROVIDER agrees to refrain from duplicate billing within thirty (30) days after submitting a bill for Covered Services to MCC or its designee.

F. MCC will make best efforts to verify a Participant's eligibility. If it is later determined that a patient was not a Participant, PROVIDER may bill patient directly.

Appendix B

Directory of America's Health Maintenance Organizations

STATE	HMO	ESTIMATED MEMBERSHIP
Alabama	**Complete Health** 2160 Highland Ave. Birmingham, AL 35205 (205) 933-7661	123,000
	Health Maintenance Group of Birmingham 936 South 19th Street Birmingham, AL 35205 (205) 985-5590	6,000
	Health Partners of Alabama Beacon Ridge Tower 600 Parkway West, Suite 500 Birmingham, AL 35209 (205) 942-5787	45,000
	Southeast Health Plan, Inc. 104 Inverness Center Place, Ste. 130 Birmingham, AL 35242 (205) 991-6000	35,000
	Health Advantage Plans, Inc. 701 Noland Parkway Fairfield, AL 35064 (205) 786-0211	2,000

STATE	HMO	ESTIMATED MEMBERSHIP
Alabama (cont.)	**Humana Health Care Plan of AL, Inc.** 303 Williams Ave., SW, Ste. 121 Huntsville, AL 35801 (205) 532-2000	12,000
	Gulf Health Plans HMO, Inc. 2700 Grant Street Mobile, AL 36606 (205) 470-5900	7,000
	The PrimeHealth Companies 1400 University Blvd., South Mobile, AL 36609 (205) 342-0022	19,000
	Humana Health Plan of Alabama, Inc. 2350 Fairlane Drive, Ste. 120 Montgomery, AL 36116-1625 (205) 270-5544	14,000
Arizona	**Aetna Health Plans of Arizona, Inc.** Pionte Corridor Center IV 7878 North 16th St., Suite 210 Phoenix, AZ (602) 395-8812	22,000
	CIGNA Private Practice Plan-Phoenix 11001 North Black Canyon Hwy., Ste. 400 Phoenix, AZ 85029 (602) 942-4462	149,000
	HMO Arizona 2444 West Las Palmaritas Drive P.O. Box 13466 Phoenix, AZ 85002 (602) 864-4400	79,000
	Humana Health Plan, Inc. 2231 East Camelback Rd., Ste. 208 Phoenix, AZ 85016 (602) 381-4300	36,000

MetLife HealthCare Network of AZ, Inc.   6,000
3020 East Camelback Road, Ste. 100
Phoenix, AZ 85016
(602) 553-1300

The Samaritan Health Plan, Inc.   42,000
5300 North Central Ave., Ste. 220
Phoenix, AZ 85012
(602) 230-1555

FHP, Inc.   169,000
1615 South 52nd Street
Tempe, AZ 85281
(602) 966-6773

CIGNA HealthCare of Arizona, Inc.   28,000
7901 East 22nd Street
Tucson, AZ 85710
(602) 290-3680

Intergroup Healthcare Corporation   277,000
1010 North Finance Center Drive
Tucson, AZ 85710
(602) 721-1122

PARTNERS Health Plan of Arizona   94,000
5210 East Williams Circle, Ste. 300
Tucson, AZ 85711
(602) 748-8020

Arkansas   **American HMO**   44,000
Three Financial Centre
Little Rock, AR 72211
(501) 221-3534

Complete Health of Arkansas, Inc.   10,000
415 North McKinley Street
Plaza West Building
Little Rock, AR 72201
(501) 664-7700

Health Advantage   47,000
10816 Executive Center Dr., Ste. 300
Little Rock, AR 72211
(501) 221-1800

STATE	HMO	ESTIMATED MEMBERSHIP
Arkansas (cont.)	**Healthsource Arkansas, Inc.** 333 Executive Court Little Rock, AR 72205 (800) 831-6654	9,000
	HMO Arkansas, Inc. P.O. Box 1460 Little Rock, AR 72203-1460 (501) 227-7776	19,000
	Prudential Health Care Plan of AR, HMO 1701 Centerview, Ste. 210 Little Rock, AR 72211 (501) 227-7776	3,000
California	**FHP, Inc. (California)** 18000 Studebaker Rd. Cerritos, CA 90701 (301) 809-5399	439,000
	CareAmerica Health Plans 20500 Nordoff Street Chatsworth, CA 91311 (818) 407-2222	201,000
	Community Health Group 740 Bay Boulevard Chula Vista, CA 91910 (619) 422-0422	31,000
	TakeCare Health Plan, Inc. 2300 Clayton Rd., Ste. 1000 Concord, CA 94520-2100 (510) 246-1300	414,000
	PacifiCare of California 5701 Katella Avenue Cypress, CA 90630 (714) 952-1121	869,000

ValuCare   57,000
P.O. Box 25790
Fresno, CA 93729-5790
(209) 435-8366

CIGNA HealthCare of California, Inc.   250,000
505 North Brand Blvd., Ste. 400
Glendale, CA 91203
(818) 500-6262

CIGNA Private Practice Plan   76,000
505 North Brand Blvd., Ste. 500
Glendale, CA 91203
(818) 500-6798

United Health Plan   96,000
3405 West Imperial Highway
Inglewood, CA 90303
(310) 671-3456

MetLife HealthCare Network of CA, Inc.   66,000
4500 East Pacific Coast Hwy., Ste. 600
Long Beach, CA 90804
(310) 498-5200

SCAN Health Plan   6,000
521 East 4th Street
Long Beach, CA 90802
(310) 435-0380

Community Health Plan   108,000
313 North Figueroa St., 6th Floor West
Los Angeles, CA 90012
(213) 240-7783

Maxicare California   108,000
1149 South Broadway St., Ste. 819
Los Angeles, CA 90015
(213) 365-3000

Contra Costa Health Plan   24,000
595 Center Avenue
Martinez, CA 94553
(510) 313-6000

STATE	HMO	ESTIMATED MEMBERSHIP
California (cont.)	**National Health Plans** 1005 West Orangeburg Ave., Ste. B Modesto, CA 95350 (209) 527-3350	49,000
	Coast Health Plan 777 Cuesta Drive, Ste. 210 Mountain View, CA 94040 (415) 988-7500	2,000
	HMO California 4675 MacArthur, #14000 Newport Beach, CA 92660 (800) 795-8753	6,000
	CIGNA HealthCare of Northern CA, Inc. 1999 Harrison St., Ste. 1000 Oakland, CA 94612-3508 (510) 273-8400	11,000
	Kaiser Foundation Health Plan, Inc./Northern CA 1950 Franklin Street Oakland, CA 94612 (510) 987-1000	2,000,000
	QualMed Plans for Health 155 Grand Ave. Oakland, CA 94612 (510) 465-9600	176,000
	Kaiser Foundation Health Plan, Inc. Southern CA Walnut Center 393 East Walnut Pasadena, CA 91188 (818) 405-5000	2,000,000
	Inter Valley Health Plan 300 South Park Ave., Ste. 300 Pomona, CA 91766 (909) 623-6333	46,000

Foundation Health, A Calif. Health Plan   500,000
3400 Data Drive
Rancho Cordova, CA 95670
(916) 631-5000

Aetna Health Plans of Southern CA, Inc.   200,000
303 East Vanderbilt Way
San Bernardino, CA 92408-3581
(800) 347-4325

Aetna Health Plans of San Diego, Inc.   49,000
7676 Hazard Center Drive, 10th Floor
San Diego, CA 92108
(619) 497-1762

CIGNA HealthCare of CA, Inc.-San Diego   36,000
9809 Scranton Rd., Ste. 400
San Diego, CA 92121
(619) 457-5402

Blue Shield of California HMO   164,000
P.O. Box 7168
San Francisco, CA 94120-7168
(415) 445-5000

Chinese Community Health Plan   6,000
170 Columbus Ave., Ste. 210
San Francisco, CA 94133
(415) 397-3190

LifeGuard, Inc.   107,000
P.O. Box 5506
San Jose, CA 95150-5506
(408) 943-9400

Valley Health Plan   4,000
750 South Bascom Ave.
San Jose, CA 95128
(408) 299-8100

Freedom Plan, Inc.   6,000
201 North Salsipuedes, Ste. 206
Santa Barbara, CA 93103
(805) 564-0072

STATE	HMO	ESTIMATED MEMBERSHIP
California (cont.)	**Health Plan of the Redwoods** 3033 Cleveland Ave. Santa Rosa, CA 95403 (707) 544-2273	83,000
	Universal Care 1600 East Hill St. Signal Hill, CA 90806 (310) 424-6200	67,000
	Omni Health Plan 1776 West March Lane, Ste. 240 Stockton, CA 95207 (209) 466-6664	79,000
	Health Net P.O. Box 9103 Van Nuys, CA 91409-9103 (818) 719-6800	900,000
	Aetna Health Plans of Northern California 201 North Civic Drive, Ste. 300 Walnut Creek, CA 94596 (415) 952-2005	130,000
	California Care P.O. Box 4089 Woodland Hills, CA 91365-4089 (818) 703-4204	600,000
	PruCare of California 5800 Canoga Ave. Woodland Hills, CA 91367 (818) 992-2093	200,000
Colorado	**Comprecare, Inc.** P.O. Box 441170 Aurora, CO 80044 (303) 695-6685	200,000

TakeCare of Colorado 95,000
12100 East Iliff Ave.
Aurora, CO 80014
(303) 695-6685

Health Network of Colorado, Inc. 12,000
555 East Pikes Peak Ave., Ste. 108
Colorado Springs, CO 80903
(719) 475-5025

CIGNA HealthCare of Colorado, Inc. 5,000
3900 East Mexico Ave., Ste. 1100
Denver, CO 80210-3946
(303) 782-1500

HMO Colorado 49,000
700 Broadway
Denver, CO 80203
(303) 831-4114

Humana Health Plan, Inc. 15,000
3900 East Mexico Ave., Ste. 800
Denver, CO 80210-3944
(303) 691-6990

Kaiser Foundation Health Plan of CO 290,000
10350 East Dakota Ave.
Denver, CO 80231-1314
(303) 344-7200

MetLife HealthCare Network of CO, Inc. 7,000
1125 17th St., Ste. 2100
Denver, CO 80202
(303) 299-9020

PruCare of Colorado 17,000
4643 South Ulster St., Ste. 1000
Denver, CO 80237
(303) 796-6100

FHP of Colorado, Inc. 4,000
6312 S. Fiddlers Green Circle, Ste. 230E
Englewood, CO 80111-4945
(303) 689-9646

STATE	HMO	ESTIMATED MEMBERSHIP
Colorado (cont.)	**Rocky Mountain HMO** 2775 Crossroads Blvd. P.O. Box 60129 Grand Junction, CO 81506 (303) 244-7760	55,000
	San Luis Valley HMO 95 West 1st Ave. Monte Vista, CO 81144 (719) 852-4055	4,000
	QualMed Plans for Health, Inc. 225 North Main Street Pueblo, CO 81003 (719) 542-0500	34,000
	Southern Colorado Health Plan P.O. Box 958 41 Montebello, Ste. H Pueblo, CO 81002 (719) 545-6272	8,000
Connecticut	**CIGNA HealthCare of CT, Inc.** and **CIGNA HealthCare of Mass., Inc.-Spr.** 5700 Bigelow Commons Enfield, CT 06082 (203) 745-2288	10,000
	ConnectiCare 30 Batterson Park Rd. Farmington, CT 06032-2574 (203) 674-5700	93,000
	Kaiser Permanente Medical Care Program 76 Batterson Park Rd. Farmington, CT 06034-4011 (203) 678-6000	115,000

U.S. HealthCare (CT)   30,000
Middlesex Corporate Center
213 Court St., 7th Floor
Middletown, CT 06457
(215) 926-8882

Community Health Care Plan, Inc.   39,000
221 Whitney Ave.
New Haven, CT 06511
(203) 773-8358

Yale Health Plan   25,000
P.O. Box 208237
New Haven, CT 06520-8237
(203) 432-0076

Constitution HealthCare, Inc.   94,000
370 Bassett Road
North Haven, CT 06473-0500
(203) 234-2011

M.D. Health Plan   111,000
6 Devine Street
North Haven, CT 06473
(800) 345-9272

Suburban Health Plan, Inc.   3,000
680 Bridgeport Ave.
Shelton, CT 06484-4748
(203) 926-8882

Physicians Health Services of CT, Inc.   109,000
120 Hawley Lane
Trumbull, CT 06611
(203) 381-6400

**Aetna Health Plans of Southern New
England**   61,000
Windsor Customer Center
80 Lamberton Rd.
Windsor, CT 06095
(800) 223-6857

STATE	HMO	ESTIMATED MEMBERSHIP
Delaware	**Principal Health Care of Delaware, Inc.** One Corporate Commons 100 West Commons Blvd., Ste. 300 New Castle, DE 19720 (302) 322-4700	74,000
	The HMO of Delaware 200 Hygeia Drive P.O. Box 6008 Newark, DE 19714 (302) 421-2466	15,000
	Aetna Health Plans (Delaware) 501 Carr Rd., Third Floor Wilmington, DE 19803 (302) 761-4910	Figure unavailable
	Aetna Health Plans of New Jersey, Inc. Rockwood Office Park 501 Carr Rd., Third Floor Wilmington, DE 19809 (302) 761-4900	Figure unavailable
	CIGNA HealthCare of Delaware, Inc. **CIGNA HealthCare of PA-Philadelphia,** and **CIGNA HealthCare of So. New Jersey** 1 Beaver Valley Rd., Ste. CHP Wilmington, DE 19803 (302) 477-3700	13,000
District of Columbia	**George Washington Univ. Health Plan** 1901 Pennsylvania Ave. N.W., Ste. 600 Washington, DC 20006 (202) 416-0400	71,000
	Group Health Association 4301 Connecticut Ave. NW Washington, DC 20008 (202) 364-2000	128,000

Florida	**Advantage Health Plans** One Alhambra Plaza, Ste. 1000 Coral Gables, FL 33134 (305) 443-3739	22,000
	CAC-Ramsay Health Plans, Inc. 75 Valencia Ave. Coral Gables, FL 33134 (305) 447-3200	127,000
	Florida Health Care Plan, Inc. 350 North Clyde Morris Blvd. Daytona Beach, FL 32014 (904) 238-3200	51,000
	PruCare of South Florida 5900 North Andrews Ave., Ste. 1000 Fort Lauderdale, FL 33309 (305) 492-8244	57,000
	Ave-Med Health Plan P.O. Box 823 Gainesville, FL 32602-0823 (904) 372-8400	158,000
	Association I.N.E.D., H.M.O., Inc. 770 West 29th St. Hialeah, FL 33012 (305) 885-8511	7,000
	Pasteur Health Plan HMO, Inc. 3233 Palm Ave. Hialeah, FL 33012 (305) 882-7701	52,000
	HIP Health Plan of Florida, Inc. 300 South Park Rd. Hollywood, FL 33021 (800) 826-1023	35,000
	Anthem Health Plan of Florida, Inc. P.O. Box 48000 Jacksonville, FL 33247-8000 (904) 363-7600	26,000

STATE	HMO	ESTIMATED MEMBERSHIP
Florida (cont.)	**Health Options, Inc.** 8900 Freedom Commerce Pkwy. Bld. #2, 3rd Fl. Jacksonville, FL 32256 (904) 363-5788	289,000
	Humana Medical Plan, Inc. (Jacksonville) 4190 Belfort Rd., Ste. 250 Jacksonville, FL 32216 (904) 281-8800	5,000
	Principal Health Care of FL, Inc.-Jksnville 1200 Gulf Life Dr., Ste. 500 Jacksonville, FL 32207 (904) 390-0935	34,000
	PruCare of Jacksonville 1200 Gulf Life Dr., Ste. 701 Jacksonville, FL 32207 (904) 346-5800	57,000
	CIGNA HealthCare of FL, Inc.-Orlando 1101 North Lake Destiny Rd., Ste. 300 Maitland, FL 32751 (407) 660-1344	17,000
	PruCare of Orlando 2301 Lucien Way, Ste. 230 Maitland, FL 32751 (407) 875-6600	80,000
	Care Florida, Inc. 7950 NW 53rd St. Miami, FL 33166 (305) 591-3311	53,000
	Century Medical Health Plan, Inc. 6101 Blue Lagoon Dr., Ste. 300 Miami, FL 33126 (305) 267-6633	288,000

Family Health Plan, Inc.   63,000
6101 Blue Lagoon, Ste. 300
Miami, FL 33126
(305) 267-6633

JMH Health Plan   9,000
1500 NW 12th Ave., JMT Ste. 1001 West
Miami, FL 33169
(305) 585-7120

Max A Med Health Plans, Inc.   5,000
1515 NW 167th St., Ste. 104
Miami, FL 33169
(305) 626-0135

Miami Dad Health Plan   20,000
2260 SW 8th Street
Miami, FL 33135
(305) 541-1400

PCA Health Plans of Florida, Inc.   34,000
6101 Blue Lagoon Dr., Ste. 300
Miami, FL 33126
(305) 267-6633

Preferred Medical Plan, Inc.   12,000
2500 SW 75th Ave.
Miami, FL 33155
(305) 667-4853

Principal Health Care of FL, Inc.-So. FL   10,000
9130 South Dadeland Blvd. #1116
Miami, FL 33156
(305) 670-9244

CIGNA HealthCare of So. FL, Inc.   8,000
15600 NW 67th Ave., Ste. 301
Miami Lakes, FL 33014
(305) 826-6200

Humana Medical Plan, Inc. (So. FL)   261,000
3400 Lakeside Dr.
Miramar, FL 33027
(305) 621-4222

STATE	HMO	ESTIMATED MEMBERSHIP
Florida (cont.)	**Humana Medical Plan, Inc. (Daytona)** 780 West Granada Blvd., Ste. 104 Ormond Beach, FL 32174 (904) 676-1800	34,000
	Principal Health Care of FL, Inc.-Pensacola One University Plaza 7282 Plantation Rd., Ste. 300 Pensacola, FL 32504 (904) 484-4000	21,000
	Capital Health Plan 2140 Centerville Place, P.O. Box 13267 Tallahassee, FL 32308 (904) 386-3161	50,000
	Healthplan Southeast 3520 Thomasville Rd., Ste. 200 Tallahassee, FL 32308 (904) 668-3000	45,000
	Aetna Health Plans of Florida, Inc. 4890 West Kennedy Blvd., Ste. 545 Tampa, FL 33609 (813) 287-7820	28,000
	CIGNA HealthCare of FL, Inc.-Tampa 5404 Cypress Center Dr., Ste. 365 Tampa, FL 33609 (813) 281-1000	45,000
	Complete Health of Florida, Inc. 5201 West Kennedy Blvd., Ste. 712 Tampa, FL 33609 (813) 286-8429	1,000
	Humana Medical Plan, Inc. (Tampa) 5401 West Kennedy Blvd., Ste. 800 Tampa, FL 33609 (813) 286-8829	127,000

PruCare of Tampa Bay   39,000
6200 Courtney Campbell Causway, Ste. 200
Tampa, FL 33607
(813) 288-0080

Well Care HMO, Inc.   Figure
11016 North Dalemabry Hwy.   unavailable
Tampa, FL 33618
(813) 963-6128

Florida 1st Health Plan   4,000
P.O. Box 9126
Winter Haven, FL 33883
(813) 293-0785

Georgia   **Aetna Health Plans of Georgia, Inc.**   39,000
3500 Piedmont Rd. NE, Ste. 300
Atlanta, GA 30305-1565
(404) 814-4330

CIGNA HealthCare of Georgia, Inc.   23,000
1349 Peachtree Street, West
Midtown Plaza II, Ste. 1300
Atlanta, GA 30309
(404) 881-9779

Complete Health of Georgia, Inc.   9,000
1455 Lincoln Pkwy, Ste. 730
Atlanta, GA 30346
(404) 698-8600

HMO Georgia, Inc.   53,000
3350 Peachtree Rd., NE
Atlanta, GA 30326
(404) 842-8400

Kaiser Foundation Health Plan of GA, Inc.   165,000
9 Piedmont Cntr., 3495 Piedmont Rd. NE
Atlanta, GA 30305-7136
(404) 364-7000

PruCare of Atlanta   77,000
2839 Paces Ferry Rd., Ste. 1000
Atlanta, GA 30339
(404) 955-8010

STATE	HMO	ESTIMATED MEMBERSHIP
Georgia **(cont.)**	**United HealthCare of Georgia, Inc.** 2970 Clairmont Rd., Ste. 300 Atlanta, GA 30329-1634 (404) 982-8800	80,000
	Master Health Plan 3604 Wheeler Rd., Unit 13 Augusta, GA 30909 (706) 863-5955	10,000
	MetLife HealthCare Network of GA, Inc. 1130 NorthHare Pkwy, P.O. Box 6187 Marietta, GA 30067-0187 (404) 980-0740	11,000
Guam	**Guam Memorial Health Plan** 142 West Seaton Blvd. Agana, Guam 96910 (671) 472-4647	42,000
	FHP, Inc. and **Health Maintenance Life Insurance Co.** P.O. Box 6578 Tamuning, Guam 96931 (671) 646-7826	36,000
Hawaii	**Community Health Program, Health Plan Hawaii,** and **HMO Hawaii** P.O. Box 860 Honolulu, Hawaii 96808 (808) 944-2110	41,000
	Island Care 500 Ala Moana Blvd. Six Waterfront Plaza, Ste. 210 Honolulu, Hawaii 96813 (808) 532-6900	14,000

Kaiser Foundation Health Plan, Inc.   191,000
711 Kapiolani Blvd.
Honolulu, Hawaii 96813
(808) 834-5333

Pacific Health Care   10,000
1946 Young Street
Honolulu, Hawaii 96826
(808) 973-3000

The Straub Plan   3,000
888 South King Street
Honolulu, Hawaii 96813
(808) 522-4540

Idaho

Idaho Preferred Healthcare   11,000
P.O. Box 7408
Boise, ID 83707
(208) 345-4550

Illinois

Dreyer Health Plans   36,000
2111 Plum St.
Aurora, IL 60506-3252
(708) 859-1100

Personal Care Insurance of Illinois   35,000
510 Devonshire Dr., Ste. G
Champaign, IL 61820
(217) 366-1226

Aetna Health Plan of Illinois   14,000
100 North Riverside Plaza
Chicago, IL 60606-1518
(312) 441-3253

Chicago HMO Ltd.   310,000
540 North LaSalle St.
Chicago, IL 60610
(312) 751-4460

COMPASS Health Care Plans   12,000
310 South Michigan Ave., Ste. 1300
Chicago, IL 60604
(312) 294-0200

STATE	HMO	ESTIMATED MEMBERSHIP
Illinois **(cont.)**	**HMO Illinois** 233 North Michigan Chicago, IL 60601 (708) 620-0176	387,000
	Humana Health Plans, Inc. 2545 Martin Luther King Jr. Drive Chicago, IL 60616 (312) 808-3810	292,000
	Illinois Masonic Community Health Plan 836 West Wellington Chicago, IL 60657 (312) 296-7014	5,000
	Maxicare Illinois 111 East Wacker Dr., Ste. 1500 Chicago, IL 60601 (312) 616-4700	30,000
	RUSH Prudential Health Plans 33 East Congress Pkwy., Ste. 600 Chicago, IL 60605 (312) 347-3430	185,000
	Union Health Service 1634 West Polk Street Chicago, IL 60612 (312) 829-4224	28,000
	University of Illinois HMO-Plan Trust P.O. Box 6998, M and C 692 Chicago, IL 60680 (312) 996-3553	6,000
	CIGNA HealthCare of Illinois, Inc. 1700 Higgins Rd., Ste. 600 Des Plaines, IL 60018 (708) 699-5600	17,000

American HMO   20,000
P.O. Box 160, 19740 Governors Hwy.
Flossmoor, IL 60422
(708) 503-5000

SHARE Health Plan of Illinois, Inc.   98,000
One Pierce Place, Suite 600
Itasca, IL 60143-1299
(708) 250-3200

**Heritage and John Deere Family
Health Plan**   286,000
1515 5th Ave., Ste. 200
Moline, IL 61265-1368
(309) 765-1200

Travelers Health Network of Illinois, Inc.   1,000
184 Shuman Blvd., Ste. 400
Naperville, IL 60563
(708) 983-2400

New York Life/Sanus Health Plan of IL, Inc.   800
1111 West 22nd Street
Oak Brook, IL 60521
(708) 573-4999

Principal Health Care of Illinois, Inc.   12,000
One Lincoln Centre, Ste. 1040
Oakbrook Terrace, IL 60181
(708) 916-6622/(800) 888-2310

TakeCare Health Plan of Illinois, Inc.   41,000
One Lincoln Centre, Ste. 700
Oakbrook Terrace, IL 60181-4260
(708) 916-8400

CliniCare, Inc.   28,000
7124 Windsor Lake Pkwy.
Rockford, IL 61111
(815) 654-3600

MetLife HealthCare Network of IL, Inc.   17,000
1900 East Golf Rd., Ste. 501
Schaumburg, IL 60173
(708) 619-2222

STATE	HMO	ESTIMATED MEMBERSHIP
Illinois (cont.)	Health Alliance Medical Plans, Inc. 102 East Main P.O. Box 6003 Urbana, IL 61801 (217) 337-8010	66,000
Indiana	Southeastern Indiana Health Organization 432 Washington St. Columbus, IN 47202 (812) 378-7000	Figure unavailable
	Physicians Health Network, Inc. 1 Riverfront Place, Ste. 400 P.O. Box 3357 Evansville, IN 47732 (812) 465-6000	25,000
	Welborn HMO, A Division of Welborn Clinic 19 NW Fourth St., Ste. 600 Evansville, IN 47708 (812) 425-3939	35,000
	Physicians Health Plan of No. Indiana, Inc. 7222 Engle Rd. Fort Wayne, IN 46804 (219) 432-6690	36,000
	Principal Health Care of Indiana, Inc. 409 East Cook Rd., Ste. 100 Fort Wayne, IN 46825 (219) 487-2000	26,000
	Anthem Health Plan of Indiana, Inc. 333 North Alabama St., Ste. 370 Indianapolis, IN 46204 (317) 262-4577	15,000

Health Maintenance of Indiana   32,000
Lockerbie Marketplace
333 North Alabama, Ste. 300
Indianapolis, IN 46204
(317) 262-4577

Healthsource Indiana   40,000
225 South East Street, Ste. 100
Indianapolis, IN 46202
(317) 685-8300

M Plan   72,000
8802 North Meridian St., Ste. 100
Indianapolis, IN 46260
(317) 571-5300

Maxicare Indiana, Inc.   71,000
Division of Maxicare Health Plans (Midwest)
9480 Priority Way West Dr.
Indianapolis, IN 46240
(317) 844-5775

PruCare of Indiana   1,000
8425 Woodfield Crossing Blvd., Ste. 301
Indianapolis, IN 46280
(317) 469-8060

Arnett HMO   22,000
3768 Rome Dr.
P.O. Box 6108
Lafayette, IN 47903-6108
(317) 448-8200

PARTNERS National Health Plans   39,000
of Indiana, Inc.
1 Michiana Square
100 East Wayne St., Ste. 502
South Bend, IN 46601
(219) 233-4899

Iowa   **Medical Associated Health Plan, Inc.**   30,000
700 Locust St., Ste. 230
Dubuque, Iowa 52001-6800
(319) 556-8070

STATE	HMO	ESTIMATED MEMBERSHIP
Iowa (cont.)	**Care Choices HMO** 600 Fourth St., Terra Centre Sioux City, Iowa 51101 (712) 252-2344	16,000
	Principal Health Care of Iowa, Inc. 4600 Westown Pkwy. Regency 6, Ste. 301 West Des Moines, Iowa 50266 (515) 225-1234	81,000
Kansas	**CIGNA HealthCare of Kansas/Missouri, Inc.** 7400 West 110th St., Ste. 600 Overland Park, KS 66210 (913) 339-4700	5,000
	Kaiser Foundation Health Plan of Kansas City, Inc. 10561 Barkley, Ste. 200 Overland Park, KS 66212 (913) 967-4600	45,000
	MetLife HealthCare Network of Kansas City, Inc. 9200 Indian Creek Pkwy., Ste. 185, Bldg. 9 Overland Park, KS 66210 (913) 451-5656	7,000
	HMO Kansas, Inc. P.O. Box 110 Topeka, KS 66601-0110 (913) 233-2751	26,000
	CIGNA HealthCare of Kansas/Missouri 101 South Webb Rd., Ste. 200 Wichita, KS 67207 (316) 687-5606	22,000

HealthCare America Plans, Inc.   14,000
331 East Douglas
Wichita, KS 67202
(316) 262-7400

Preferred Plus of Kansas   15,000
345 Riverview
Ste. 103, P.O. Box 49288
Wichita, KS 67201-9288
(316) 268-0390

Kentucky   **Blugrass Family Health, Inc.**   Figure
651 Perimeter Park, Ste. 2B   unavailable
Lexington, KY 40517
(606) 269-4475

HealthWise of Kentucky, Ltd.   56,000
489 East Main Street
Lexington, KY 40507
(606) 259-1771

Humana Health Plans, Inc.   34,000
101 Prosperous Place, Ste. 300
Lexington, KY 40509
(606) 263-1400

Lexington Health Advantage   9,000
701 Bob O Link Drive, Ste. 120
Lexington, KY 40504
(606) 276-0306

Alternative Health Delivery Systems, Inc.   112,000
10100 Linn Station Rd.
Louisville, KY 40223
(800) 955-3035

HMO Kentucky   33,000
P.O. Box 23795
Louisville, KY 40223
(502) 423-2282

STATE	HMO	ESTIMATED MEMBERSHIP
Kentucky (cont.)	**Humana Health Care Plan, Inc.** The Waterside Building 101 E. Main Street, 11th Floor Louisville, KY 40202 (502) 580-5005	160,000
Louisiana	**CIGNA HealthCare of Louisiana, Inc.** Sherwood Oaks Office Park 4354 South Sherwood Forest Blvd., Ste. D240 Baton Rouge, LA 70816 (504) 295-2800	13,000
	Community Health Network of LA, Inc. 2431 South Acadian Thruway, Ste. 350 Baton Rouge, LA 70808 (504) 923-0550	44,000
	Gulf South Health Plans, Inc. 5615 Corporate Blvd., Ste. 3 Baton Rouge, LA 70808 (504) 927-7212	92,000
	CIGNA HealthCare of Louisiana, Inc. 3838 No. Causeway Blvd, Ste. 2800B Metairie, LA 70002 (504) 832-3004	Figure unavailable
	Maxicare Louisiana, Inc. 3850 North Causeway Blvd. 2 Lakeway Center, Ste. 990 Metairie, LA 70002 (504) 836-2022	34,000
	Ochsner Health Plan 1 Galleria Blvd., Ste. 1224 Metairie, LA 70001 (504) 836-6600	74,000

Principal Health Care of LA, Inc.   23,000
3421 North Causeway Blvd., Ste. 600
Metairie, LA 70002
(504) 834-0840

Travelers Health Network of LA, Inc.   6,000
3900 North Causeway Blvd., Ste. 600
Metairie, LA 70002
(504) 832-7655

Aetna Health Plans   Figure
3900 North Causeway Blvd., Ste. 410   unavailable
New Orleans, LA 70002-7283
(504) 295-7833

Aetna Health Plans of LA, Inc.   29,000
3900 North Causeway Blvd., Ste. 410
New Orleans, LA 70002-7283
(504) 830-5600

CIGNA HealthCare of Northern Louisiana   9,000
6425 Youree Drive, Ste. 200
Shreveport, LA 71105-4625
(318) 798-4740

Maine   **Healthsource Maine, Inc.**   42,000
174 South Freeport Rd., P.O. Box 447
Freeport, ME 04032-0447
(207) 865-6161

HMO Maine   21,000
2 Gannett Dr.
South Portland, ME 04106-6911
(207) 822-7000

Maryland   **Aetna Health Plans of the Mid-Atlantic, Inc.** 71,000
1829 Reisterstown Rd., Ste. 270
Baltimore, MD 21208
(703) 903-7030

Chesapeake Health Plan, Inc.   39,000
814 Light Street
Baltimore, MD 21230
(800) 487-7391/(410) 539-8622

STATE	HMO	ESTIMATED MEMBERSHIP
Maryland (cont.)	**Free State Health Plan, HealthCare Corp. of the Mid-Atlantic,** and **HealthCare Corp. of the Potomac** 100 South Charles St., Tower II, 6th Floor Baltimore, MD 21201-2707 (410) 528-7000	111,000; 68,000; 9,000
	PHCP of the Mid-Atlantic 2800 North Charles St. Baltimore, MD 21218 (410) 554-7200	156,000
	Preferred Health Network of Maryland, Inc. 5700 Executive Dr. Baltimore, MD 21228 (410) 747-9060	33,000
	Total HealthCare 1501 Division St. Baltimore, MD 21217 (410) 383-8300	24,000
	CIGNA HealthCare of the Mid-Atlantic, Inc. 9700 Patuxent Woods Dr. Columbia, MD 21046 (410) 720-5800	7,000
	Columbia Medical Plan, Inc. Two Knoll North Drive Columbia, MD 21045 (410) 997-8500	75,000
	Delmarva Health Plan, Inc. 106 Marlboro Rd. Easton, MD 21601 (410) 822-7223	22,000
	HealthPlus 7601 Ora Glen Dr. Greenbelt, MD 20770 (301) 441-1600	248,000

Kaiser Foundation Health Plan   321,000
of the Mid-Atlantic
2101 East Jefferson
Rockville, MD 20852
(301) 816-2424

Mid-Atlantic Medical Services, Inc.   440,000
4 Taft Ct.
Rockville, MD 20850
(800) 638-8898

Principal Health Care
of the Mid-Atlantic, Inc.   4,000
1801 Rockville Pike, Ste. 110
Rockville, MD 20852
(301) 881-4903

Massachusetts **HMO BLUE**   461,000
100 Summer St.
Boston, MA 02110
(617) 956-2000

MetLife HealthCare Network of Mass.   2,000
99 High St., 21st Floor
Boston, MA 02110-2310
(617) 574-3911

Neighborhood Health Plan   41,000
253 Summer St.
Boston, MA 02210
(617) 772-5500

Harvard Community Health Plan   460,000
10 Brookline Place West
Brookline, MA 02146
(617) 431-1070

U.S. Healthcare (Massachusetts) and
U.S. Healthcare of New Hampshire   52,000
3 Burlington Woods Dr.
Burlington, MA 01803
(215) 628-4800

STATE	HMO	ESTIMATED MEMBERSHIP
Massachusetts (cont.)	**Bay State Health Care** 101 Main St. Cambridge, MA 02142 (617) 868-7000	165,000
	Harvard University Group Health Program 75 Mt. Auburn St. Cambridge, MA 02138 (617) 495-2008	14,000
	MIT Health Plans 77 Massachusetts Ave., Bldg. E-23, Room 308 Cambridge, MA 02139 (617) 253-1322	10,000
	CIGNA HealthCare of MA, Inc. 20 Spreen St., Third Floor Framingham, MA 01701 (508) 935-2100	1,000
	Community Health Plan/MA Region 163 Conz Street Northampton, MA 01060 (413) 584-0600	34,000
	Pilgrim Health Care, Inc. 10 Accord Executive Dr., P.O. Box 9102 Norwell, MA 02061 (617) 871-3950	292,000
	Health New England One Monarch Place Springfield, MA 01144-1006 (413) 787-4000	48,000
	Tufts Associated Health Plans, Inc. 333 Wyman St., P.O. Box 9112 Waltham, MA 02254-9112 (617) 466-9400	238,000

	Central Massachusetts Health Care	79,000
	300 Mechanics Tower, 100 Front St.	
	Worcester, MA 01608-1449	
	(508) 798-8667	

Fallon Community Health Plan   168,000
Chestnut Place, 10 Chestnut St.
Worcester, MA 01608
(508) 799-2100

Michigan   **M-Care**   58,000
3601 Plymouth Rd.
Ann Arbor, MI 48105
(313) 747-8700

Comprehensive Health Services, Inc.   123,000
6500 John C. Lodge Freeway
Detroit, MI 48202
(313) 875-4200

Health Alliance Plan of Michigan   393,000
2850 West Grand Blvd.
Detroit, MI 48202
(313) 872-8100

Life-Choice Quality Health Plan   28,000
2401 20th
Detroit, MI 48216
(313) 496-0610

OmniCare Health Plan   95,000
1155 Brewery Park Blvd., Second Floor
Detroit, MI 48207
(313) 259-4000

Total Health Care, Inc.   24,000
2500 Fisher Bldg.
Detroit, MI 48202
(313) 871-2000

Care Choices Health Plans   137,000
34605 Twelve Mile Rd.
Farmington Hills, MI 48331-3221
(313) 489-6202

STATE	HMO	ESTIMATED MEMBERSHIP
Michigan (cont.)	**HealthPlus of Michigan** 2050 South Linden Rd., P.O. Box 1700 Flint, MI 48501-1700 (313) 230-2000	80,000
	Blue Care Network, Great Lakes 611 Cascade West Pkwy. SE Grand Rapids, MI 49546-2143 (616) 957-5057	146,000
	Grand Valley Health Plan, Inc. 829 Forest Hill Ave., S.E. Grand Rapids, MI 49546 (616) 949-2410	23,000
	Priority Health 2025 East Beltline, SE, Ste. 500 Grand Rapids, MI 49546 (616) 942-0954	91,000
	Blue Care Network-Health Central 1403 South Creyts Rd. Lansing, MI 48917 (517) 322-4000	68,000
	Physicians Health Plan, Inc.- Michigan P.O. Box 30377 Lansing, MI 48909 (517) 349-2101	158,000
	Blue Care Network of East Michigan 4200 Fashion Square Blvd. Saginaw, MI 48603 (517) 791-3200	76,000
	Blue Care Network of Southeast Michigan 25925 Telegraph Rd, P.O. Box 5043 Southfield, MI 48086-5043 (313) 354-7450	151,000

NorthMed/HMO   13,000
109 East Front St., Ste. 204
Traverse City, MI 49684
(616) 935-0500

SelectCare HMO   87,000
2401 West Big Beaver, Ste. 700
Troy, MI 48084
(810) 637-5300

Minnesota   **HealthPartners**   500,000
8100 34th Ave. South, P.O. Box 1309
Minneapolis, MN 55440-1309
(612) 883-6000

MEDICA   473,000
5601 Smetana Dr., P.O. Box 1587
Minneapolis, MN 55440
(612) 936-1200

Metropolitan Health Plan   33,000
822 South 3rd St., Ste. 140
Minneapolis, MN 55415
(612) 347-8557

NWNL Health Network, Inc.   35,000
20 South Washington Ave.
Minneapolis, MN 55440-0358
(612) 672-8400

Mayo Health Plan   4,000
21 First St. SW, Ste. 401
Rochester, MN 55902
(507) 284-8274

Central Minnesota Group Health Plan   20,000
1245 North 15th St.
St. Cloud, MN 56303
(612) 253-5220

Blue Plus   67,000
3535 Blue Cross Rd., P.O. Box 64179
St. Paul, MN 55164
(612) 456-8000

STATE	HMO	ESTIMATED MEMBERSHIP
Minnesota (cont.)	**UCare Minnesota** 2550 University Ave. West, Ste. 330N St. Paul, MN 55114 (612) 627-4301	24,000
	First Plan HMO 1010 Fourth St. Two Harbors, MN 55616 (218) 834-7207	10,000
Mississippi	**Complete Health of Mississippi, Inc.** 607 Corrinne, Ste. B4 Hattiesburg, MS 39401 (601) 543-0500	3,000
Missouri	**MetLife HealthCare Network, Inc.** 14500 South Outer 40 Rd., Ste. 500 Chesterfield, MO 63017 (314) 542-1400	23,000
	CIGNA HealthCare of St. Louis, Inc. 8182 Maryland Ave., Ste. 900 Clayton, MO 63105 (314) 726-7700	8,000
	PruCare of St. Louis 12312 Olive Blvd., Ste. 500 Creve Coeur, MO 63141 (314) 542-4500	19,000
	Blue Advantage, Inc. P.O. Box 41930 Kansas City, MO 64141 (816) 395-2131	18,000
	Blue Care P.O. Box 419169 Kansas City, MO 64141-6169 (816) 395-2222	21,000

BMA Selectcare, Inc.   4,000
One Penn Valley Park
P.O. Box 419458
Kansas City, MO 64141
(800) 262-5433

Humana Prime Health Plan   96,000
10450 Holmes, Ste. 330
Kansas City, MO 64131
(816) 941-8900

Principal Health Care of Kansas City, Inc.   46,000
1001 East 101st Terrace, Ste. 230
Kansas City, MO 64131
(816) 941-3030

PruCare of Kansas City   15,000
4600 Madison Ave., Ste. 300
Kansas City, MO 64112
(816) 756-5588

Total Health Care   36,000
P.O. Box 413163
Kansas City, MO 64141
(816) 395-3777

Aetna Health Plans of St. Louis   Figure
City Place One   unavailable
One Cityplace Dr., Ste. 670
St. Louis, MO 63141
(504) 830-5600

Blue Choice   67,000
1831 Chestnut St.
St. Louis, MO 63103-2275
(314) 923-6225

GenCare Health Systems   155,000
969 Executive Pkwy. Dr., Ste. 100
St. Louis, MO 63141-6301
(314) 434-6114

STATE	HMO	ESTIMATED MEMBERSHIP
Missouri (cont.)	**Group Health Plan, Inc.** 940 Westport Plaza, Ste. 300 St. Louis, MO 63146 (314) 453-1700	129,000
	Physicians Health Plan of Greater St. Louis, Inc. 77 Westport Plaza, Ste. 500 St. Louis, MO 63146 (314) 275-7000	97,000
	Principal Health Care of Kansas City, Inc. 12312 Olive, Ste. 150 St. Louis, MO 63141 (314) 434-6990	1,000
	St. Louis Labor Institute 300 South Grand Blvd. St. Louis, MO 63103 (314) 658-5613	12,000
	The Medical Center Health Plan City Place One One City Place Dr., Ste. 670 St. Louis, MO 63141 (504) 830-5600	41,000
Montana	**HMO Montana** P.O. Box 8004 Helena, MT 59604 (406) 444-8250	13,000
Nebraska	**Mutual of Omaha Health Plans of Lincoln** 220 South 17th St. Lincoln, NE 68508 (402) 475-7000	18,000

Exclusive Healthcare, Inc. and **Mutual**   37,000;
of Omaha Companies, HMO Health Plan   17,000
Mutual of Omaha Plaza
Omaha, NE 68172
(402) 978-2700

HMO Nebraska   20,000
2421 South 73rd St.
Omaha, NE 68124-2359
(402) 392-2800

Principal Health Care of Nebraska, Inc.   24,000
10810 Farnum Dr., Ste. 325
Omaha, NE 68154
(402) 333-1720

SHARE Health Plan of Nebraska, Inc.   34,000
302 South 36th St.
Omaha, NE 68131
(402) 345-9900

Nevada   **FHP, Inc.**   26,000
2300 West Sahara Ave., Box 14, Ste. 700
Las Vegas, NV 89102-4354
(702) 871-4441

Health Plan of Nevada, Inc.   107,000
P.O. Box 15645
Las Vegas, NV 89114-5645
(702) 242-7303

Humana Health Plan, Inc.   15,000
3107 South Maryland Pkwy.
Las Vegas, NV 89109
(702) 737-7211

Hospital Health Plan/Coordinated Care   27,000
Option
400 South Wells Ave.
Reno, NV 89502
(702) 329-0101

STATE	HMO	ESTIMATED MEMBERSHIP
New Hampshire	**Healthsource New Hampshire, Inc.** 54 Regional Dr., P.O. Box 2041 Concord, NH 03302-2041 (603) 225-5077	73,000
	Matthew Thornton Health Plan 410 Amherst St. Nashua, NH 03063 (800) 774-7122	77,000
New Jersey	**CIGNA HealthCare of Northern NJ, Inc.** 3 Stewart Court Denville, NJ 07834 (201) 361-3444	74,000
	HMO of New Jersey/U.S. Healthcare 55 Lane Rd. Fairfield, NJ 07004 (215) 628-4800	425,000
	MetLife HealthCare Network of No. NJ 485 Route 1, South, Ste. 120, Bldg. B Iselin, NJ 08830 (908) 602-6500	26,000
	HMO Blue 3 Penn Plaza East Newark, NJ 07101-0820 (201) 466-8100	78,000
	Aetna Health Plans of New Jersey, Inc. 20 Waterview Blvd. Parsippany, NJ 07054 (201) 334-2200	134,000
	HIP/Rutgers Health Plan One Worlds Fair Dr. Somerset, NJ 08873 (908) 560-9898	175,000

Garden State Health Plan   16,000
CN 712
Trenton, NJ 08625-0712
(609) 588-3526

HMOBlue Health Center   18,000
416 Bellvue Ave.
Trenton, NJ 08618
(609) 396-4600

New Mexico   **FHP of New Mexico, Inc.**   36,000
4300 San Mateo Blvd., NE
Albuquerque, NM 87110
(505) 889-8500

Health Plus of New Mexico   Figure
P.O. Box 27489   unavailable
Albuquerque, NM 87125
(505) 823-0700

HMO New Mexico, Inc.   16,000
12800 Indian School Rd., NE
Albuquerque, NM 87112
(505) 291-6902

Lovelace Health Systems, Inc.   127,000
5301 Central Ave. NE, Ste. 400
Albuquerque, NM 87108
(505) 262-7000

QualMed Plans for Health, Inc.   30,000
6100 Uptown Blvd., NE, Ste. 400
Albuquerque, NM 87110
(505) 889-8800

New York   **Capital District Physicians' Health Plan**   151,000
One Columbia Circle
Albany, NY 12203
(518) 452-1941

Health Services Medical Corp. of Cntrl NY 51,000
8278 Willett Pkwy.
Baldwinsville, NY 13027
(315) 638-2133

STATE	HMO	ESTIMATED MEMBERSHIP
New York (cont.)	**Elderplan, Inc.** 6323 Seventh Ave., 3rd Floor Brooklyn, NY 11220-4711 (718) 921-7990	5,000
	Community Blue, the HMO of Blue Cross/ Blue Shield 1901 Main St., P.O. Box 159 Buffalo, NY 14240-0159 (716) 884-2800	194,000
	Health Care Plan 900 Guaranty Building Buffalo, NY 14202 (716) 847-1480	85,000
	Independent Health 511 Farber Lakes Dr. Buffalo, NY 14221 (716) 631-3001	296,000
	Community Health Plan of Bassett One Atwell Rd. Cooperstown, NY 13326 (607) 547-9244	Figure unavailable
	Travelers Health Network of NY, Inc. 5015 Campuswood Dr., Ste. 303 East Syracuse, NY 13057 (315) 433-5700	15,000
	CIGNA HealthCare of New York, Inc. 1010 Northern Blvd., Ste. 324 Great Neck, NY 11021 (516) 466-1000	48,000
	MetLife HealthCare Network of NY, Inc. 2929 Express Dr. North Hauppauge, NY 11787 (516) 348-4200	61,000

Sanus Health Plan of Greater NY/NJ   101,000
75-20 Astoria Blvd.
Jackson Heights, NY 11370
(718) 899-5200

Mid-Hudson Health Plan   17,000
Park West and Harley Ave., P.O. Box 3786
Kingston, NY 12401-3786
(914) 338-0202

Community Health Plan/Capital Area Reg.   166,000
1202 Troy-Schenectady Rd.
Latham, NY 12110
(518) 783-1864

ChoiceCare-Long Island   47,000
Corporate Center
395 North Service Rd.
Melville, NY 11747-3127
(516) 694-4000

Empire Blue Cross & Blue Shield   122,000
622 Third Ave.
New York, NY 10017
(212) 251-3981

Health Insurance Plan of Greater NY   952,000
7 West 34th St.
New York, NY 10001-8190
(212) 630-5000

Metropolitan Health Plan   15,000
500 Fifth Ave., 27th Floor
New York, NY 10110
(212) 626-8300

Oxford Health Plan of New York   240,000
521 5th Ave.
New York, NY 10175
(212) 599-2266

WellCare of New York, Inc.   71,000
130 Meadow Ave.
Newburgh, NY 12550
(914) 566-0700

STATE	HMO	ESTIMATED MEMBERSHIP
New York (cont.)	**Community Health Plan/Hudson Valley Region** 160 Union St. Poughkeepsie, NY 12601 (914) 471-2368	38,000
	MVP Health Plan (Mid-Hudson) 385 South Rd., Beechwood Office Park Poughkeepsie, NY 12601 (914) 473-1762	33,000
	Aetna Health Plans of New York 2700 Westchester Ave., Ste.102 Purchase, NY 10577-2554 (914) 251-0600	73,000
	Blue Choice 150 East Main St., Gateway Center Rochester, NY 14647 (716) 454-1700	485,000
	Preferred Care 259 Monroe Ave. Rochester, NY 14607 (716) 325-3920	158,000
	MVP Health Plan (North); MVP Health Plan (South Central); MVP Health Plan-East 111 Liberty St. Schenectady, NY 12305 (518) 370-4793	13,000; 11,000; 98,000
	PruCare of Connecticut, Inc.; PruCare of New Jersey; PruCare of New York 400 Rella Blvd., Ste. 300 Suffern, NY 10901 (914) 368-4497	4,000; 71,000; 78,000

HMO-CNY, Inc. 37,000
344 South Warren St.
Syracuse, NY 13202
(315) 448-6820

Patients' Choice, Inc. 22,000
P.O. Box 1498
Syracuse, NY 13201-1498
(315) 449-1100

Independent Health-Hudson Valley 26,000
200 White Plains Rd.
Tarrytown, NY 10591
(914) 631-0939

Managed Health, Inc. 7,000
EAB Plaza
Uniondale, NY 11556-0162
(516) 683-1010

U.S. Healthcare (New York) 397,000
Nassau Omni West, 333 Earle Ovington Blvd.
Suite 502
Uniondale, NY 11553
(215) 628-4800

BlueCARE Plus 16,000
12 Rhoads Dr., Utica Business Park
Utica, NY 13502-6398
(315) 798-4399

Physicians Health Services of NY, Inc. 22,000
Crosswest Office Center
399 Knollwood Rd., Ste. 212
White Plains, NY 10603-1900
(914) 682-8006

Travelers Health Network of NY, Inc. 15,000
701 Westchester Ave.
White Plains, NY 10604
(914) 761-9102

STATE	HMO	ESTIMATED MEMBERSHIP
New York (cont.)	**MVP Health Plan - Central** 4947 Commercial Dr. Yorkville, NY 13495 (315) 736-1625	31,000
North Carolina	**CIGNA Health Care of North Carolina, Inc.** 7400 Carmel Executive Park Charlotte, NC 28226 (704) 544-4350	2,000
	Maxicare North Carolina, Inc. 5550 77 Center Dr., Ste. 380 Charlotte, NC 28217-0700 (704) 525-0880	14,000
	PruCare of Charlotte 2100 Rexford Rd., Ste. 314 Charlotte, NC 28211 (704) 365-8088	38,000
	Winston-Salem Health Care Plan 250 Charlois Blvd. Winston-Salem, NC 27103 (910) 768-4730	31,000
	Blue Cross & Blue Shield of North Carolina P.O. Box 2291 Durham, NC 27702-2291 (919) 489-7431	33,000
	Personal Care Plan of North Carolina, Inc. P.O. Box 30004 Durham, NC 27702 (919) 489-7431	8,000
	Physicians Health Plan, Inc. 2307 West Cone Blvd. Greensboro, NC 27408 (910) 282-0900	81,000

Carolina Physicians' Health Plan, Inc.   74,000
4000 Aerial Center Pkwy.
Morrisville, NC 27560
(919) 460-1610

CIGNA HealthCare of North Carolina, Inc.   3,000
4011 Westchase Blvd., Ste. 290
Raleigh, NC 27607
(919) 839-7800

Kaiser Foundation Health Plan of NC   118,000
3120 Highwoods Blvd.
Raleigh, NC 27604-1018
(919) 981-6000

PARTNERS National Health Plans of NC   68,000
Forsyth Corporate Center
2000 Frontis Plaza Blvd., Ste. 200
Winston-Salem, NC 27103
(910) 760-4822

North Dakota   **Northern Plains Health Plan**   1,000
1000 South Columbia Rd.
Grand Forks, ND 58201
(701) 780-1600

Heart of America HMO   3,000
802 South Main
Rugby, ND 58368
(701) 776-5848

Ohio   **Advantage Health Plan of Ohio and West**   11,000
Virginia
3000 Guernesey St.,
Bellaire, OH 43906
(614) 676-4623

Aetna Health Plans - Ohio Valley   600
615 Elsinore, Ste. 800
Cincinnati, OH 45202
(513) 579-3310

STATE	HMO	ESTIMATED MEMBERSHIP
Ohio (cont.)	**ChoiceCare** 655 Eden Park Dr., Ste. 400 Cincinnati, OH 45202 (513) 784-5200	181,000
	CIGNA Health Care of Ohio 36 East Seventh St., Ste. 2301 Cincinnati, OH 45202 (513) 629-2640	2,000
	Health Maintenance Plan 4665 Cornell Rd., Ste. 300 Cincinnati, OH 45241 (513) 247-6600	142,000
	Humana Health Plan of Ohio, Inc. 8044 Montgomery Rd., Ste. 460 Cincinnati, OH 45236 (513) 792-0511	10,000
	MetLife Health Care Network of Ohio, Inc. Northmark III, Ste. 150 4501 Erskine Rd. Cincinnati, OH 45242 (513) 745-9700	16,000
	PruCare of Cincinnati 312 Elm St., Ste. 1400 Cincinnati, OH 45202 (513) 784-7500	18,000
	TakeCare Health Plan of Ohio, Inc. 11260 Chester Rd., Ste. 800 Cincinnati, OH 45246 (513) 772-7325	36,000
	Aetna Health Plans of Ohio, Inc. 3690 Orange Place, Ste. 200 Cleveland, OH 44122 (216) 464-2722	35,000

CIGNA Health Care of Ohio-Cleveland   10,000
5005 Rockside Rd., Ste. 700
Cleveland, OH 44131
(216) 642-2920

HMO Health Ohio   220,000
2060 East Ninth St.
Cleveland, OH 44115-1355
(216) 687-7000

Kaiser Foundation Health Plan of Ohio   198,000
North Point Tower, 1001 Lakeside Ave.
Cleveland, OH 44114
(216) 621-5600

Personal Physician Care of Ohio, Inc.   27,000
1255 Euclid Ave., Bank 1 Building, Ste. 500
Cleveland, OH 44115
(216) 687-0015

PruCare of Northern Ohio   30,000
1228 Euclid Ave., Halle Building, Ste. 750
Cleveland, OH 44115
(216) 241-5623

Total Health Care Plan   24,000
12800 Shaker Blvd.
Cleveland, OH 44120
(216) 991-3000

CIGNA Health Care of Ohio-Columbus   20,000
455 Hutchinson Ave., Ste. 900
Columbus, OH 43235
(614) 847-7100

Health Power of Columbus, Inc.   32,000
560 East Town St.
Columbus, OH 43215
(614) 461-9900

PHP Ohio   197,000
3650 Olentangy River Rd.
Columbus, OH 43214-3459
(614) 442-7100

STATE	HMO	ESTIMATED MEMBERSHIP
Ohio (cont.)	**Principal Health Care of Ohio, Inc.** 8101 North High St., Ste. 380 Columbus, OH 43235 (614) 841-1240	26,000
	DayMed Health Maintenance Plan P.O. Box 1236, Mid City Station Dayton, OH 45402 (513) 224-5646	33,000
	Dayton Area Health Plan One Dayton Centre One South Main St., Ste. 440 Dayton, OH 45402 (513) 224-3300	28,000
	Western Ohio Health Care Corporation 6601 Centerville Business Pkwy. P.O. Box 591208 Dayton, OH 45459-8028 (800) 231-2918	188,000
	PruCare of Central Ohio 485 Metro Place South, Ste. 450 Dublin, OH 43017 (614) 761-0002	35,000
	HealthFirst 372 East Center St. Marion, OH 43302 (614) 387-6355	27,000
	Hometown Hospital Health Plan 876 Amherst Rd. Massillon, OH 44646 (216) 837-6880	14,000
	Licking Memorial Hospital Health Plan 1320 West Main St., Ste. HP Newark, OH 43055 (614) 366-0533	15,000

Health Plan of the Upper Ohio Valley   75,000
52160 National Road East
St. Clairsville, OH 43950
(614) 695-3585

Family Health Plan   22,000
1001 Madison Ave.
Toledo, OH 43624
(419) 241-6501

Medical Value Plan   34,000
415 Madison Ave., P.O. Box 2147
Toledo, OH 43603-2147
(419) 244-2900

Paramount Care, Inc.   31,000
1715 Indian Wood Circle
P.O. Box 928
Toledo, OH 43697-0928
(419) 891-2500

Toledo Health Plan   33,000
P.O. Box 6298, 3401 Glendale Ave.
Toledo, OH 43614
(419) 382-8600

InHealth, Inc.   33,000
200 East Campus View Blvd., Ste. 300
Worthington, OH 43235
(614) 888-2223

Oklahoma   **CIGNA Health Care of Oklahoma, Inc.**   4,000
5100 North Brookline, 9th Floor
Oklahoma City, OK 73112
(405) 943-7711

PacifiCare   65,000
525 Central Park Dr., Ste. 200
Oklahoma City, OK 73105
(405) 525-9200

STATE	HMO	ESTIMATED MEMBERSHIP
Oklahoma (cont.)	**PruCare of Oklahoma City** NW Medical Center 3330 North West 56th St., Ste. 500 Oklahoma City, OK 73112 (405) 942-2200	35,000
	CIGNA HealthCare of Oklahoma-Tulsa 9810 East 42nd St.,Ste. 220 Tulsa, OK 74146 (918) 664-0168	600
	Community Care HMO, Inc. 4720 South Harvard, Ste. 202 Tulsa, OK 74135 (918) 749-1171	Figure unavailable
	GHS Health Maintenance Organization 1400 South Boston Tulsa, OK 74119-3618 (918) 561-9900	29,000
	PacifiCare of Oklahoma 7666 East 61st St., Ste. 400 Tulsa, OK 74133 (918) 459-1111	70,000
	PruCare of Tulsa 7912 East 31st Court, Ste. 300 Tulsa, OK 74145 (918) 624-4600	29,000
Oregon	**PACC Health Plans** P.O. Box 286 Clackamas, OR 97015-0286 (503) 659-4212	49,000
	SelectCare 600 Country Club Rd. Eugene, OR 97401 (503) 485-1850	86,000

PacifiCare of Oregon   95,000
Five Centerpointe Dr., Ste. 600
Lake Oswego, OR 97035-8650
(503) 620-9324

Health Maintenance of Oregon   266,000
100 SW Market
Portland, OR 97201
(503) 225-5321

Kaiser Foundation Health Plan   379,000
of the Northwest
2701 NW Vaughn, Ste. 300
Portland, OR 97210-5398
(503) 721-3800

Liberty Health Plan, Inc.   Figure
825 Northeast Multnomak, Ste. 1900   unavailable
Portland, OR 97232
(503) 234-5345

Qual-Med Oregon Health Plan, Inc.   22,000
4800 SW Macadam Ave., Ste. 400
Portland, OR 97201
(503) 222-5217

Sisters of Providence Health Plan in Oregon 96,000
1235 NE 47th Ave., Ste. 220
Portland, OR 97213-2196
(503) 249-2981

HMO Oregon   197,000
P.O. Box 12625
Salem, OR 97309
(503) 364-4868

Pennsylvania   **HMO of Pennsylvania; U.S. Healthcare**   622,000;
                 (Delaware)   29,000
                 980 Jolly Rd., P.O. Box 1109
                 Blue Bell, PA 19422
                 (215) 628-4800

STATE	HMO	ESTIMATED MEMBERSHIP
Pennsylvania (cont.)	**Keystone Health Plan Central** P.O. Box 898812 Camp Hill, PA 17089-8812 (717) 763-3458	114,000
	Geisinger Health Plan 100 North Academy Ave. Danville, PA 17822-3020 (717) 271-8760	159,000
	HealthAmerica of Central Pennsylvania 2601 Market Place St. Harrisburg, PA 17110-9339 (717) 540-4260	92,000
	PruCare of Philadelphia 220 Gibraltar Rd., Ste. 200 Horsham, PA 19044 (215) 672-1944	29,000
	HealthGuard of Lancaster, Inc. 280 Granite Run Dr., Ste. 105 Lancaster, PA 17601 (717) 560-9049	32,000
	Greater Atlantic Health Service 3550 Market St. Philadelphia, PA 19104 (215) 823-8600	81,000
	Keystone Health Plan East 1901 Market St., P.O. Box 7516 Philadelphia, PA 19101-7516 (215) 241-2001	502,000
	Advantage Health Plan of Pennsylvania 121 Seventh St., Ste. 500 Pittsburgh, PA 15222 (412) 391-9300	10,000

Aetna Health Plans of Western Pennsylvania, Inc.   25,000
5700 Corporate Dr., Ste. 300
Pittsburgh, PA 15237
(412) 366-9000

HealthAmerica Pennsylvania, Inc.   187,000
Five Gateway Center
Pittsburgh, PA 15222
(412) 553-7300

Keystone Health Plan West, Inc.   113,000
Foster Plaza VI, 6th Floor, 681 Andersen Dr.
Pittsburgh, PA 15220
(412) 937-4300

U.S. Healthcare (Pittsburgh)   41,000
Two Marquis Plaza
5313 Campbells Run Rd., Suite 300
Pittsburgh, PA 15205
(215) 628-4800

Aetna Health Plans of Central and Eastern   73,000;
Pennsylvania; Aetna Health Plans of New   79,000
Jersey, Inc.
Chesterbrook Corporate Center
955 Chesterbook Blvd., Ste. 200
Wayne, PA 19087-5693
(610) 644-3800

HMO of Northeastern Pennsylvania   63,000
70 North Main St.
Wilkes-Barre, PA 18711
(717) 831-3500

Rhode Island   **Harvard Community Health Plan**   84,000
of New England
One Hoppin St.
Providence, RI 02903
(401) 331-3000

STATE	HMO	ESTIMATED MEMBERSHIP
Rhode Island (cont.)	**HMO Rhode Island, Inc.** 30 Chestnut St. Providence, RI 02903 (401) 459-5500	14,000
	United Health Plans of New England, Inc. 475 Kilvert St., Ste. 310 Warwick, RI 02886 (401) 737-6900	170,000
South Carolina	**Healthsource South Carolina, Inc.** 215 East Bay St., Ste. 401 Charleston, SC 29401 (803) 723-5520	61,000
	Companion Health Care Corporation I-20 at Alpine Rd. Columbia, SC 29219 (803) 786-8466	36,000
	Physicians Health Plan of South Carolina 110 Centerview Dr., Ste. 301 Columbia, SC 29210 (803) 750-7400	23,000
	Maxicare South Carolina 535 North Pleasantburg Dr., Ste. 108 Greenville, SC 29607 (803) 233-7437	13,000
South Dakota	**DakotaCare** 1323 South Minnesota Ave. Sioux Falls, SD 57105 (605) 334-4000	21,000
Tennessee	**Tennessee Health Care Network, Inc.** P.O. Box 1407 Chattanooga, TN 37401-1407 (615) 755-5662	19,000

Healthsource Tennessee, Inc. 16,000
625 South Gay St., Ste. 300
Knoxville, TN 37902-1656
(615) 546-2529

CIGNA HealthCare of Tennessee, Inc. 10,000
6555 Quince Rd., Ste. 215
Memphis, TN 38119
(901) 755-7411

Complete Health of Tennessee, Inc. 25,000
5865 Ridgeway Center Pkwy., Ste. 202
Memphis, TN 38120
(901) 681-9197

PruCare of Memphis 29,000
845 Crossover Lane, Ste. 220
Memphis, TN 38117
(901) 766-7908

Southern Health Plan, Inc. 53,000
600 Jefferson, P.O. Box 97
Memphis, TN 38101-0097
(901) 544-2202

Aetna Health Plans of Tennessee, Inc. 7,000
Palmer Plaza, 1801 West End Ave., Ste. 500
Nashville, TN 37203-2518
(615) 322-1600

CIGNA HealthCare of Tennessee, Inc. 16,000
1801 West End Ave., Ste. 800
Nashville, TN 37203
(615) 340-3059

PruCare of Nashville 30,000
227 French Landing Dr., Ste. 300
Nashville, TN 37228
(615) 248-7100

Tennessee Primary Care Network 365,000
205 Reidhurst Ave., Ste. N104
Nashville, TN 37203
(615) 329-2016

STATE	HMO	ESTIMATED MEMBERSHIP
Texas	**Southwest Health Alliances, Inc.** 3310 Danvers Amarillo, TX 79106 (806) 356-5151	34,000
	Harris Methodist Health Plan 611 Ryan Plaza Dr. Arlington, TX 76011-4009 (817) 462-7000	143,000
	PCA Health Plans of Texas, Inc. 8303 MoPac, Ste. 450 Austin, TX 78759 (512) 338-6100	147,000
	PruCare of Austin 9050 Capital of Texas Hwy., State Route 325 Austin, TX 78759 (512) 465-6661	73,000
	Travelers Health Network of Texas, Inc. 9442 Capital of Texas Hwy. North, Ste. 600 Austin, TX 78759 (512) 338-6800	31,000
	Coastal Bend Health Plan 2502 Morgan, P.O. Box 3457 Corpus Christi, TX 78463-3457 (512) 887-0101	27,000
	Humana Health Plan of Texas 5350 South Staples, Ste. 301 Corpus Christi, TX 78411 (512) 994-2000	26,000
	Anthem Health Plan of Texas, Inc. 5055 Keller Springs Rd., Building 1 Dallas, TX 75248 (214) 732-2000	600

Kaiser Foundation Health Plan of Texas   129,000
12720 Hillcrest, Ste. 600
Dallas, TX 75230
(214) 458-5000

PruCare of North Texas   51,000
4100 Alpha Rd., Ste. 400
Dallas, TX 75244-4327
(713) 993-0014

Rio Grande HMO, Inc.   26,000
4150 Pinnacle, Ste. 203
El Paso, TX 79902
(915) 542-1547

Aetna Health Plans of Texas, Inc.   22,000
2900 North Loop West, Ste. 200
Houston, TX 77092
(713) 683-7599

CIGNA Health Care of Texas-Houston   17,000
1360 Post Oak Blvd., Ste. 1100
Houston, TX 77056
(713) 796-8422

MetLife HealthCare Network   32,000
of Texas, Inc.
5 Post Oak Park, Ste. 550
Houston, TX 77027
(214) 751-0777

Sanus Health Plan, Inc.   207,000
3800 Buffalo Speedway, Ste. 300
Houston, TX 77098
(713) 624-5000

Travelers Health Network of Texas, Inc.   4,000
10800 Richmond Ave.
Houston, TX 77042
(713) 268-7800

CIGNA HealthCare of Texas-Dallas   29,000
600 East Las Colinas Blvd., Ste. 1100
Irving, TX 75039
(214) 401-5200

STATE	HMO	ESTIMATED MEMBERSHIP
Texas (cont.)	**Sanus Texas Health Plan** 4500 Fuller Dr. Irving, TX 75038-6597 (214) 791-3900	163,000
	Southwest Health Plans, Inc. 2350 Lakeside Blvd., Ste. 500 Richardson, TX 75082 (214) 470-7608	51,000
	Travelers Health Network of Texas, Inc. 2270 Lakeside Blvd., Ste. 600 Richardson, TX 75082 (214) 437-3074	3,000
	Humana Health Plan of Texas Med Center Plaza 8431 Fredericksburg Rd. San Antonio, TX 78229 (210) 617-1000	73,000
	PacifiCare of Texas 8200 IH-10 West, Ste. 1000 San Antonio, TX 78230-3878 (210) 366-1921	87,000
	PruCare of San Antonio 40 NW Loop 410, Ste. 600 San Antonio, TX 78216 (216) 366-1921	35,000
	PruCare of Houston One Prudential Circle, Mail Stop 100 Sugarland, TX 77478 (713) 276-0311	185,000
	Scott and White Health Plan 2401 South 31st St. Temple, TX 76508-3000 (817) 742-3000	101,000

| Utah | **Educators Health Care**
852 East Arrowhead Lane
Murray, UT 84107-5298
(801) 262-7476 | 800 |

CIGNA HealthCare of Utah, Inc.
5295 South 320 West, Ste. 280
Salt Lake City, UT 84107
(801) 265-2777

14,000

FHP of Utah, Inc.
35 West Broadway
Salt Lake City, UT 84101
(801) 355-1236

159,000

HealthWise
2505 Parley's Way, Box 30804
Salt Lake City, UT 84130-0804
(801) 481-6177

23,000

IHC Care, Inc.; IHC Group, Inc.;
IHC Health Plans, Inc.
36 South State St.
Salt Lake City, UT 84111
(801) 538-5000

62,000;
59,000;
115,000

United Health Care of Utah
7910 South 3500 East
P.O. Box 21409, Ste. 100
Salt Lake City, UT 84121
(801) 942-6200

70,000

Vermont **Community Health Plan/Vermont Region**
7 Park Ave.
Williston, VT 05495
(802) 878-2334

64,000

Virginia **CIGNA HealthCare of Virginia, Inc.-**
Richmond
4050 Innslake Dr.
Glen Allen, VA 23060
(804) 273-1100

Figure
unavailable

STATE	HMO	ESTIMATED MEMBERSHIP
Virginia (cont.)	**Peninsula Health Care, Inc.** 606 Denbigh Blvd., Ste. 500 Newport News, VA 23602 (804) 875-5760	Figure unavailable
	HealthKeepers of Virginia, Inc. P.O. Box 26623 Richmond, VA 23261 (804) 354-3860	71,000
	HMO Virginia Inc.; Physicians Health Plan, Inc. P.O. Box 26623 Richmond, VA 23261 (804) 354-3860	13,000
	PruCare of Richmond 1000 Boulders Pkwy. Richmond, VA 23225 (804) 323-0900	17,000
	Southern Health Services, Inc. P.O. Box 85603 Richmond, VA 23285-5603 (804) 747-3700	41,000
	CapitalCare 1921 Gallows Rd., 9th Floor Vienna, VA 22182-3929 (703) 761-5400	92,000
	CIGNA HealthCare of Virginia, Inc. Reflections II, Ste. 450 200 Golden Oak Ct. Virginia Beach, VA 23452 (804) 463-8606	54,000

OPTIMA Health Plan; Sentara Health Plan, Inc.   68,000; 46,000
4417 Corporation Lane
Virginia Beach, VA 23462
(804) 552-7400

Washington   **Qual-Med Washington Health Plan, Inc.**   95,000
520 Corporate Center, Building C
2331 130th Ave. NE, Ste. 200
Bellevue, WA 98005
(206) 869-3500

CIGNA HealthCare of Washington, Inc.   3,000
701 Fifth Ave., Ste. 2940, 2940 Columbia Cntr.
Seattle, WA 98104
(206) 625-8800

Good Health Plan of Washington   34,000
1501 Fourth Ave., Ste. 500
Seattle,WA 98101-1621
(206) 622-6111

Group Health Cooperative of Puget Sound   483,000
521 Wall Street
Seattle, WA 98121
(206) 448-6565

HealthPlus   72,000
P.O. Box 327
Seattle, WA 98111-0327
(206) 670-7400

HMO Washington   14,000
1800 Ninth Ave.
Seattle, WA 98101
(206) 340-6600

Pacific Health Plans   30,000
600 University St., Ste. 700
Seattle, WA 98101
(206) 326-4645

STATE	HMO	ESTIMATED MEMBERSHIP
Washington (cont.)	**Virginia Mason Health Plan** 1100 Olive Way 1580 Metropolitan Park West Tower Seattle, WA 98101-1828 (206) 223-8844	41,000
	Group Health Northwest P.O. Box 204 Spokane, WA 99210-0204 (800) 497-2210	100,000
Wisconsin	**Group Health Cooperative of Eau Claire** 2503 North Hillcrest Pkwy. Altoona, WI 54720 (715) 836-8552	16,000
	United Health of Wisconsin Insurance Co. P.O. Box 507 Appleton, WI 54912-0507 (414) 735-6300	36,000
	Valley Health Plan 2270 Highland Mall, P.O. Box 3128 Eau Claire, WI 54702-3128 (715) 832-3235	18,000
	Employers Health Care Plan Employers Health Insurance Co. 1100 Employers Blvd. Green Bay, WI 54344 (414) 336-1100	31,000
	HMO Midwest 502 Second St. Hudson, WI 54016 (612) 456-8434	11,000
	Greater LaCrosse Health Plans, Inc. P.O. Box 38 LaCrosse, WI 54602-0038 (608) 781-9692	9,000

Group Health Cooperative of South Central 38,000
Wisconsin
P.O. Box 44971
8202 Excelsior Dr.
Madison, WI 53744-4971
(608) 251-4156

Physicians Plus HMO   78,000
340 West Washington Ave.
Madison, WI 53703
(608) 282-8900

Q Care   5,000
P.O. Box 8190
Madison, WI 53708-8190
(608) 221-4711

U-Care HMO, Inc.   22,000
444 Science Dr., Ste. 200
Madison, WI 53711-1056
(608) 238-7887

Security Health Plan of Wisconsin, Inc.   54,000
1000 North Oak Ave.
Marshfield, WI 54449
(800) 472-2363

Network Health Plan of Wisconsin, Inc.   36,000
1165 Appleton Rd., P.O. Box 120
Menasha, WI 54952
(414) 727-0100

DeanCare HMO   141,000
2711 Allen Blvd., P.O. Box 56099
Middleton, WI 53562
(608) 836-1400

Compcare Health Services Insurance Corp. 152,000
401 West Michigan St., P.O. Box 2947
Milwaukee, WI 53201-2947
(800) 242-7312

STATE	HMO	ESTIMATED MEMBERSHIP
Wisconsin (cont.)	**Maxicare Health Insurance Company** 790 North Milwaukee St. Milwaukee, WI 53202 (414) 271-6371	23,000
	PrimeCare Health Plan, Inc. 1233 North Mayfair Rd. Milwaukee, WI 53226 (414) 453-9070	185,000
	Wisconsin Health Organization Ins. Corp. 111 West Pleasant St.; P.O. Box 12359 Milwaukee, WI 53212-0359 (414) 223-3300	90,000
	HMO of Wisconsin Insurance Corporation 840 Carolina St. Sauk City, WI 53583-1371 (608) 643-2491	38,000
	Eau Claire-Chippewa Health Protection Plan 2000 Westwood Dr. Wausau, WI 54401 (715) 847-8970	90
	Greater Wisconsin Rapids Health Protection Plan 2000 Westwood Dr. Wausau,WI 54401 (715) 842-6844	600
	Green Bay Health Protection Plan 2000 Westwood Dr. Wausau, WI 54401 (715) 842-6896	15,000
	North Central Health Protection Plan 2000 Westwood Dr. Wausau, WI 54401 (715) 847-8866	37,000

Oshkosh Area Health Protection Plan 3,000
P.O. Box 8017
Wausau, WI 54402-8017
(715) 842-6896

Family Health Plan Cooperative 105,000
11524 West Theodore Trecker Way
P.O. Box 44260
West Allis, WI 53214-4260
(414) 256-0006

Appendix C

Treatment Summary

SUBSCRIBER INFORMATION

Name:_____ D.O.B.:_____

Address:_____

Employer:_____Insurance:_____

Subscriber:_____Group Number:_____

PATIENT INFORMATION: (if different from subscriber)

Name:_____D.O.B.:_____

Address:_____

Primary Care Physician:_____

ASSESSMENT/DIAGNOSIS INFORMATION:

A. Current symptoms and impairment in social/occupational functioning:

_____
_____
_____
_____
_____
_____
_____
_____

B.   Use of mood-altering substances, including alcohol or other illicit drugs and family history of same. Indicate if problematic:

_____

_____

_____

_____

_____

_____

_____

_____

C.   Present prescribed medication for medical or psychiatric condition:

_____

_____

_____

_____

Is there need for evaluation for medication, psychological testing, or physician evaluation? _____yes _____no

If YES explain:_____

_____

_____

D.   DSM-III-R Diagnosis (include code)
Axis 1:_____
Axis 2:_____
Axis 3:_____
Axis 4:_____
Axis 5:_____

TREATMENT PLAN:

A.   Objective of Treatment:_____

_____

_____

_____

B.   Interventions (refer to the following as relevant: theme of focus of sessions, techniques to be used, assignments outside therapy, use of community resources, use of chemotherapy):

_____

_____

_____

_____

_____

_____

_____

_____

C.   Mode of treatment (i.e., group, individual, etc.):_____

_____

D.   Frequency of sessions:_____Length of sessions:_____

E.   Number of sessions already conducted (this enrollment year):

_____

F.   Estimated number of sessions needed to complete objectives:___

_____

PERSON PROVIDING TREATMENT: (Print)_____

Signature:_____ Date:_____

MCC COMPANIES, INC.
TREATMENT UPDATE

Patient Name:_____D.O.B.:_____

Describe response to treatment (achievement of or progress toward treatment goals):

_____

_____

_____

Number of sessions previously authorized by MCC:_____

Number of sessions completed to date:_____

Number of additional sessions requested:_____

Frequency of sessions:_____

Current DSM-III-R Diagnosis:_____

Current Symptoms:_____
_____
_____
_____

Modification to treatment goals:_____
_____
_____
_____

Rationale for additional sessions:_____
_____
_____
_____

Name of Therapist:_____

Signature:_____Date:_____

MCC Companies, Inc.
7702 Parham Road, Suite 104
Richmond, VA 23294
(804) 747-MCC2

MCC COMPANIES, INC.
CLOSING SUMMARY

PATIENT'S NAME:_____ DATE OF CLOSING:_____
DATE OF BIRTH:_____

I. Extent of Contact

A) Client seen from_____to_____

B) Number of appointments_____

C) Number of "no shows" or cancelled appointments_____

II. Presenting Problems

_____
_____
_____

III. Brief Description of Course of Treatment

_____
_____
_____

IV. Reason for Closing

_____
_____
_____

V. Diagnosis at End of Treatment, Prognosis, and/or Recommendations

_____
_____
_____

Signature:_____

Title:_____

Return to: **MCC Companies, Inc., 7702 Parham Rd., Ste. 104,
Richmond, VA 23294, Attn: Medical Records Dept.**

_____

_____
_____
_____

RE:_____
Dear:_____

This patient was seen for an evaluation on_____. Our Intake Team has carefully evaluated this patient and determined that the primary diagnosis is_____
_____.

We are referring this patient to you for _____
therapy and have identified the treatment goals as:

1._____
2._____
3._____

_____ visits are authorized and we believe these will be suffi-cient to resolve the patient's presenting problem. If you have any addition or disagreement to these treatment goals, or number of sessions autho-rized, please submit a written diagnostic report and treatment summary by the fourth visit. On completion or termination of treatment, for any rea-son, please submit the enclosed closing treatment summary.

     The MCC case manager is_____ .

Cordially yours,

Norman Winegar, LCSW, CEAP
Executive Director

Appendix D

S.O.A.P Process Note
Recording Format

S (Subjective)

What the patient says
Basic history (first session)
Major focus of session–content

O (Objective)

Mental status exam
Appearance
Speech
Nonverbal behavior
Defenses

A (Assessment)

5 axis diagnosis DSM–III–R (initial session)
Subsequent sessions:
–Improvement vs. regression
–Motivation
–Relapse behavior

P (Plan)

Any further assessment needed
Use of community resources
Homework
Goals of treatment
Spacing of sessions
Contract for length of treatment
Development of support systems
Techniques to be used

Appendix E

Managed Care Directory, 1995

Access Care
2203 North Lois Avenue
Suite 1150
Tampa, Florida 33607
800-458-6139
813-876-5036
813-872-8666 fax

ACORN Behavioral Healthcare Management Corporation
ACORN Building
134 N. Narberth Avenue
Narberth, Pennsylvania 19072
800-223-7050
215-660-0634 fax

Behavior Health, Inc.
6160 Perkins Road, #200
Baton Rouge, Louisiana 70808
504-769-5400
504-767-2065 fax

Behavior Management Associates, Inc.
Four Commerce Park Square
23200 Chagrin Boulevard, #325
Beechwood, Ohio 44122
216-292-6007
216-292-7352 fax

Behavioral Health Services
619 Oak Street, #750
Cincinnati, Ohio 45206
513-569-5434
513-569-5440 fax

Behavioral Health Systems, Inc.
485 South Frontage Road, #305
Burr Bridge, Illinois 60521-7110
708-655-4440
708-655-4558 fax

Behavioral Healthcare Options
P.O. Box 15645
Las Vegas, Nevada 89114-5645
702-364-1484
702-364-0843 fax

Benesys Managed Mental Health Services
1775 St. James Place, #200
Houston, Texas 77056
800-324-0800
713-871-6301 fax

California Psychological Health Plan
5750 Wilshire Boulevard, #490
Los Angeles, California 90036-3697
213-965-4870
213-937-9688 fax

CMG Health
25 Crossroad Drive
Owings Mills, Maryland 21117
410-581-5000
410-581-5007 fax

CNR Health, Inc.
2400 South 102nd Street, #100
Milwaukee, Wisconsin 53227
414-327-5197
414-327-0886 fax

ComPsych Behavioral Health Corporation
515 North State Street, #2310
Chicago, Illinois 60610
312-245-2699
312-245-2767 fax

Family Enterprises, Inc.
11700 West Lake Park Drive
Milwaukee, Wisconsin 53224
414-359-1040
414-359-1074 fax

First Mental Health, Inc.
501 Great Circle Road, #300
Nashville, Tennessee 37228
615-246-3400
615-256-0786 fax

Florida Psychiatric Management
1276 Minnesota Avenue
Winter Park, Florida 32789
407-647-1781
407-647-0668 fax

Green Spring Health Services, Inc.
5565 Sterrett Place
Columbia, Maryland 21044
800-245-7013
410-740-9501
410-740-8573 fax

Health Management Strategies International, Inc. (HMS)
1725 Duke Street, #300
Alexandria, Virginia 22314
703-706-4100
703-706-4803 fax

HMA Behavioral Health, Inc.
255 Park Avenue, #800
Worcester, Massachusetts 01609-1946
800-248-9908
508-757-2290
508-754-3616 fax

Human Affairs International (HAI), a division of AETNA
5801 South Fashion Boulevard
Salt Lake City, Utah 84107
801-268-0553
801-268-9716 fax

Integra, Inc.
320 King of Prussia Road
Radnor, Pennsylvania 19087
215-688-2700
215-688-5399 fax

Integrated Behavioral Care (IBC)
8316 Arlington Boulevard, #600
Fairfax, Virginia 22031
703-698-5220
703-573-2351 fax

Integrated Behavioral Health
P.O. Box 30018
Laguna Nigel, California 92607-0018
714-588-2688
714-588-0832 fax

LifeLink, Inc.
23046 Avenida De La Carlota #700
Laguna Hills, California 92653
714-859-7971
714-859-9824 fax

Managed Health Network, Inc. (MHN)
5100 West Goldleaf Circle, #300
Los Angeles, California 90056
213-299-0999
213-298-2777 fax

Medco Behavioral Care Corporation
400 Oyster Point Boulevard, #306
South San Francisco, California 94080
415-742-0980
415-742-0988 fax

Mid-Atlantic Psychiatric Services, Inc. (MAPSI)
4 Taft Court
Rockville, Maryland 20850
301-738-1803
301-762-6132 fax

Occupational Health Services Corporation (OHS)
125 East Sir Francis Drake Boulevard, #300
Larkspur, California 94939-1860
415-461-8100
415-925-9728 fax

OPTIONS Mental Health
240 Corporate Boulevard
Norfolk, Virginia 23502
800-451-3581
804-459-5218 fax

Perspective
111 North Wabash Avenue, #1620
Chicago, Illinois 60602
708-932-7788
708-932-2315 fax

Plan 21, Inc.
4550 Post Oak Place, #341
Houston, Texas 77027
713-621-6500
713-621-6560 fax

Prudential Psychiatric Management, a division of Prudential
56 North Livingston Avenue, #250
Roseland, New Jersey 07068
201-716-8663
201-716-8497 fax

Sentara Mental Health Management
4417 Corporation Lane, #250
Virginia Beach, Virginia 23461
804-552-7500
804-552-7508 fax

Sheppard Pratt Preferred Resources
6501 North Charles Street
P. O. Box 6815
Baltimore, Maryland 21285-6815
410-938-3445
410-938-3406 fax

United Behavioral Systems, Inc. (UBS), a division of United Healthcare
9705 Bata Park
Minnetonka, Minnesota 55343
800-433-0519
612-945-6699 fax

U.S. Behavioral Health (USBH)
2000 Powell Street, #1180
Emeryville, California 94608
510-601-2200
510-547-2336 fax

Value Behavioral Health, Inc. (VBH)
P. O. Box 1570
Merrifield, Virginia 22116
703-528-2255
703-205-7290 fax

Vista Health Plans
2355 Northside Drive, 3rd Floor
San Diego, California 92108
619-563-0184
619-491-5270 fax

Appendix F

Brief Therapy Reading List

Bennett, M. J. and Wisneski, M. J. (1979). Continuous psychotherapy within an HMO. *American Journal of Psychiatry, 136,*
1283-1287.

Bennett, M. (1984). Brief psychotherapy and adult development.
Psychotherapy, 2, 171–177.

Budman, S. H. and Clifford, M. (1979). Short-term group therapy
for couples in a health maintenance organization. *Professional
Psychology: Research and Practice, 10,* 419-429.

Budman, S. H. and Bennett, M. J. (1983). Short-term group psychotherapy. In H. Kaplan and B. Sadock (Eds.), *Comprehensive
Group Psychotherapy* (rev. ed., pp. 138-144). Baltimore: Williams & Williams.

Budman, S. H. and Gurman, A. S. (1983). The practice of brief
therapy. *Professional Psychology: Research and Practice, 14,*
277-292.

Budman, S. H. and Gurman, A. S. (1988). *Theory and Practice of
Brief Therapy.* New York: Guilford Press.

Davanloo, H. (Ed.). (1978). *Basic Principles and Techniques in
Short-term Dynamic Psychotherapy.* New York: Spectrum.

Davanloo, H. (1980). A method of short-term dynamic psychotherapy. In H. Davanloo (Ed.), *Short-term Dynamic Psychotherapy*
(pp. 43-71). New York: Jason Aronson.

De Shazer, S. (1982). *Patterns of Brief Therapy.* New York: Guilford Press.

De Shazer, S. (1985). *Keys to Solution in Brief Therapy.* New York:
Norton.

De Shazer, S. (1988). *Clues: Investigating Solutions in Brief Therapy.* New York: Norton.

Fisch, R., Weakland, J. H., and Segal, L. (1982). *The Tactics of Change: Doing Therapy Briefly.* San Francisco: Jossey-Bass.

Flegenheimer, W. V. (1982). *Techniques of Brief Psychotherapy.* New York: Jason Aronson.

Haley, J. (1973). *Uncommon Therapy: The Psychiatric Techniques of Milton H. Ericson, M.D.* New York: Norton.

Haley, J. (1976). *Problem Solving Therapy.* San Francisco: Jossey-Bass.

Madanes, C. (1981). *Strategic Family Therapy.* San Francisco: Jossey-Bass.

Mann, J. (1973). *Time-Limited Psychotherapy.* Cambridge, MA: Harvard University Press.

Mann, J. and Goldman, R. (1982). *A Casebook in Time-Limited Psychotherapy.* New York: McGraw-Hill.

O'Hanlon, W. H. (1987). *Taproots: Underlyin Principles of Milton Erickson's Therapy and Hypnosis.* New York: Norton.

O'Hanlon, W. H. and Weiner-Davis, M. (1989). *In Search of Solutions: A New Direction in Psychotherapy.* New York: Norton.

Parad, H. J. and Parad, L. G. (1968). A study of crisis oriented planned short-term treatment: Part I. *Social Casework, 49,* 346-355.

Parad, L. G. and Parad, H. J. (1968). A study of crisis oriented planned short-term treatment: Part II. *Social Casework, 49,* 418-426.

Pekarik, G. (1989). *Brief Therapy Training Manual.* Unpublished manuscript.

Sifneos, P. E. (1979). *Short-Term Dynamic Psychotherapy: Evaluation and Technique.* New York: Plenum Press.

Small, L. (1979). *The Briefer Psychotherapies.* New York: Brunner/Maze.

Talmon, M. (1990). *Single Session Therapy.* San Francisco: Jossey-Bass.

Watzlawick, P., Fisch, R., and Segal, L. (1982). *The Tactics of Change.* San Francisco: Jossey-Bass.

Weakland, J. H., Fisch, R., Watzlawick, P., and Bodin, A. (1974). Brief therapy: Focused problem resolution. *Family Process, 13,* 141-168.

Wells, R. H. and Giannetti, V. J. (Eds.). (1990). *Handbook of the Brief Psychotherapies*. New York: Plenum Publishing Corporation.

Wolberg, L. R. (1980). *Handbooks of Short-Term Psychotherapy*. New York: Grune & Stratton.

Developed by and provided courtesy of Dr. John Bistline.

Appendix G

Managed Care Market Share Estimates, 1995

Organization	Enrollment, in Millions
1. Value Behavioral Health	16.5
2. Medco Behavioral Care	12.0
3. HAI	11.5
4. HMS	7.2
5. Green Springs Health Services	6.7
6. UBS	5.7
7. First Mental Health	5.6
8. MCC Behavioral Care	5.0
9. Family Enterprises	3.8
10. U.S. Behavioral Health	3.1

MANAGED CARE MARKET SHARE ESTIMATES, NON-RISK POPULATION, 1995*

Organization	Enrollment, in Millions
1. Value Behavioral Health	8.3

2. Green Springs Health Services	1.5
3. HAI	1.4
4. MCC Behavioral Care	1.2
5. OPTIONS Mental Health	.5

* Excludes EAP only populations and Utilization Review/Precertification only populations.

MANAGED CARE MARKET SHARE ESTIMATES, AT-RISK POPULATION, 1995

Organization	Enrollment, in Millions
1. Medco Behavioral Care	6.0
2. MCC Behavioral Care	3.0
3. UBS	2.5
4. Value Behavioral Care	1.6
5. CMG Health	1.4
6. Green Springs Health Services	1.9
7. OHS	.6
8. First Mental Health	.5
9. MNN	.4
10. LifeLink	.4

Glossary

Administrative Services Only (ASO) fee: A type of capitation fee arrangement in which a provider organization is paid a fixed fee per covered life, per month for the provision of administrative services, such as preadmission certification, care management, utilization reviews, eligibility determination, claims administration (additional fees per claim paid may also be charged), and data reporting. This type of financial arrangement may be employed when the purchaser wishes to retain the responsibility for the financial risk of actual services provided. The successful administration of an ASO contract pre-supposes an existing, efficient administrative infrastructure and the opportunity for the vendor organization to gain fee-for-service revenues from the provision of clinical services.

Administrative Services Only (ASO) fee, with risk sharing: In addition to the above characteristics, this arrangement between the purchaser and vendor organization stipulates one or more service targets, which if not met result in a penalty usually in the form of a monetary rebate to the purchaser. Targets may involve inpatient or outpatient utilization, claims payment turnaround time or accuracy, or customer service targets such as telephone answering responsiveness. The term Guaranteed Cost, meaning that the payor of the clinical services will be assured that the actual cost of the services will not exceed a target level, can also be applied to this type of contracting.

At-Risk Capitation: In this arrangement the provider organization is paid by the purchaser of managed care services a fixed fee per covered life (or member) per month and in return the managed care organization is at-risk for the administrative as well as clinical service delivery costs associated with the provision of care to an identified consumer population group eligible for specified behavioral care benefits. The monthly payment fluctuates only as the size of the population changes, allowing the purchaser–an HMO or employer–to predict and budget its mental health/substance abuse care costs, while providing incentives to the managed care organization to provide cost-effective care along a continuum of service offerings.

Carve-Outs: A benefit strategy in which an employer separates ("carves out") the mental health and substance abuse portion of health care benefits from others and hires a MBC company to manage or provide these benefits through its networks. Affords the employer with specialized management for this portion of the overall benefits package.

Case Management: A coordinated set of professional activities focused on treatment planning and the assurance of treatment delivery that addresses patients' biopsychosocial needs and achieves quality, cost effective outcomes. Also termed *care management.*

Claimant: Enrollee or covered person that files a claim for benefits.

Certification: A determination by a utilization review organization that an admission, extension of stay, or other clinical service has been reviewed (based on the available information) to meet the requirements for medical necessity, level of care placement, or effectiveness under the auspices of the applicable benefit plan.

Claims Administrator: Any entity that reviews and pays claims to enrollees or providers of care on the behalf of health benefit plans. May be insurance companies, managed mental health care companies, third-party administrators, self-insured employers, or other contractors.

Clinical Review Criteria: The written screens, decision-trees, or other protocols used by a Utilization Review organization to determine medical necessity and level of care decisions.

Community Rating: A premium rating methodology frequently used by HMOs. The HMO using this method must charge the same amount of money per member for all members of a plan. The methodology does not allow for employer account-specific variables to influence pricing. Contrasts with *Experience Rating.*

Cost of Services Ratio (COS Ratio): The ratio between the cost incurred by the managed care entity that is directly related to service delivery, and the amount of revenue acquired. A COS ratio of 75 percent or more is common in MBC operations, and excludes administrative or overhead costs.

Current Procedural Terminology (CPT) Codes: Sets of five-digit codes frequently used for billing professional services.

Disenrollment: A process by which an HMO may exclude a member, after due process, from a health plan due to non-payment of required copayments to providers or repeated failure to adhere to reasonable treatment plans.

Employee Assistance Program (EAP): An employer-sponsored counseling and consultation service aimed at assisting employees or family members experiencing emotional, substance abuse, family, or other problems that can interfere with productivity or worker safety. EAPs pursue goals by ensuring the provision of appropriate and cost-effective services.

EAPs may be offered by employers as an integral part of the benefit plan, or as an entirely separate program. The EAP may be voluntary or mandatory. In mandatory EAPs the benefit plan reimburses only care that is delivered by a clinician associated with the EAP's provider network. Incentivized EAPs feature a higher level of reimbursement when care is rendered by a member of the EAP provider network. In addition to provider networks, EAPs may also offer utilization management and other managed care functions.

Enrollee: An individual who is eligible for benefits under a health care plan. Frequently used in connection with indemnity insurance.

Enrollment Period: A specified time period provided by an employer and a health care organization during which employees may select a health care benefit plan or offering from within a plan. Selection may be done in person or electronically and may be based on literature distributed by the vendors or through information obtained in meetings conducted by vendor representatives.

Experience Rating: A premium rating methodology that adjusts as an account's rate based on the utilization experience and other factors specific to the account. This system allows for lower premiums for employers who have healthy workforces, and contrasts with *Community Rating* methodology which averages data for multiple groups of employees.

Fiduciary: Under ERISA, any person or entity that exercises discretionary control over the administration of a benefit plan. Self-insured employers can delegate this responsibility to MBC or UR firms concurring Mental Health and Substance Abuse benefits.

HMO Act of 1973: Amended in 1988. This law allowed HMOs to become "federally qualified" by meeting various standards. Once so designated, the HMO has the right to ask any local employer of twenty-five or more employees to offer it as a health care benefit option. HMOs were required to charge the same "community rate" to all employers, pooling all employers together for risk purposes. In 1988, Congress amended the Act. The right of HMOs to put themselves on the benefit menu of local employers was scheduled to expire in 1995. HMOs were allowed to adjust premiums by actual employer group experience, no longer adhering to a community rating system. Caps were placed in charges to smaller employer groups. HMOs were also permitted to provide services through non-HMO physicians, charging extra fees when members utilize such services.

Integrated Health Plans: A type of benefit plan in which all employees are enrolled into a single managed care system for all health care services. Members may have options to utilize non-network providers, but at an increased cost.

Managed Care or Managed Behavioral Care (MBC): Refers to any of a variety of systems and strategies aimed at marshalling appropriate clinical and financial resources to ensure needed care for consumers. It features increased structure and accountability for providers and the overall coordination of care, while eliminating duplicative or unnecessary services.

Managed Care Organization (MCO): A term that describes any HMO or managed behavioral care entity.

Management Information System (MIS): The computer hardware, software, and automated systems that provide support for the management of a business.

Mandated Benefits: Minimal benefit levels established by statutes enacted by state legislatures. These vary from state to state and can add to overall health care costs. ERISA exempts employers who are self-insured from these mandates. Other exceptions have been made for "basic," low cost, insurance products that can be offered to the uninsured segment of the workforce.

Medical Reimbursement Account: An increasingly popular feature of new employer sponsored health benefit plans designed to assist employees with the increased cost sharing associated with these plans. The employee annually sets aside pre-tax dollars into the medical reimbursement account which may be used for expenses such as copayments, deductibles, eyeglasses, well-baby care, or child care expenses. Employers sometimes contribute to these accounts.

Member: An individual who is eligible for benefits under a health care plan, particularly an HMO or other prepaid system.

Network or Provider Network: A group of providers, organized, accredited, and administered by a MBC firm. Members agree to practice in an effective, cost-conscious manner utilizing the MBC firm's clinical guidelines or standards. Members also agree to discounted fee arrangements. In turn, they are eligible for referrals, through the MBC firm, of members of employer groups contracting with the firm. Providers agree to the MBC firm's quality management program. The network may include both inpatient and outpatient providers. It is increasingly important for providers to join networks in order to allow access to their services by large numbers of potential patients. This requires providers to become familiar with goal-oriented, solution-focused therapies, to manage practices efficiently, and to develop innovative practice styles in order to compete successfully for referrals.

Open Enrollment Period: The time period during which an employee may change or join a health care plan. This usually occurs once per year for each employer group. Most HMOs have about half their accounts available for open enrollment in the Fall, with an effective date of January 1.

Out-of-Pocket Maximum: The maximum amount an insured person will have to pay for a covered health care expense. Often this amount is $500, $1,000, or more, or a percentage of annual salary. Usually calculated on a yearly basis.

Per Diem Reimbursement: A system used most commonly with hospitals or partial hospital programs and based on a predetermined set rate per day of care, rather than usual charges. This system is a cost containment measure, usually assuring the facility of referral volume and the managed care entity of discounted fees.

Per Employee, Per Year (PE PY): A payment method used in financing Employee Assistance Programs on a pre-paid, per capita basis.

Per Member, Per Month (PM PM): A payment method used in financing managed care arrangements under which the vendor is paid for each enrollee each month.

Practice Guidelines: Recommended therapies and procedures for the treatment of specific disorders so as to achieve optimum results as efficiently as possible. They are not rigid standards, but rather suggestions which offer supportive guidance to clinicians. Many MBC organizations use such guidelines for quality assurance or accountability purposes. Practice guidelines are developed from the clinical literature, professional societies, and/or through other clinician input forums.

Preadmission Review (PAR): Also known as precertification for admission. A common function in various managed care systems. This term is also commonly used to denote a "participating" facility, one that is contracted with a managed care entity to participate in its utilization management activities, including preadmission review.

Preferred Provider Arrangement (PPA): An agreement between a business entity and a provider or group of providers. Differs from a PPO, which is an actual organization.

Preferred Provider Organization (PPO): An arrangement by which an entity contracts with an organization of providers for specified services. These services are delivered on a discounted fee basis, and the providers are guaranteed a volume of referrals, prompt claims payment, etc. The providers also agree to comply with utilization management procedures.

Primary Care Physician (PCP): Usually internists, family physicians, general practitioners, and pediatricians. Some managed care plans require PCP screening and referral of members in need of mental health or substance abuse treatment services.

Provider: A professional who delivers clinical services to a managed care member. Facility provider refers to hospitals or other institutional entities.

Provider Relations Manager: A coordinating position, found in some HMOs, which has responsibility for the recruitment and credentialing of PCPs or other providers. Provider relations is a function in all managed behavioral care systems that utilize Provider Networks.

Quality Management Program: A structured program that monitors and evaluates the quality and effectiveness of a health care system's services. Minimal components include the monitoring of: utilization of services, accessibility of services, patient satisfaction, provider credentialing, and treatment outcomes. May include chart audits and case reviews. Provider contracts with health care systems usually stipulate compliance and cooperation with Quality Management Program activities.

Reasonable and Customary Charge: Also known as usual, customary, and reasonable charge (UCR). The maximum amount an insurer will consider as eligible for reimbursement. A claims cost control device.

Reviews:

>Concurrent Review: Utilization review conducted during the patient's course of treatment. Also termed Continued Stay Review.
>
>Initial or First Level Review: The initial review of a request for benefit coverage.
>
>Retrospective Review: Review conducted after services have been provided.
>
>Second Level Review: An appeal review conducted by a clinical peer of a request for benefit certification that was denied by the Initial Review.

Utilization Management (UM) or Utilization Review (UR): Any of several techniques and procedures used to monitor and evaluate the necessity or appropriateness of care for the purposes of insurance coverage or provider reimbursement.

Index

Page numbers followed by the letter "t" designate tables; those followed by "f" designate figures.

Termination, 189-190,219-220,
293-295
Third-party payors/payment. *See*
Insurance; Reimbursement
Transition visits, 172-173
Treatment orientation, 105-106
Treatment outcomes, 108-110,
163-164
case study, 110-112
Treatment planning, 77-80,179
Treatment summary form, 297-302

URAC (Utilization Review
Accreditation Committee),
34-35
U.S. Healthcare, 34
Utilization
data reporting, 91
history of, 82
hospital admissions, 101-102
inpatient hospitalization, 98-100
length of stay in substance abuse
treatment, 161-162
outpatient services, 102
rate calculation formulas, 100-101

Utilization management, 26-27,324
denials and appeals, 130-131
employment opportunities in, 147
legal issues in
implications for employers,
140-141
major cases, 135-139
state regulation and ERISA,
141-142
medical necessity and, 129-130
procedural alternatives, 132-134
procedures
benefit interpretation, 122
concurrent review, 125-128
eligibility determination, 122
precertification, 123-125,
130-134
typical decisions, 128
Utilization review, 34-35,324
Utilization Review Accreditation
Committee (URAC), 34-35

Wellness model of health care, 74
Wenzel, Lee, 60-61
Wickline v. California, 136-139
*Wilson v. Blue Cross of Southern
California*, 139